Eastern Horizons

Also by Levison Wood

Walking the Nile
Walking the Himalayas
Walking the Americas

Eastern Horizons

Hitchhiking the Silk Road

Levison Wood

HODDER &
STOUGHTON

First published in Great Britain in 2017 by Hodder & Stoughton
An Hachette UK company

1

Copyright © Levison Wood 2017

A CIP catalogue record for this title is available from the British Library

ISBN 9781473676268
eBook ISBN 9781473676282
Trade Paperback ISBN 9781473676275

Typeset in Bembo by Hewer Text UK Ltd, Edinburgh
Printed and bound by CPI Group (UK) Ltd, Croydon, CR0 4YY

Hodder & Stoughton policy is to use papers that are natural, renewable
and recyclable products and made from wood grown in sustainable forests.
The logging and manufacturing processes are expected to conform
to the environmental regulations of the country of origin.

Hodder & Stoughton Ltd
Carmelite House
50 Victoria Embankment
London EC4Y 0DZ

www.hodder.co.uk

For my parents, who had no idea where I was most of the time

In memory of Arthur Conolly

Contents

Author's note

This is an account of a journey taken at the age of twenty-two, fresh out of university with the dregs of a student loan. I set off on a trek that, unbeknown at the time, was to become a defining point of reference for perhaps all my subsequent expeditions.

The year 2004 was a seminal one in my own life, and one of great social upheaval and change on the fringes of Europe, in Russia, and along the countries of the old Silk Road. However, this book does not purport to present a geo-political narrative, or indeed a comprehensive history of the ancient overland routes to the Indian subcontinent. Nor does it seek to analyse the complexities of Western foreign policy in the region, or the inter-tribal conflicts that have marred the paths of high Asia for centuries. There are other books that already do that very well. This is simply an account of my own youthful wanderings in a general easterly direction - albeit with a sprinkling of the kind of anecdotal history that interested me at the time.

The book was written over a two-year period after I left the army in 2010, some six years after the events had occurred. It was my first attempt at writing. It relies for the most part on my journals and notes kept at the time. The manuscript lay dormant for a subsequent six years until I was fortunate enough to retrace a part of my earlier adventures for a television documentary and it seemed an appropriate time to dust off the diaries.

The text itself is largely unchanged, therefore I should probably apologise for the perambulating style and literary immaturity of the narrative. But, rather than change it, I have chosen to keep it as it is and retain the essence of the memory. Because for me, that is what travel is all about: good memories – whichever direction they take you.

I travel not to go anywhere, but to go. I travel for travel's sake. The great affair is to move . . . to come down off this featherbed of civilisation and find the globe granite underfoot and strewn with cutting flints . . . [It] is no great industry, but it is one that serves to occupy and compose the mind. And when the present is so exacting, who can annoy himself about the future?

Robert Louis Stevenson, *Travels with a Donkey in the Cévennes*, 1878

Preface

Taybad/Dogharoun, November 2004

The border post appeared as a mirage on the horizon, disfigured by the heat of the desert, rising like a phantom flame from the road. There was little but sand in all directions and the only reminder at all that life existed here was the group of speckled figures in the distance. Rifles were slung over their shoulders and dark beards concealed their faces. But even these shadowy apparitions did not seem real, and the entrance to Afghanistan appeared like a figment of my imagination. Wild, dangerous and romantic.

A rusty barbed-wire fence disappeared into the scrubby desert to the north and south, separating Iran from Afghanistan; by several centuries, it appeared. Bearded and turban-clad tribes-men squatted on their haunches like a scene from the Arabian nights. A shepherd eyed his flock of skinny goats, and the soldiers, dressed in a ragtag array of grey caps, woollen jumpers and old Russian greatcoats, sat in the shade of the immigration office – a crumbling shed with a painting of the Afghan flag on one white-washed wall. It would have seemed quaint had it not been pock-marked with bullet holes.

As it was, I felt a combination of fear and excitement at the prospect of entering a country notorious for bloodshed and a predilection for disposing of foreigners by the most grisly of means. War was never far away; this was 2004 and as allied soldiers were pouring in from the West, so too were Islamic jihadists from the East. The stage was set for a resurgence of violence, and another ten years of bloody fighting. I had not planned on going to Afghanistan, but there I was: young, alone and penniless in the Khorasan desert, sixty miles away from Herat – the nearest thing to civilisation, and you could hardly call it that.

This sunbaked no-man's-land was the place where Zoroastrianism and Buddhism prevailed in the centuries before Islam; where Alexander conquered the Persians and Babur began his epic journey across the Hindu Kush. It is the geographical transition between the Middle East and Central Asia – the heart of the Silk Road – and a place of mystery and wilderness since recorded travel began. For me, too, this was more than just another border crossing: it was the last great frontier before the Indian subcontinent, and one step closer to my dream.

Part 1

I

A Letter

. . . and above all, travel.

Those words, written in a letter, had resounded in my imagination ever since I first read them. Second Lieutenant James Whitehurst of the Royal Artillery has a lot to answer for.

It's funny how small things can change your life in such big ways. Little was I to know when I lost my wallet at the age of sixteen, that it would have such a great influence on the rest of my life.

It was a pretty normal Saturday afternoon for a teenage boy from Staffordshire. We'd planned it for a while; the attractions of Alton Towers were too strong to resist and one day a few of us from school cycled the fourteen miles through the Moorlands to try and sneak into the theme park. We set off, past the chip shop on the high street and the pub where gruff men smoked and drank pints of cheap lager. It only took an hour along the twisting country lanes, over the rolling hills before the looming gates emerged at the side of the road. We went straight past, another half a mile or so to where a little trail led off into the woods. We knew it like the back of our hands, given the fact we'd all worked there over the summer, selling hot dogs and pressing the go button for the monorail. We hid our bikes in the bushes and covered our tracks. There was a little hole in the fence where we could climb in; and from there it was a simple case of avoiding the security guards with their big dogs and emerging out of the rhododendron bushes without any of the staff noticing. Not that they'd care though. We all made it, and found ourselves dusting off twigs inside the castle grounds before lunch. Mission accomplished. Now we were at liberty to go on the rides and have a fun afternoon in the park without spending all of our pocket money on the entry ticket. Karma got me back though when, an hour later, having enjoyed being hurled around on the corkscrew rollercoaster, I wobbled off, only to discover, much to my horror, that my wallet was gone. Had it fallen out? Perhaps it had been stolen. Either way, it was extremely annoying at the time and a severe blow to my finances, especially since my bus pass was in there and it would mean paying the full fare on the number seven to Cheadle.

Luckily for me, though, the wallet turned up in the post a week after I lost it. Surprisingly, it was complete with all of its contents, including the bus pass, and with it came a short letter from the man who'd found it. I was impressed by its style and politeness, and the way Second Lieutenant James Whitehurst of the Royal Artillery addressed me as an adult. It was on smart paper complete with an embossed watermark. He threw in, dryly, that he'd written it in the early hours of the morning, apologising if the writing was untidy – he was up at that time because, as an officer in the army, he had very important duties to attend to. I pictured a dashing young soldier dug in a shell scrape on manoeuvres in some secret location, preparing his men for war.

Eager to find out more about my new hero, I wrote back immediately, thanking him for his integrity and having taken the time to write at all, when even the most honest of folk these days would have simply handed the wallet in to the local police station and let them deal with it. I'd been interested in a career in the army ever since I was a kid, but nobody I knew had joined, especially as an officer, and I hadn't the first clue how to go about applying, so, seeing the opportunity I asked if he wouldn't mind offering me some tips.

The reply came by return of post in the form of six full pages of sound and practical advice: *Learn to read a map and a compass, get fit, run a mile and a half in nine minutes, join the TA, read the news, know your military history . . . take a gap year, and above all, travel.*

There it was in black and white – a plan for the future, who'd have thought it? Determined on my new path, I set about following this advice to the letter for the next two years. Whilst finishing off my A Levels at school by day, at night I studied contours and ridgelines; went running and started doing press ups, I read the broadsheets and tried my best to keep up to date with political scandal. I got stuck into history and read anything I could get my hands on. It wasn't hard; I'd always loved history, especially tales of adventure from foreign climes. I devoured the diaries of explorers and ancient navigators who had journeyed to the east.

And, above all, I travelled. I remember showing my parents the letter when I turned eighteen.

'Look, Dad, it says what I have to do right here, travel.'

'And what about university?' They didn't seem too impressed and stared at me disapprovingly.

'I'll go next year. I promise.'

My father looked unconvinced and my mother distraught.

'A *gap year*. Whatever is one of those anyway? Your mother and I never had *gap years* in our day.'

'Yes, you did. You had the hippy trail.'

'Well, we weren't bloody hippies.'

'Neither am I. I just want to see a bit of the world.'

They studied me in silence, shaking their heads in resignation. Finally, my father broke the tension.

'Well, you can bloody pay for it. And you can start paying rent while you're at it.'

I was ecstatic. I got a job. In fact, I got a lot of jobs. I became a labourer, warehouse assistant, rail-track layer, burger-flipper, supermarket shelf-stacker, and van driver; I even went back to work at Alton Towers for a while, where I repaid my debt of sneaking in through long hours dressed in an orange uniform selling keyrings and stuffed toys to Chinese tourists.

With a few quid in my pocket and a brand-new rucksack, I set off alone. I was under no illusion that six months in Africa, Australia and South-East Asia was considered trail-blazing. I didn't explore any uncharted peaks or walk across any deserts or paddle to the source of any rivers. I did, however, learn the basics of independent travel and the benefits of trying to understand other cultures, rather than staying put in isolated ghettos with other tourists. I found that one of the best ways to meet people was to hitchhike. It was generally unpredictable, often lonely, sometimes fun and frequently downright dangerous. But it was always interesting. Travel is by its very nature fascinating; an education. And I was eager to learn.

Much to my parents' relief, on my return from my gap year, I enrolled at the University of Nottingham to continue my passion and study history. But all the way through university, I carried on travelling; each time, in an insatiable search of adventure, I would spend a month or two roaming the wilds, sometimes alone and sometimes in the company of a like-minded student. I trekked through the highlands of Scotland and the plains of Eastern Europe. Once, in a fit of juvenile irresponsibility, I even hitchhiked home from Cairo, by way of Jerusalem and Baghdad, in the middle of the Second Gulf War. That was my real education. Looking back, I was driven not only by a real desire to learn about the world, but also a fear of missing out. I didn't want to get old without seeing the world.

Mark Twain puts it nicely:

> *Twenty years from now you will be more disappointed by the things that you didn't do than by the ones you did . . . So throw off the bowlines. Sail away from the safe harbour. Catch the trade winds in your sails. Explore. Dream. Discover.*

The only times that my trade winds were disrupted were during the first two weeks of each summer holiday, when I would be obliged to complete a fortnight's summer camp with the Officer Training Corps. I had enrolled in my first year of studies, following the advice of the letter I'd received three years before, and it was here that I met Winfield.

Jon Winfield hailed from the craggy moors of the Peak District. Although we became friends in the vaguely military environment of the deceptively serious-sounding 'East Midlands Universities Officer Training Corps', Jon had no designs on joining the army, unlike me. In fact, among military circles he was identified for his very unmilitary behaviour. EMUOTC was technically a unit in the Territorial Army and therefore to the uninitiated, quite stern stuff, but in reality, it was a drinking club for students who were contemplating joining the real army – and of course people like Jon, who merely fancied the social scene. He would often turn up to training unshaven, with his hair way beyond regulation length. I don't recall him ever ironing his uniform and on exercise in Wales, his water canteen would regularly be replaced with a good bottle of port. Jon was a natural rebel; I knew he would make an excellent travelling companion.

Knee deep in mud in the Lake District, we would talk about travelling together. Backpacking through Thailand, bartending in Greece, volunteering in Kenya ... cliché after cliché. Until one particularly wet soldierly day on the immense green slopes of Helvellyn, my thoughts turned to a book I'd stumbled across in the university library called *The Great Game*. Quite why I was reading that when the module I was supposed to be writing about was Frankish knights I don't recall, but the distraction proved fortuitous. It told stories of bold young Englishmen sneaking over high mountain passes to defend the Empire, with India as its centrepiece, against brutish Russian marauders.

One person in particular stood out. I think I must have been impressed with the beard. Contemporary portraits show a barrel-chested man with immense facial fuzz and a turban that would have put the Ayatollah to shame. It belonged to Arthur Conolly, a dashing young officer in the British East India Company, who was the first person to coin the term 'the Great Game'. I wondered if he and his mates had made their travel plans whilst training in the green fields of Blighty? Conolly undertook several forays into the far south of Russia, as well as the khanates of the Muslim Central Asian states – often in disguise, rarely with official permission, and always at great personal risk. One day, in the summer of 1839, he set off on an overland trip from England to India, to see if it was possible to travel along the Silk Road in the age of Empire.

I suddenly had the urge to do the same. I shouted through the mist to Jon, 'India?'

'Hmmm,' he mused. 'I do enjoy a good curry, but I was thinking I'd like to tick Russia off first. It'd give me an excuse to read

War and Peace.' It wasn't quite the answer I'd hoped for, but I could see I'd tickled his fancy.

'How about both?' I stuttered, out of breath as we climbed a steep gorge, the square-jawed Sergeant Major now shouting at us to stop chattering and get on with the march.

'And everything in between?' I said, just as the soldiers' stick narrowly missed the back of my head.

We marched on in silence, but the seed had now been planted. I can still remember the feeling of restlessness and excitement that was born from that misty epiphany. I got home to my grimy flat on Kimbolton Avenue and thoughts of travel bounced around my mind. That night I lay awake, staring up at the flickering lightbulb and listening to the familiar sounds of the student flat. It was a cold December night and a drunk outside had begun singing merrily to himself before stopping abruptly, probably to vomit. In the distance, a faint siren could be heard, heralding pub closing time in the town centre. Finally, I drifted into unconsciousness and a journey began to unfold.

I traced the route on a mental globe, a bold scarlet line over a smooth surface of azure oceans and dark green continents. A booming horn signalled the departure of a monstrous ferry, which glided away from the familiar chalky cliffs of Dover and then, in an instant, I was soaring high above the Paris skyline, then low, skimming like a smooth pebble over red-tiled Germanic rooftops and castles. Soon enough, as the plains of Central Europe gave way to the pine forests and onion domes of the edge of Christendom, I felt nothing more than the rough texture of a mountain or two as I soared joyfully over the Caucasus and then, in a second, I glided down, out of the wilds of Circassia and into the scorching deserts of Persia.

Deep canyons and towering passes showed me that Bactria was close. Was this the route taken by Alexander the Great? I could almost hear the trickle of the River Oxus in the north, but no, I was still going east; more mountains. This time bigger – the Himalayas. But even these Tibetan thrones could not stop my strident progress, as I plunged into deepest India with its jungles, paddy fields and tea plantations. Within a moment I came to an abrupt halt. I was lost, alone, amongst the masses, in a frenzy of oriental commerce and mystical intrigue. I saw turbaned ancients amidst a sea of multicoloured rugs and carpets. Animals – humped-back cows, oxen and fettered chickens – fighting for their very existence amongst the busy throng of Punjabis. A kohl-eyed Pathan swathed in thick black robes scurried into the shadows before a platoon of Sikhs marched through the bazaar causing the crowd to part wildly . . .

I woke up with a start, finding it still dark, but the sounds of morning were already whispering through the curtains. I realised that it was time to face the winter chill, and with it, revision, exams and reality. At the back of my mind, though, I remembered the scene, and, unusually, none of its vividness had faded with the night. I left the house without eating breakfast, too excited and too full of thoughts of travel.

The eastern road towards the Indian subcontinent has lured travellers from the west since time immemorial. Thomas, apostle of Jesus, is believed to have travelled from the Holy Land to India in AD 52. But even he was no trail-blazer. Four hundred years before him, in the spring of 326 BC, Alexander the Great set off from Greece with an army of Europeans, bent on conquering the lands of Hind across the Indus river.

Since ancient times, a succession of armies, merchants, missionaries, and that most vague of breeds, travellers, have been tempted to make the overland journey from the fringes of Europe to the Indian subcontinent – travelling by foot, horse, mule and camel. Sea travel was increasingly common, even two thousand years ago, and it was feasible to journey from the civilised ports of the Middle East to India in only a few months. But for many explorers, sea travel wasn't satisfactory; it didn't allow them the riches of the Silk Road, or the glory of exploring new and uncharted lands in the name of kings and queens.

Before the modern age, the Middle East and South Asia were perhaps the best-charted regions in the world outside Europe. The newly discovered Americas were vast unknown quantities, full of savage jungle dwellers. Africa was still the 'dark continent', fearsome and threatening. In contrast, the Holy Lands, Arabia and Persia were centres of learning and civilisation. Even the lowliest of peasants in an Irish bog had heard of Jerusalem and Babylon. They, too, had heard stories of the ruthless Genghis Khan, whose barbarian hordes and their descendants had chewed away at the outskirts of Europe until very recently. Asia was a place of danger and awe and mystery, but it was also full of charm and romance. Stories abounded: *One Thousand and One Nights* confirmed what the inquisitive European already believed – that the East was magical, its women beautiful and seductive, its horses magnificent and its men untrustworthy.

While Europe was still hauling itself out of the Middle Ages, India was flourishing. Vast empires traded goods and technology; science and creativity bloomed. But a barrier still existed between East and West. There were vast tracts of endless desert and freezing mountain ranges, populated by increasingly hostile tribes and religious fanatics – as well as the powerful menace of the Mongols. Despite the growing commercial promise of the

East, only the most intrepid Europeans dared to travel the perilous overland route. It wasn't until the establishment of the East India Companies in the eighteenth century that large-scale commercial activity became viable between Europe and the subcontinent, and most of that was conducted by sea.

Only when the landlocked Central Asian states hit the headlines of London and St Petersburg, during the Russian expansionism of the nineteenth century, did it become necessary for Europeans – namely British and Russian political agents – to venture into the mountainous no-man's-land in order to protect their respective empires against invasion. The Great Game became a byword for this exploration and overland travel in Asia. The bearded Conolly was only one of many adventurers who put their lives on the line in the name of empire and eternal fame. And he, for one, paid the ultimate price.

The few individuals that did make the overland journey, when not being attacked, murdered, robbed, starved or forcibly converted, became part of an exclusive club of travellers. They saw with their own eyes what most people were content to read about in fantastic stories, where dog-headed men, mermaids and fire-breathing dragons regularly entered the arena.

It wasn't really until the twentieth century, and the advent of motorised transport and the social upheaval of the Second World War, that a new breed of travellers emerged who were able to observe, with a greater degree of objectivity, the reality of traversing a continent by clinging to its dusty caravan tracks. These strange, long-haired, spiritual sandal wearers, known to posterity as hippies, achieved what generations of travellers before them had failed to do. They popularised overland travel in Asia and made India accessible to the European masses. For the first time in history, the route was open to those whose livelihoods did not depend on spices, silk or spying.

Then suddenly, in 1979, it all changed once again. The Russians invaded Afghanistan, Iran was taken over by a theocratic regime, and the overland trail was again off limits to all but the most intrepid wanderers. The year 2001 brought another dimension. On that bright September morning when the twin towers came crashing down, the world changed forever. East and West were forced apart yet again, this time in a battle over a way of life. The Silk Road countries bear the brunt of this struggle and only time will tell how they fare. In the opening years of the twenty-first century, it is sad to think that overland travel from Europe to India is probably more disrupted and hazardous, and less viable, than it was when Marco Polo did it.

Encouraged by romantic notions of adventure, however, I saw my new task as a completion of my studies: a personal journey into the past as well as the future. In the university library, I searched the shelves for a copy of Arthur Conolly's overland diary and began to scribble down routes and dates and prices. How long would it take? Where would I start? Where would I finish?

I had already spent a very brief spell in the Indian subcontinent when I backpacked around the world before university, and it wasn't a pleasant experience. I spent two weeks hiding in the mountains of Nepal in 2001, when the Nepali royal family was massacred in Kathmandu and the whole country went into lockdown. There were Maoist riots in the countryside and a nine o'clock curfew across the cities. People were getting shot in the streets and my passport had been stolen.

Luckily, I was taken in by a local farmer named Binod, who kept me away from the violence until things subsided. I finally retrieved my passport and embarked on a gruelling fifty-three-hour bus journey to Delhi. In India, I got violently sick and had to fly home after only two days, having seen little more than the inside of my $2 hotel room – and the shared toilet.

Still, despite this, and perhaps because of it, I knew that I had to return to India. It has always been a part of the British consciousness. I thought back to childhood days of cricket in the park in Stoke-on-Trent, of being sent by my grandmother to the local corner shop, where I gazed in wonder at the rows of spices and exotic tins, with a smiling Bengali behind the counter. And, of course, there were my grandfather's stories from the war – of docking in Calcutta, fighting the Japanese in Burma, and marching through thick, jungle-clad mountains alongside his Gurkha allies into Kohima.

And then I realised. It was the same fascination with Britain's past that had caused me to set off when I was eighteen. But this time I was more focused. I held those childhood images dear and wanted to see first-hand if the reality would live up to my expectations, whether Marco Polo's tall tales and my grandfather's gruesome stories, and those of Alexander the Great and Arthur Conolly, would bear any resemblance to the modern-day truth in an age of relentless change. It was the draw of the East, of the Silk Road and the Great Game. The same allure of the mystical Orient that has sent generations of British travellers to the subcontinent for hundreds of years.

So, I had a plan. It was a very vague one, but it was a plan, nonetheless. I called Jon.

'India overland. I'm being serious. Let's do it.' There was a silence at the end of the phone for a few seconds.

'You're mad,' he said.

'June.'

'I can't,' he said. 'I'm doing a work placement until September. And anyway, what about Russia? I told you, I want to read *War and Peace*.'

'We'll do it all,' I said, imploring him to see the importance. 'Russia first, then overland through God-knows-where, till we get to the beach in Goa. It's fail-safe. Tell you what. I'm going to hitchhike. Let's meet up somewhere in Eastern Europe when you're done faffing about in London and we'll go to Russia together and see where we end up.'

Romantic notions of being on the road took hold, and in June the next year, with exams out of the way, I set off to hitchhike to India, wild and carefree, and thoroughly unprepared for my journey.

That summer was one of the best of my life. Time flew by in a hazy mixture of warm afternoons, snoozing in parks and staying with old friends. France was little more than a quick escape from the dingy dockyards of Calais, followed by shortcuts through vineyards in Champagne, but Germany passed by slowly and in vivid detail. The dream was suddenly a reality.

Red-tiled roofs jutted skyward and colourful flowers danced on the eves of half-wood, half-brick houses. White carnations dangled in Teutonic uniformity from symmetrical hanging baskets on wooden balustrades and evenly mowed green lawns – all at the peak of their pride in midsummer. The thought of the Black Forest mountains with their emerald lakes still sends a shiver down my spine.

In Nuremberg, all the details – the angular city walls, the immaculate drawbridges and the towering castles remain silhouetted against a clear sky. On top of ancient battlements, the red-tiled spires rose upwards to the heavens, and concealed in their torsos – unseen attics, filled with bats. The shadows crept beyond the city walls and the red and white panels that under-pin the massive eves faded into oblivion. The streetlights flick-ered on, and at the end of steep, cobbled streets, the castles began to glow a deep red with their impossibly thick walls. Further east, pink hues of Czech villages stood proudly against back-drops of coniferous hedgerow, a shield from the untamed forests beyond.

I travelled mostly at night and usually in the company of sullen lorry drivers. The stars would fade into the atmosphere as the dim light of dawn gradually approached, and it got wilder and more romantic as I went east. I was always delighted to be greeted with ever more attractive scenes of Swabian medieval-ism on entering a new town. I had breakfast in cobbled alley-ways with the aroma of freshly baked pretzels, and lunches of Bratwurst, served by Bohemian girls with deep grey eyes. Days and weeks passed by. I hitched from town to town. Sleep would come rough, more often than not; next to rivers, hedgerows and even roundabouts. And when I became sick of the mosquitoes or slugs that were my constant bed partners, I would sometimes pay for the cheapest bed in a dormitory, but often find it worse. When the dorms became too loud, I would return to the streets or the parks, and disused factories.

I met many interesting people. There was a Buddhist monk from Thailand undertaking his version of the European Grand Tour dressed ascetically in his orange robes; Kurt, a great German photographer, took me in for three days. Marta showed me places in rural Poland that no tourists would ever see. Christian put me up in his university and introduced me to the delights of

German beer. And then there was Marc Engberg, the American scholar and comedian whose charm and intellect fed my imagination, and whose conversation ensured many a pleasant afternoon drinking coffee in Warsaw Central Square.

Halcyon days. It was life at its freest. I wandered about Eastern Europe for a while. Places with strange names sucked me in: Szepietowo, where I fell in love, and Suwalky where I was almost robbed of my only pair of shoes by a gang of feral thieves. There were lots of castles. Castles on lakes, castles in forests, castles by the sea. Sometimes I would sleep on their walls or in little enclaves removed from view. When not being arrested for vagrancy, I was blissfully happy.

I got to Estonia, where I dined with diplomats by day and slept on the ancient ramparts of the city walls by night. I would eat bread and soup at the National Library canteen, and write emails and letters to embassies trying to chase up my visas, and when I tired of that, I took the bus to the beach at Pirita, where the most beautiful girls in Europe gathered to bathe in the surprisingly warm Baltic Sea. I was an Englishman alone, before it became popular for stag parties, sitting in the beer gardens of the central Tallinn square, or overlooking the harbour from the upper town. I could have stayed for the rest of the summer and in fact almost two weeks passed by, hardly noticed.

But one beautiful afternoon, as I sat reading and drinking coffee, the realisation dawned on me that it was looking less likely that I would get any further.

'Your Iranian visa will be ready in Warsaw,' the officials said in Tallinn.

'Not here,' they said in Warsaw. 'Try in Moscow.'

And as for a Russian visa: 'Only in London,' they said. 'You have to collect in person.'

It became more and more clear that no matter how many phone calls I made or letters I wrote, I would have to return to England to get the paperwork sorted.

It was my own fault, of course, but I still felt a sense of dread at the thought of having to admit defeat. How could I face my family and friends who had bade me farewell, when I hadn't even left the confines of Europe? To all concerned, I'd been lazing about on a mere beach holiday. Those long days of walking down motorways and sleeping under hedges – taunted all the while by threats from the police and criminals alike – had all been in vain.

I felt like a fraud and it was hard to hide my feelings of disappointment. What about Kurt, Christian, Marta and Marc – all the people that I'd told I was going to India? Most importantly, what would Winfield say?

But in the end, there was nothing to be done. The summer was coming to an end; the beach at Pirita was empty. I resolved to go home and start again as soon as I had obtained the necessary clearance. Next time I would be more thorough, I promised myself. Things weren't so bad. Above all, at least I had travelled.

2

Tramps Abroad

Blackened lorries trundled by, interrupting the silence of a September Sunday morning. To the west, endless fields rolled away like a patchwork quilt of green and brown. In the east, a Lincolnshire town was just about visible. Roofs pointed out from the tall hedgerow, and, in the distance, the spire of a church gave away that this was rural England. I already saw in my imagination the onion domes of Moscow, the jagged peaks of Georgia, the eternal deserts and minarets of Persia and the golden palaces of India.

I had a combination of hope and dread in anticipation of continuing my journey from where I had broken it off. By now it was nearing the start of autumn and already cold gusts of wind were blowing through the streets – reddening leaves were starting to take on a crisper appearance, marking the end of a fine summer. Six weeks had passed since I turned back from the Baltic Sea, embarrassed and chastened, and although I had kept myself busy chasing around the embassies, earning a little money, and generally avoiding having to explain myself, I was getting restless now and knew it was time to get back on the road. I'd gone to see Jon and explain myself at having retreated from the expedition, but my worries had been in vain.

I watched as Jon's boots pounded up and down, transfixed by the gentle monotony. He had taken the lead and was now a few paces in front. Jon was the same age as me, twenty-two. He had finished his placement and recently moved to London, where he had been offered work with a big company starting in the New Year. He seemed happy to tag along – after all, Russia had been his idea. He hadn't given me too much hassle about not making it further than Estonia and, in fact, told me himself that he was glad we'd be starting again, this time together.

Winfield had already travelled quite a bit in Europe and across the United States and despite his nonchalant demeanour, he was quite capable of looking after himself. He was interesting and well read; a large part of his rucksack (which bounced in front of me with each of his springing steps) was filled with an unabridged volume of *War and Peace,* which he aimed to finish by the end of the trip. I was glad not to be setting off alone again.

High above, I noticed the white vapour trail from an aeroplane, cutting through the clouds. Back on earth, cows munched lazily on the far side of the hedge; their tails swatting away invisible flies. A life of ignorant contentment. I looked down as torn sheets of a newspaper danced in the wake of another truck and one of them flapped a while, caught around Jon's leg. 'NHS in crisis,' warned the muddy rag. 'Blair plans cabinet reshuffle as minister quits,' announced page four. 'Pensioners march on Westminster,' proclaimed the headline.

For ten million commuters, something was always going on in London. There was enough mild scandal and drama to fill the newspapers, but to the eyes of a graduate with no money and no job it all appeared rather tame. All I seemed to be able to think about was the unfolding excitement abroad. *Abroad.* Outside of the confines of western civilisation, that was where the real drama was. These were interesting times.

Iraq took centre stage. Despite the military successes of the previous year, it looked like it was going to turn nasty after all. Various insurgent groups had begun to rise up against the allied occupation in the struggle for power following the toppling of the *Ba'athist* regime. Saddam Hussein had recently been captured down a hole in Tikrit and was awaiting trial. Osama bin Laden was still at large somewhere in the mountains of Afghanistan or Pakistan.

Violence seemed to be on the increase and that year saw an unprecedented rise in the use of suicide bombers across the whole region and even in Europe: Madrid became the victim of an al-Qaeda attack, when a bomb exploded on one of its trains, and Spain quickly withdrew its troops from Iraq after the world's most wanted man offered peace to those countries that capitulated. In Britain, the USA and Canada, there were a series of outrages at so-called prisoner abuse in Iraqi jails, culminating in some high-profile investigations and even military trials. Moreover, the UN had declared the war illegal and Blair's Britain had become embarrassed.

Closer to home, Eastern Europe was gaining a foothold in the new world order as NATO expanded to include seven new countries and the EU also admitted ten new member states from former Soviet territories, much to the annoyance of Vladimir Putin. Russia was further upset after a series of bombings across the country, proving that the rebellion in Chechnya was still not over. Afghanistan, on the other hand, with its medieval warlords, had largely gone from people's minds since the destruction of the Taliban in 2002.

I was eager to see something of the state of affairs that we read so much about; this turbulent East, with its bombings and uprisings, its assassinations and jihads.

Jon and I hadn't said a word in over half an hour. A cattle bridge loomed overhead; its underbelly, daubed in vulgar graffiti, was the only entertainment. The road seemed to go on forever. Things weren't promising – in over an hour, nobody had stopped to pick us up. Still, my thoughts were of nothing but utter freedom and eager anticipation. Trucks and coaches rumbled past. Jon suddenly chuckled to himself – he did that often. I knew that despite his silent protests, he felt the same as me. Looking out over the gusty fields to the east, a flock of geese hurriedly worked their way across the sky and I felt a shiver of excitement. We were going to India.

I had promised myself – and Jon – that things would be different. This time I, or we, would make it. The visas had eventually come through. Russia, Iran, Pakistan, they were all there: big, vulgar stamps that took up a page each.

'I'll come to Georgia or Turkey, maybe a bit further, but there's no way I'm going anywhere near Iran,' Jon said, as another lorry sprayed the road with brown sludge. Winfield was an avid traveller, but had the added virtue of common sense as well.

'All right, we'll see.' I thought that once he was on the road, I'd persuade him to forget about his job and come all the way to the Himalayas.

'And anyway, at this rate we won't even get as far as France,' he said with a sardonic smirk, as we plodded along the hard shoulder. It was a Sunday and there wasn't much traffic.

We'd started the journey that morning, waking up from a boozy slumber on someone's couch in a student flat. I remember wincing at the time; it was ten-thirty and we were supposed to be catching a flight from Stansted airport the following morning. We'd banked on hitchhiking down the east coast of Britain that day. Alex, my housemate from university, had offered to drop us off on the dual carriageway somewhere near to Grantham.

'Try not to get yourself on Al Jazeera,' Alex said with a grin. For a second, I imagined a newsreel of us being captured by Islamic militants and paraded on the Qatar news channel. 'You lucky bastards,' he added, evidently jealous. Alex was never averse to a spot of danger and I thought back to the year before, when he and I had hitchhiked home from Cairo, accidentally passing through Iraq in the middle of the war.

'We'll try not to,' I grinned back, before reminding him of our usual arrangement.

'Remember, keep your phone on. If we get in the shit – you'll be the one bailing us out. You know the score, if you don't hear from us within five days after entering anywhere dodgy, then get on the blower to the Foreign Office. We'll keep you posted.'

We waved goodbye to Alex and Jon peered down at the passing trucks as they flew underneath the concrete bridge. I looked into the distance as the road disappeared over the horizon to the south, flanked by English countryside in all its glory.

'Shall we?'

Jon nodded and we started to walk down the slip road. It was an odd way to begin a journey. We were hitchhiking down a motorway to an airport so we could fly back to Eastern Europe, all because I'd had to turn back from there a few weeks before. It was pedantic, but I was adamant we'd pick up the trail properly where I had left it, in Estonia – and Winfield didn't seem to mind.

Cars and lorries flew by, dangerously close, honking their horns indignantly. I remembered how the French police had almost arrested me on a motorway in Champagne for vagrancy and that the best thing to do was to find a service station and wait for a lift there.

After a few miles, we came across a desolate truck stop near to the village of Stretton. It was a bleak, prefabricated outpost, with a miserable old woman who looked like a wartime dinner lady. Inside the tiny café, on plastic white chairs, fat lorry drivers spilled their midriffs over the armrests and fought to understand each other's regional dialects.

This is where it starts, in this little service station, I thought. Looking east, ten thousand miles of road would lead us to India. It seemed an insurmountable distance. It was hard to imagine how this wretched motorway would take us beyond the furthest reaches of Europe and on to the Silk Road. Visions of camel trains and date palms came to mind. Then, a horn blared and quickly faded as it sped past, snapping me quickly back to reality. All of that, of course, was a long way off. First of all, we needed a lift.

Some people think that hitchhiking is dangerous, or mad, or stupid. They might be right, but actually, when you think about it, hitching is no more dangerous than taking a taxi, insomuch as you are accepting a lift from a perfect stranger. In the past, I had hitchhiked all around England, in Southern Africa, Australia and the Middle East, and everywhere I went people had stopped and offered their help – eventually.

Standing at the edge of the car park next to a motorway, keeping an eye on the truck drivers inside, hoping that one would leave soon, it took a while to forget about the embarrassment at being so vulnerable and at the mercy of other people's pity. Hitchhiking, I had long understood, is not for the proud.

Cars passed by at a hundred miles per hour. I sometimes caught a glimpse of the drivers as they shot past. They always seemed to have the same aloof stare, looking intently at the road ahead, even though I know they always saw me. They didn't want the unpleasant feeling of meeting my gaze and then having to experience a pang of guilt afterwards. For them it was better to concentrate on the central reservation, accidentally glancing away as they passed by, deluding themselves into ignorance and inventing an excuse for why they didn't stop.

I was going too fast, there's no way I could have stopped in time . . . probably would have caused an accident or something. There's nowhere to stop, anyway. No room in the car. I'm only going down the road . . . and besides, he's probably a maniac murderer or a thief or a Greenpeace activist . . .

Of course, by the time all this has passed through the motorist's head, the hitchhiker is pleasantly out of view and he can forget all about it. The guilt rarely lasts long, and he is certain *someone else* will pick him up anyway.

Generally, if people give you a lift, they either feel sorry for you or have been in the same situation themselves. I've been picked up by the most unlikely people: a motorist whose car was completely full of furniture, but nevertheless stopped and rearranged it all, and in Australia, a mother who had her three children in the back of the car – at night! And people have driven miles out of their way to take me to my destination.

After ten minutes, a small red Ford Fiesta pulled over in the car park next to where we were loitering and its driver peered out of the window.

'Where are you fellows off to?'

He was about fifty and wore a smart, brown woollen suit. Thin grey hair was combed over a balding scalp and wispy eyebrows jerked erratically from a weathered forehead. His eyes were piercingly blue. He barked out of the window in a regal accent with the air of a university professor: 'Well? Don't just stand there – get in!'

Jon and I looked at each other for a second before rushing to cram our bags into the boot.

'I always pick up hitchhikers,' said the man. 'I was one myself many years ago. So, where are you going?'

'Anywhere so long as it's south. We want to get to Stansted,' said Winfield.

'Where are you going? You look like a pair of tramps, they won't let you in any nightclubs on the Costa del Sol looking like that.'

'Estonia,' I told him. 'Then we're hitching to India.'

'*India*,' he repeated dreamily. Furry white eyebrows twitched up and down in a way that betrayed his admiration.

'Bugger me. Well, I suppose I shall have to take you to Stansted then. You've got a long journey ahead of you.'

We squeezed into the tiny motor, grateful for such a stroke of luck, but at the same time a little suspicious. I looked around the cramped car as we sped off down the motorway. Jon and I were both on the back seat, taking second place to a large pile of brown envelopes and packages sealed roughly with shiny parcel tape. The driver must have noticed me eyeing his cargo.

'Hunter,' he said.

'Excuse me?' Jon replied.

'My name is Rogers – Hunter Rogers. And who are you two?'

We introduced ourselves to the eccentric driver. I could see that Winfield was as intrigued as I was. Here was this perfect aristocrat in a three-piece tweed outfit reduced to driving a clapped-out Ford Fiesta filled with unmarked packages.

'Went across Asia myself in the sixties. A lot safer then, though, of course.' He pondered ruefully before continuing, 'Never been to Moscow, though. I tell you what. In exchange for me taking you to the airport, you must send me a postcard when you get there.'

'Fair enough,' said Jon. 'What would you like? Red Square? The Kremlin?'

'No,' Hunter bellowed, raising a finger like an ancient philosopher. 'I want that beastly Lenin's corpse.'

Jon looked at me from the corner of his eye and flashed a smile. 'Certainly.'

About halfway down the motorway, at another dismal truck stop, Hunter insisted on buying us 'high tea'. Surrounded by hairy lorry drivers in dirty white vests reading crumpled copies of the *News of the World*, we sipped on polystyrene cups full of a grey, milky brew. Hunter barely seemed to notice them. I couldn't help but wonder what misfortune had befallen this relic of a bygone age.

'I used to travel a lot in my youth. All over,' Hunter said thoughtfully. He sat like a proud old artist and I tried to imagine him as a young man exploring the world; sketching, seducing, thinking. He was quintessentially English, but even a stiff upper lip couldn't quite disguise his melancholy.

'And now I drive around delivering parcels. That's what happens in life, you'll find out one day.' It was a depressing thought.

We arrived at the airport at dusk. Hunter had driven fifty miles out of his way and despite evidently being quite odd, his generosity went a long way in reminding me of the joy of hitch-hiking. We took our intriguing driver's address and promised him his picture postcard of Lenin's stuffed cadaver.

Part 2

Part 2

3

Back on the Road

Tallinn. Four days of drinking, travelling and catching the tail-end of a summer that was almost over – but I was back where I left off.

The beach in Pirita was deserted this time around. In summer, I'd been full of hope and excitement and the kind of enthusiasm that comes with arriving at a place with so many expectations. I remembered how, in July, the sea had been invitingly warm and the soft sands host to a throng of the young and beautiful. But now the sea took on a darker, more sinister appearance and a cold bluster ran through the tall pines that lined the promenade. The hordes of Baltic partygoers had finished their season of hedonism and gone home, back to the forests and villages. The riotous summertime atmosphere was replaced by a strange feeling of emptiness and disappointment. Almost like the sense of lonely depression that goes hand in hand with a lingering hangover.

'I think it's time we get on with this,' said Jon.

Bleary eyed, we took a bus to the outskirts of the city and hitched eastwards towards the Russian border.

The countryside closed in as our road travelled deeper into the Baltic hinterland. A twenty-two-year-old Arthur Conolly also passed along this road in the month of September, making covert notes on the state of the Russian army and the lay of the land as he, too, vagabonded his way to India in 1829. I imagined how much had changed. At least the landscape would have been familiar to my Victorian hero.

'I wonder if he started growing his beard before the trip?' said Jon, as I told him the story and showed him a picture of the little-known explorer. 'It seems pretty good for a bloke our age.' The road was narrow and both sides were enclosed in deep pine forests, impenetrable to all but the wolves and bears that inhabited their black depths. There were a few villages *en route* with names like Koogu and Loobu, but the afternoon sun wasn't bright enough to make them distinguishable from the surrounding woodland.

Born in 1807, Arthur Conolly had a tumultuous childhood and then was orphaned when he was twelve. After schooling at Rugby, he set sail for India at the tender age of sixteen. A boy amongst men, he was sent to join the Bengal Light Infantry. Without any parental guidance, the young Conolly – suddenly thrown into the alien world of Calcutta – adopted the army as his new family, and threw himself into service wholeheartedly. After a strict boarding school education it must have been liberating to bear the respect and honour of a British Officer's rank abroad. Seasons of polo, field exercises and society balls would intertwine with frequent long marches into the hills, patrolling the plantations and keeping order amongst the native tribes.

Like many others, the experience of life as a young officer on the plains of India instilled in him a taste for adventure, but Conolly wasn't satisfied with mere regimental duty, he wanted more. The eager soldier yearned to make a name for himself amongst his fellow officers and superiors through exploration, and, with little to lose, he decided to aim high. His plan was simple: to go where few Europeans had ever been and attempt to chart the vast no-man's-land between British India and the age-old foe – Russia.

In those days, large parts of the Indian subcontinent were ruled by the British East India Company. Not by Britain itself, but a commercial enterprise with its own civil service and army, staffed by British expatriates and served by native contingents. It was a profitable business that enticed thousands of young British men to leave their homes and seek their fortunes in the East. But in the 1820s, there were still vast tracts of land, especially in the northern regions of India – now Pakistan, Kashmir, Nepal and Tibet – that remained completely uncharted by Europeans.

Central Asia was at that time totally unexplored and remained as a wild, neutral buffer zone between the East India Company and Tsarist Russia. In fact, the impending fear that the Imperial Empire was encroaching, year by year, into what was seen as the British sphere of influence worried many, including the patriotic Conolly.

During a spell of home leave in 1829, the young Irishman determined to explore the hinterlands and while he was at it, indulge in a spot of spying on behalf of his chiefs. He knew that it would be his best chance of securing a reputation and future promotion. Armed with little more than his natural charm and splendid whiskers, he set off alone across Europe towards Moscow, where his adventure would begin in earnest. Travelling by horse, Conolly rode south on almost exactly the same route that I planned to take with Jon.

In the early nineteenth century, the two nations of Britain and Russia were technically allies, after the Napoleonic wars had seen France defeated and Bonaparte die in exile nine years before Conolly set off. But it was an uneasy truce. Nevertheless, Conolly was treated well by the Russian aristocracy and was allowed to pass freely through the Imperial domain, where he made covert notes on the state of his host's army.

He observed their equipment, tactics and morale and was impressed by their stoic hardiness and resilience to cold weather. It was an important task – after all, these were the troops that he thought would be sent over the mountains into India when the time came, and someone needed to keep an eye on them.

Conolly reached the Caucasus and left the relative safety of Europe to enter the wilds of Circassia. With only a small band of Cossacks as an escort, he made more notes on the local tribes before crossing into Persia. His plan had been to reach Khiva across the Karakum desert, but this was thwarted when the caravan he was travelling in was threatened by bandits. Undeterred, he traversed Persia and in disguise, under the name of 'Khan Ali' – a clever play on his name – he became the first non-Muslim to enter the holy shrine of Ali Reza at Mashad.

Continuing east, Conolly passed through Afghanistan and over the Bolan Pass, so that on 14 January 1831, he finally crossed the Indus into British India, just over a year after he had departed Dover. He wasn't yet twenty-four years old. At regimental level, he was hailed as a hero and acclaimed as the triumphant adventurer who had mapped the potential Russian invasion route. He was subsequently promoted and tasked with future secret missions across Central Asia, where he spent months at a time negotiating deals with fierce tribes and winning them over to the side of Britain.

But it is sad to say his success was short-lived. Only eleven years after his epic overland journey, Conolly was sent on a mission that would cost him his life. Charged with a task to rescue a brother officer, Colonel Stoddard, who had been imprisoned by the Emir of Bukhara, Conolly found himself thrown into the same dungeon almost immediately on entering the famed city. The Emir had the pair beheaded in the central square in June 1842, as a warning to other potential 'spies'. Despite his ill-fated end, Conolly will forever embody the spirit of the Great Game, where hundreds of young men, barely out of their teens, risked everything for the sake of adventure and glory.

By the time we reached the outskirts of the city of Narva, in Estonia, it was already dark and we hadn't eaten in hours. Thanking the driver, we walked through the suburbs of the murky town towards the river, a bridge over which forms the border with Russia.

'There's no lights on there,' Winfield said, pointing to the bridge.

He was right, the border post was clearly closed for the night, and a big gate that blocked the entrance to the bridge confirmed our suspicions.

'We'll have to sleep this side tonight.'

'Well, the good news is there won't be any more travelling today. I'm starving, let's find something to eat.'

What we found was our first introduction to borscht, a kind of beetroot soup. We later discovered that it varies depending on where you get it, and even now I can't think of the Baltics or Russia without pining for a taste of it.

'It's not bad at all,' said Jon, slurping the purple liquid from a chipped bowl, as a stray dog limped past the door.

I looked out of the café window and took stock of our surroundings. By night, the town looked like the worst kind of Soviet backdrop. Monstrous chimneys and industrial plants daubed the skyline. Drab tower blocks built to house the masses filled most of the city. Its only redeeming feature, from what I could tell, was the fortress that overlooked the great Narva River and once kept the menacing Russian armies at bay.

I peered through the darkness at the silhouetted castle, which was as ancient as it looked. It was founded in the thirteenth century, when the Danish kings ruled the country. But before the great grandchildren of the Vikings had settled here, the town was a mere village surrounded by deep forests. Since then, it has grown to become Estonia's third largest city.

As we plodded along the bleak streets, Narva appeared an eerie place. We walked the poorly lit avenues attempting to negotiate broken pavements and unpredictable potholes. Filthy concrete towers loomed menacingly on both sides and little of its glorious history remained. Gone were the magical wooden Danish fortresses or baroque Swedish mansions, and thanks to German bombs, even the might of Imperial Russian architecture had almost vanished. Only the castle remained. Cars that hadn't been driven in years rotted by the wayside, missing wheels and windows. Gangs of drunks shouted obscenities as we passed by hurriedly in search of somewhere to stay.

'Well,' said Jon. 'Any ideas for accommodation?'

'Not really. I don't fancy the look of these grimy flats, though. Did you bring the guidebook?'

'No. I think I left it in that bloke's car on the way to the airport.'

'You idiot!' I snapped.

'Chill out, mate. Let's head back to the bridge,' said Jon, calm as you like. 'We can sleep rough somewhere, it'll be an adventure. That's what you wanted, isn't it? And that way we can get up early in the morning and cross the border as soon as it opens. I'm not that keen on staying in this dive either.'

'Fine. Do you still have that whisky?'

'Got plenty,' said Jon, patting the side of his rucksack with a conspiratorial smirk.

'Good, I think we're gonna need it.'

We retraced our steps through the town, guided by the gentle rumblings of the Narva River. Behind a three-storey building, the silhouette of the fortress came into view. The square outline of the Hermann tower dominated the banks of the river. It rose squarely out of the cliff face on the west bank, with a huge buttress supporting the immense walls. On the western wall, the white tower rose majestically above the rest of the feature and had a distinctive Teutonic flavour. It reminded me of Bavaria.

Despite being dark, there was a bright full moon that illuminated the tower and guided us around the walls to its base on the southern side. The river glistened benignly in the moonlight. I suggested that we climb down the grassy mound and inspect a disused building in the waste ground at the bottom of the hill. From our vantage point, it looked like an ideal place to squat for the night. The stone building was quite big and the weed-infested garden had a high brick wall around it. Ideal lodgings, I thought.

'Yeah, looks okay, we shouldn't be disturbed down there,' said Jon, who led the way across the pasture and through a bramble-stricken paddock. We pushed through some broken wooden panels that served as the only entry point, as the wall looked too precarious to scale in the dark. Entering the grounds silently, we took a look around. It looked like it used to be a small factory, or a mill perhaps. Rusting machinery littered the courtyard and piles of debris cluttered the path to the building itself.

The wrought-iron door wouldn't budge and so I climbed onto a window ledge. The glass itself had long been smashed through, but razor-edged shards pointed viciously from the corners, and I carefully manoeuvred myself through the small hole. Despite my best efforts, I managed to get a trouser leg caught on one of the shards, and in an attempt to free myself, plunged helplessly through the hole into the room on the far side; crashing noisily into a pile of what I guessed by the tremendous smell to be fox excrement. I was unhurt, but to my dismay, found that Jon had succeeded in forcing open the door and stood chuckling in the shadows.

'That bloody stinks. I'm not sleeping anywhere near you tonight.'

In the darkness, I could make out that the room was full of rubble, like the courtyard outside. Broken bricks, pottery and planks of charred wood lay scattered about the floor. I looked down and saw that there were syringe needles lying only centimetres from where I had fallen. Suddenly from the bowels of another room there was a deep groaning noise. Both of us froze and looked at each other. The awful clatter of my landing and resultant profanities must have caused a racket, because whoever the current occupant of this den was, they were now awake. A cough, and then footsteps grew nearer. After a moment of terrifying hesitation, Jon and I quickly scarpered out of the door, back through the garden, over the wall and dashed across the wasteland towards the castle and its safety.

'It's a bloody crack den. Don't even think of having any more ideas like that again,' Jon growled angrily. 'And you still stink of fox shit.'

Having roughed it all summer, I should have known better. It's always best to sleep high on a vantage point, rather than hide away in a crumbling hut or lowly crevice, where the risk of drunken louts stumbling on you is increased tenfold. As it happened, the parks here seemed to be more popular with the native alcoholics than anywhere I had vagabonded before, and the moat was busy with every kind of illicit activity you could imagine. A car spun across the grass down below and three shady characters got out, then began pointing to the mill. We quickly hid behind a bush, but couldn't understand what they were saying. Under the cover of a rough hedge, we climbed back up the grassy *motte* to the shadows of the castle walls.

'There's nothing for it. We'll have to sleep here. That was a close call.'

We agreed that we were better off in the open air, where in the event of being mobbed, we could escape more easily. At the top of the bank, underneath the base of the castle walls, it was high enough to overlook the riverside path and far enough away from the pimps and gangs of youths who were dealing drugs and setting fire to oil drums.

'No one can see us here, let's crack open the whisky,' I suggested, to make up for my poor judgement about the mill.

With that, Jon produced a bottle of single malt and we drank a good half of it from the comfort of our sleeping bags and hoped that it wouldn't rain. All through the night I had visions of packs of wild dogs, made all the more real by the nightmarish howls that emanated from the dark streets below. An unnatural siren sounded intermittently from across the river, inside the bowels of the Ivangorod fortress, where I imagined Soviet soldiers in long greatcoats and Cossack fur hats patrolling its walls. But those days were long gone. Or were they? A search-light flickered from a tower, its beam bouncing off the black rapids whirling in the river below. I didn't sleep a great deal that night. Winfield, on the other hand, didn't flinch once and snored like a bear.

In the morning, we woke before daybreak so as not to be accosted by the early morning drunks. I was glad to discover that we hadn't been relieved of our belongings or savaged by wild animals – although I still smelled like one. I peeled myself reluctantly out of the damp sleeping bag and stuffed it deep into my rucksack, still yawning. Jon did the same and we plodded in semi-consciousness towards the bridge that spanned the river. The gate was open and we were the first to cross that day. After getting stamped out of Estonia and walking through a hundred metres of no-man's-land, a wiry Russian official eyed us suspiciously and barked something incomprehensible. We presented our visas, smiled and hailed an enthusiastic '*Dobraye utra*' – 'Good morning!' He warmed just enough to stamp our passports with a militant thump and waved for us to move on.

'Cheery bunch, the Russians,' Jon smirked, as he wrapped the collar of his fleece tight around his neck to keep away the early morning chill.

4

Venice of the North

Russia ... I could hardly believe I was there! For someone born towards the end of the Cold War, that two-syllable word was highly charged. As I trudged across the border, thoughts of Stalin, the Berlin Wall, and nuclear missiles in a slow procession across Red Square filled my mind. The grey and grimy apartment blocks along the horizon hinted at a mood of – what? Something too evasive to be squared in a hurry. Churchill famously described the place as 'a riddle wrapped in a mystery inside an enigma'.

The road that led out of the town was cracked. Jon looked rough and squinted through sleep-filled eyes. I sensed his feeling of trepidation at having entered the Federation. The early morning light gradually filtered over the horizon and the wild fields had a golden sheen. The fortress of Ivangorod that had made menacing sounds the night before was veiled behind a line of tall birch trees, which appeared from afar to be thin giants gazing nonchalantly across the horizon. We walked some distance to a widening in the road, which we hoped would entice drivers going to St Petersburg to pull over and offer us a lift.

An elderly man with a set of deep wrinkles, and wearing a full-length, brown woollen overcoat, stood hunched over a scruffy leather carry-all bag, apparently waiting for a bus. Jon and I began to take turns standing at the side of the road, thumbs facing upwards, smiling expectantly as the occasional rusty car rattled on by. From the look on their oblivious faces, these drivers had none of the guilt – or even the interest – of their western European counterparts. A sullen grimace could be seen fleetingly as they passed on by without so much as an acknowledgement.

The old man watched our vain attempts at getting attention and I thought I could make out a smirk amongst his ancient furrows. Soon enough, a yellow bus that reminded me of the kind used by American schoolchildren arrived and the old man stepped on, grasping the handrail with deliberate precision. Jon ran up to the open door and addressed the driver in his best Russian.

'*Privyet!* We don't have any roubles.' The driver scowled through mousy whiskers, as he inspected the tramp before him.

'Will you take dollars?' Jon implored, producing a few weathered bills. The driver, either not understanding, or more likely, not caring, was impatient and waved us off with an aggressive '*Nyet*', no. The bus groaned off, leaving a cloud of unsettled dust in its wake, as Jon hurled profanities at its diminishing shape.

An hour passed, and then another. We walked a little further in search of a better stopping place, but as we left the edge of the town and entered the wooded countryside, it became evident that there wasn't anywhere better. All was quiet. In the distance behind us, the haunting shape of Narva Castle could be seen jutting into the grey sky. Although it was cold, there was no frost yet and murky puddles of water were a warning to the pedestrian of the cavernous holes underfoot. In a matter of weeks, these same puddles would be frozen solid with the onset of the bitter northern winter.

Jon picked up a small stone and threw it across the road into one such pool, creating a disruptive splash. From a nearby birch tree, a dove fluttered off in disgust. It was one of those moments that I felt a brooding sense of responsibility and, I suppose, guilt, for convincing Jon to join my venture.

'We'll get something soon,' I proffered, attempting to reassure him – since it had been my idea to hitchhike in the first place, and in all likelihood, he was wishing that he had never come along.

At last a lorry pulled over. I was relieved. It seemed old and its front bumper looked like it had been the cause of death for innumerable wild animals, guessing by the number of dents in it. There was a fracture in the windscreen and the trailer was covered in a dusty green tarpaulin that gave away no indication of its cargo. The driver, a man in his thirties, with piercing green eyes and a double chin, shouted from the window, '*Privyet!*'

We hailed him with an enthusiastic '*Kak dela?*' – how are you? – and jumped in.

'Peter?' he asked, nodding his head expectantly as Jon slammed the door shut.

'Lev,' I replied. He frowned and looked vaguely confused. '*Nyet* . . . Peter?' he said, this time with emphasis on the name.

'*Minya zavoot* Lev,' I introduced myself formally. He remained baffled and shook his head. Maybe he was confused by my Slavic-sounding name.

Perhaps he was a bit simple, or he hadn't understood my abysmal Russian.

'Lev,' I tried again, pointing at myself. 'Jon,' I jabbed Winfield in the chest, who was squashed next to the window and trying to avoid being dragged into the monotonous conversation. The driver tutted and repeated slowly, 'Peters–burg . . . Peter?'

All became clear. 'Ah, um, yes,' I replied, suddenly realising my mistake. I felt momentarily embarrassed, but Jon chuckled away unconcerned. We set off. The pitted road passed forests and immense fields of maize and the occasional village. Despite the jolting ride, I dozed fitfully most of the way.

We arrived in the cold dullness of late morning and thanked our driver (whose name was Boris), apologetically handing him the last of our Estonian kroonis as a gift. The outskirts of St Petersburg were screened by a low haze that seemed to envelop the buildings in a perpetual shade of grey.

It could simply be hindsight, but there must be some truth in my memory of everything in Russia being grey. The gravel-coloured trees that lined the boulevards only added to the gloom of Russian urban sprawl. Behind the veil of an occasional park or well-kept garden, the concrete facades were cracked and discoloured. Here and there, between faceless apartment blocks, the architecture of a former glory intruded with a sad grace, like chipped antiques thrown into a pile at a jumble sale.

We were both exhausted after being rattled over every pothole on the road from Narva and were glad of the walk up the main street of Nevsky Prospekt. Neither of us knew where we were going and we contemplated getting a cab. I immediately noticed how every car in the city would offer its services as a taxi. The Russians were clearly proud of their ability to drive and moreover, to own a vehicle, and would gladly pick up anyone bold enough to poke a hand into the busy street. We decided to walk, having sat still for most of the morning, and shook our heads at the soliciting motorists, then strolled slowly under the weight of our rucksacks towards the city centre.

Our Russian was limited to a few words, and our understanding of the strange, angular Cyrillic script non-existent. I was dreaming the traveller's arrogant dream, of understanding things by ignorant distant observation and brief glances. What I knew

44

of Russia was from studying its violent, chaotic and often unfathomable history. I knew next to nothing of its present. Therefore, Russia interpreted itself to me only in clichés – fur hats, uniformed soldiers, hard-faced peasants and beautiful women.

The old capital of the Russian Empire, known as Peter, has had a short but turbulent past. The grandeur of the old town emerged out of the mist and history seemed to come alive.

The swirling waters of the Neva crashed around the fortress of Peter and Paul. You could almost hear the whips of Peter the Great's henchmen against the cold skin of his army of serfs and prisoners who built the city that was to become the Imperial capital for one hundred and eighty-six years. Despite the majesty of its flanking buildings, Nevsky Prospekt was fairly dismal in September. We passed the Church of the Savior on Spilled Blood, the Kazan Cathedral and the Winter Palace in rapid succession, as we stomped about in search of somewhere to stay.

'Let's leave off with sightseeing until tomorrow, shall we? It isn't going anywhere.'

I agreed with Winfield's suggestion and upon reaching the river, we turned back and went in search of the 'St Petersburg Hostel International'. We eventually found it down a side street and though it was expensive at fifteen Euros, neither of us wanted to spend another night sleeping rough. Especially not in the confines of a city where we would likely be arrested as vagrants by the police, who had already asked to see our passports three times within the hour. A sour-faced man, who reminded me of a prison guard, gave us bunk-beds in a dormitory room that was half-empty. There was no one else in the room as we dumped our bags on two free beds.

'Looks like you've got a girl on top.'

Jon nodded at the bunk above me, and I looked around at the possessions scattered liberally about the place. There was a travel towel folded neatly on the end of the bed, presumably to ward away anyone contemplating usurping this prize spot in the corner of the room, and nearby a black sports bra hung freely from the window sill, held in place by the weight of a fat guidebook.

I looked around the room curiously; inquisitiveness gets the better of me in a dormitory. In such communal surroundings, it is difficult not to have a little peek at who is sleeping only a couple of feet away.

'The rucksack always gives away the type of traveller.' Jon motioned towards a new, brightly coloured camping bag.

'This belongs to a novice,' he continued. 'You can tell. No proper traveller worth his salt would ever be seen with something like this.'

'I mean take this one for example.' Near to the open door, he patted a prehistoric, green canvas daypack leaning solidly against the bunk bed, which looked like it had more patches than original material. 'Now that belongs to a *long hair.*'

'*Long hair?*'

'Yes, a long hair. A hippy. A vagabond. A true veteran hobo.'

'And this is almost certainly a Yank.' Jon pointed at another rather large, blue rucksack, with a handkerchief tied around the handle.

'How do you know that?' I asked, intrigued.

'Because it has a Canadian flag stitched on it,' Jon smiled. 'All the Americans do it . . . Stops awkward questions and keeps the Bush-bashers at bay.'

Dinner was a buffet and we ate a meagre helping of cold beetroot soup and cuts of salami, under the watchful eye of the old babushka that ran the kitchen, keen to stop us from overindulging. In fact, a lot of people seemed to stare at us – especially out in the street. We put it down to looking too Western, although I suspect it may have been the trampish parka jackets that caused a stir. We agreed that it would be a good idea to try and blend in as best as possible, so that we wouldn't present an obvious target for police inquisitiveness and subsequent 'fines'.

Reluctantly, away went our warm walking fleeces and cargo trousers, in exchange for cheap, stonewashed jeans and fake leather jackets from the local market. It seemed to do the trick. With a smattering of Russian and a stern look we made a fine Slavic pair. To consolidate our position as clandestine natives, we attempted the local way of shopping by way of slamming the desired goods on the shop counter without a word of acknowledgement. It seemed to meet with success, as from now on we paid the local rate, rather than the exorbitant prices reserved for tourists.

The next day we duly observed the custom of registering at the local police station. We were supposed to do this at every town and city visited within forty-eight hours of arrival. We'd been warned that failure to do so may result in fines and arrest, or even deportation. So, armed with every manner of documentation, we sought out the municipal police station and met a sinister-looking official in a very bare office. Paint was peeling away from breeze-block walls, and in the corner a solitary bookshelf was adorned with a Russian flag. He was about fifty years old and the weathered, swarthy face showed that he was used to sunnier climes. Perhaps he was from the Transcaucasus. His neat, grey moustache belied a distinctly rough appearance. The policeman seemed surprised to see us looking as we did, but after inspecting our passports and finding that we were English, he greeted us with a broad smile and lit a cigarette.

'Hallo, Englishmen. Greetings to Russia. Not so many tourist these days. Why then you travel?' he asked as he blew a steady stream of smoke that gradually dissipated into a yellow haze.

'We hope to see the sights of Russia,' I declared.

'So you stay only in Peter?'

'No, we want to visit many places.'

'No? Hmmm. Well then you must tell me where you go.'

'We want to travel to Moscow and then south, perhaps to Volgograd.' Not wanting to solicit suspicion by indicating the full extent of our plans.

'No. This not possible,' barked our man. 'You cannot go south. It is now forbidden for tourists.'

'Why's that?' I was genuinely surprised by his tone.

'Chechens. Muslims. Very bad peoples, they come and kill many peoples in our cities in south.' The policeman took on a more solemn appearance and sounded serious. There was a long pause as he stared at us.

'Good advice. We'll stick to Moscow then,' I lied, not wanting to endanger our journey.

'Yes. It is best.'

He relieved us of twenty-five Euros for the 'registration' and his sage advice, and put the cash immediately into his breast pocket. As we left, fuming at having been robbed, he called after us, grinning once again.

'Hey, Englishmen. Be careful in Moscow . . . Very bad police.'

With that we decided not to bother registering again. We reckoned that paying the forfeiture bribe would be cheaper than paying the official rates.

Back on Nevsky, we visited one of St Petersburg's more sobering experiences. Distastefully located next door to the Vodka museum is the Leningrad siege museum, and although small, it

48

was stuffed with artefacts from the infamous battle. During the Second World War, the city, then called Leningrad, was besieged by Nazi Germany and their Finnish allies. It lasted from September 1941 until January 1944 – an incredible 872 days. The siege was the longest and most destructive of major cities in modern history. Over a million civilians died, mainly from starvation. Only a small number escaped or were evacuated, so that for a while the city was almost wholly depopulated.

The economic destruction and human losses on both sides exceeded those of the battle of Stalingrad, the battle of Moscow, or indeed the atomic bombings in Japan. One cemetery alone holds the remains of half a million civilians from the siege.

One of the museum's cabinets had a display of items that were described as food during the harrowing winter of 1941–42; the only rations available to citizens were small blocks of 'bread', which was actually sixty-per-cent sawdust. Even this was only given to those defending the city, with none for women and children. Although the Soviet relief effort did attempt to provide food kiosks, there was no transport, so those in the suburbs would have to walk several kilometres into the centre, in temperatures that fell below minus thirty degrees Celsius. Thousands perished every day and bodies were left to freeze in the streets.

It wasn't long before almost the entire animal population had been eaten. The city's zoo was raided. Household pets came next. Children were sent out to catch rats and crows. Wallpaper paste was stripped from the walls and boiled together with leather thongs to make a kind of foul soup. Eventually and probably inevitably, cannibalism prevailed. Corpses from the streets were collected by the starving families and there were reports of murder. Thousands probably succumbed to the temptation, and the practice was only halted when a special police unit was established to combat the desperate act.

In January 1944, the Nazi siege fell when the Red Army broke through the German line and the blockade was lifted. The city was awarded the Order of Lenin and was the first to receive the new Russian title of Hero City for its dogged resistance.

As we sat in the little café next door pondering the scale of the calamity, an old lady brought us the cake we had asked for. It was hard and brown and looked very much like it was made of sawdust. We ate it regardless.

Outside, the temperature had dropped considerably. We spent a couple of days exploring the city and admiring the omnipresent Neva, which despite the conditions, had barely begun to ice over. Jon suggested that we visit one of the city's *banyas* or public baths to warm up. I'd heard of Swedish saunas and Turkish *hamams*, but never of a Russian banya, but Jon assured me that they were highly recommended.

'I met a Russian chap once in Brixton, he was always complaining that we didn't have public baths in London. They're a bit like a Turkish hamam, he said, but less sordid,' added Winfield, as his breath turned to an icy vapour.

We found one near to the hostel, up a dark alleyway with no signs to indicate its presence. It was only after much gesticulating and writing the word in Russian on the back of a cigarette packet that a local showed us the way – clearly this one was for the locals, as the entrance was nothing more than a seedy side door. It looked more like a brothel.

'This is the place for us,' said Jon with a conspiratorial wink, as we made our way down a dingy staircase. Inside we paid the thirty-rouble entry fee and were given towels and shown to the communal area. We immediately disrobed in accordance with the groups of fat, hairy men who did not pay us the least bit of attention. We pretended to know what we were doing, but any thoughts of silently fitting in went out of the window when I slipped on a wet tile and landed with a loud and painful slap on my backside.

Winfield bent double laughing, but the Russians simply looked on without so much as a little chuckle. Even this barely registered as humorous. I thought of how different it would have been in England – I imagined roars of laughter, or at the very least a suppressed smirk, before shows of assistance – but here nothing.

I gathered my dignity and following the lead of another newcomer, we dipped ourselves in each of the small pools. The first was utterly and spine-chillingly cold and it was accepted that ten seconds was more than enough, so feeling extremely inadequate, we plunged happily into the next, which although supposed to be only lukewarm, felt like a pool of lava after the iciness of the last one. Once the body had gradually recovered and sensed the true temperature, we quickly accompanied our unsuspecting guide into the next, which was ragingly hot. Here we were expected to endure the scolding molten lava for an unbearable five minutes before rushing brazenly into the final pool, which for masochism's sake was colder than the first.

Gladly we pulled ourselves out and made a beeline for the sauna. It was scorching, and just as we were trying to sit down without touching our naked backs against the sizzling wooden bench, the fat man sitting in front of me, with a head the size of a melon, thrust a handful of twigs into my hand and grunted expectantly. I looked at Winfield, who merely shrugged. Melon-head was clearly impatient, as he turned around and took the twigs back out of my hand and began thrashing the poor soul next to him. With a jut of his chin and a gesture that said something along the lines of 'Get it now?' he handed me the birch once again and flexed his enormous neck in preparation. Winfield shrugged again and I thought it only polite to oblige.

The sauna was the hottest I have ever had, and after another plunge in the cold pool, we left this masochist's delight. Too exhausted by the rigours of the bath to endure a night on the town, we slept like babies that night.

It was time to move on and the next day we risked a ticketless ride on the overnight train bound for Moscow. It was dark, so we saw little but the occasional faded street light that indicated that we were rattling slowly through the small towns and high pine forests that dotted the North Russian steppe. True blackness suggested high pine forests; a glimmer of luminosity perhaps the moon's midnight reflection off a cold lake. Somewhere in the darkness was the city of Tver straddling the Volga river. We settled down for the night in the woollen sheets of the cozy bunk, where I dreamed of borscht, cardboard biscuits and birch whips.

5

Urban Wanderings

Leningradsky station appeared out of the shadows just before first light. The capital had not yet roused and so after getting off the train, we walked through the deserted streets in search of a hostel. Imposing Stalinist tower blocks formed monstrous barricades at every turn. Moscow has none of the European splendour of St Petersburg, but it has a baser charm. The smell and feel of raw humanity was everywhere. This was a city to touch rather than think about.

'Look, there should be something on here.' Jon was clearly intent on finding somewhere to stay as a matter of priority, as he produced a page torn from a guidebook with the address of a cheap hotel, in a suburb a couple of kilometres from the centre.

'Perfect.' We walked on as the faint sun diffused a kind of half-light across the greyness. The only people awake were the street sweepers. Decrepit men and women, easterners mainly by their Mongol looks, and armed with brooms home-made out of straw, swept the leaves in utter futility as they fell from the trees.

'At least they're working,' muttered Jon, flicking his head in the direction of one poor wretch.

Theirs was the unfortunate lot of sweeping the same spot of clean pavement over and again in perpetuity. Turning the corner, into what reminded me of a rough south London estate, we arrived at our destination – the Hotel Central – to find the not-so-central hotel locked up.

'*Privyet?*' We banged noisily on the gates, but no one was awake. Nearby was a tiny spot of green; a children's playground occupied the space between two identical apartments and we sat down expectantly in the morning chill. A mangy dog scavenged fruitlessly, the sweepers having deprived this forsaken creature of its meagre rations.

For the first time in a while, I began to think of home. Not in a homesick way, but actually quite the opposite. The journey had only just begun and I felt that sense of spine-tingling exhilaration at the sheer fun of being in an unknown place. Home to me was irrelevant, it was the here and now that mattered. It's not that I didn't miss my family, of course I did. But the physical sense of place relating to one house or home was to me anathema. Domesticity, relationships, home life appalled me.

I'd watched friends with potential, good guys who could have gone far, sucked into the recesses of a stable life. I thought back to when I was about sixteen – around the time I got that letter – when I first decided that I wanted to make a life on the road, and I vowed to myself that I wouldn't settle down before the age of thirty, no matter how special a woman I met. Pulling my coat tightly around my neck, I broke the sombre silence.

'It's quite an exciting place to be, isn't it?'

'What, this park?' frowned Jon, clearly annoyed at finding himself homeless yet again.

'No ... Moscow, Russia. In fact, being away from England generally.'

'Yes, I suppose. You know me – always up for a trip.'

'But this is more than a trip. This is real travelling. This is what it's all about. Young, free and poor. We're like the wandering hermits. Even here, in this park, in this freezing bloody cold, I feel so incredibly free. We're men of the road, we can do whatever we want to, go anywhere ...'

'I saw that my life was a vast, empty page and I could do anything I wanted,' said Jon.

'Who's that?'

'Jack Kerouac,' said Jon. 'He took a lot of drugs.'

I checked my starry-eyed mutterings. Jon smiled sympathetically and offered a cigarette. I only smoked on rare occasions of boredom and sometimes when drunk. This time I was neither, in fact I was soberly content, but I accepted nonetheless, feeling it fitted in with my present philosophical mood. As I took a drag on the cheap Russian tobacco, I stroked the formative whisperings of a beard and carried on, 'I think I could go on forever. Travelling, I mean. Who was it? Someone in the Bible – or was it a Greek? – condemned to wander the earth forever. Well, it wasn't such a bad punishment. I mean there's so much to see and so many people to meet.'

'What about settling down? Getting married?'

'Perhaps one day. I'd rather not think about it just yet.'

'I agree, about the marriage bit, anyway' nodded Jon, contentedly puffing out a stream of blueish smoke, which dissipated with a gentle breeze in the direction of a plastic rocking horse that had something strangely apocalyptic about it.

'Far too many pretty girls to meet first,' he smiled.

From behind a wall, a door clanked disturbing the stillness and a pair of crows fluttered away, croaking noisily as if to express their severe displeasure at having been roused. A toothless old woman wielding a broom peered curiously out of the gate at us.

'Do you have any rooms?' asked Jon in slow, deliberate pidgin English.

'*Nyet,*' growled the miserable geriatric, waving her hand dismissively. It was followed by a fast, incomprehensible drawl and a rude closing of the gate. A scruffy dog barked as if to reiterate the old woman's resolve.

We took our leave from the park and carried on despondently, until eventually finding a grubby hostel on Mira Prospekt in an incongruously wealthy suburb. It was described in the page of the guidebook as 'dirty, with rude staff and bad borscht'. It would have to do. So far Moscow had met with my expectations, but I was surprised at it being far more affluent than I had previously imagined. Of course, the city contained its fair share of stereotypes: fake-leather-clad proletariat and wailing babushkas; belligerent policemen dressed in navy blue uniforms and peaked caps prowling the corners; and peroxide-blonde women with big hair looking like they belonged to a music video from the nineteen-eighties, strutting about with undisguised contempt. Yet, despite these theatrical typecasts, there was evidence of the much talked-about 'new Russia' in abundance.

BMWs and Mercedes seemed to be found parked on every street. Attractive model types dressed in designer clothes and improbably tall heels were talking into their mobiles. Shops advertised expensive laptops. Jon read aloud from the guidebook, 'It has the most billionaires and the most expensive cups of coffee ... Moscow is the most expensive city on earth and, according to one poll, it is also the most unfriendly.' So far, it's accurate. Churchill was right – Russia is an enigma.

After settling down to some accurately described borscht, we took a wander to Red Square, almost like homing pigeons, to satisfy a deep longing to see the Kremlin and the picturesque Saint Basil's Cathedral. It was grey and overcast, but it only seemed to enhance the scene and reinforce childhood fantasies formed from grainy news footage. So far, our disguises had proved a success, and the only time we met with any problem was outside of Red Square, when we were imprudent enough to be speaking English within earshot of a policeman.

'Tourists?' the young man in uniform asked in a shifty manner, his small beady eyes scanning the crowds. '*Da*,' we replied in unison.

'Show me your passports.' I looked at the small individual, whose immense peaked cap, harking back to the days of the Red Army, seemed to topple its wearer.

'Why have you not registered?' He barked, thumbing through our documents.

It was a fair question, but there was something not quite right about his manner. He seemed edgy, almost nervous.

'You need to pay me two hundred roubles each.' He continued glancing around and over his shoulder with his palm outstretched.

Jon looked at me and raised his eyebrows. I thought we may as well test the water here. The words of the official in St Petersburg rang in my head, '... very bad policemen in Moscow.'

'Listen, we registered in St Petersburg. We didn't realise we had to do it here,' I said.

I thought to myself, well I'd better stick to my guns now. I stuck out my chest and adopted my best grimace. 'Show me your badge,' I demanded. The policeman seemed taken aback and looked around, shiftier than before.

'*Kak vas zavoot?*' What is your name? I repeated deliberately.

He appeared dumbstruck and began mumbling, less forcefully this time. 'You must pay the fine. OK, one hundred then.'

I took out a pen and notepad. 'Your name, and badge number.' He took a step backwards as I tried to decipher the Cyrillic on his name badge. He raised a hand and broke into a forced smile.

'I'll let you off, tourist.' He slipped away and disappeared into the crowd, clearly disappointed by his humiliating defeat at not extracting some vodka money from us. Jon slapped me on the back and congratulated me on the victory. 'That'll teach him.'

We went to spend our money on our own vodka to celebrate our triumph over the crooked copper. It seemed the most appropriate thing to do.

Later in the afternoon I received an email from Marc Engberg, the American I had met in Warsaw back in the summer, who was now – by a stroke of luck – studying in the city. We arranged to meet that evening.

With a couple of hours to kill, Winfield suggested that we explore the famous underground transport system and attempt to negotiate some of the one hundred and eighty-five miles of subterranean splendour. Opened in 1935, the Moscow subway is celebrated for its distinctive stations and inimitable character. I was impressed with how weird and unique the stations are. Each one has a different theme in a similar fashion to rooms at an amusement park hotel. The Moscow metro is one of the most used systems in the world and carries over seven million passengers daily. At each of the main stations, a train arrives promptly every minute almost to the second.

As we descended the seemingly endless escalator into the belly of the majestic Komsomolskaya–Koltsevaya station, I found it hard to imagine a more ornate platform. Some stations have incredible mosaics dedicated to Lenin. Others have intricate bas reliefs or statues commemorating the 'great patriotic war'. Yet more house a variety of dazzling baroque ornamentation – chandeliers and so on. I tried, and failed, to picture the same on the District and Circle line.

How it works in this manic city, I have no idea. Another curious feature of the metro that we discovered was the reverse method of ticket barriers. Unlike the London Underground, where the barriers remain closed until a ticket is inserted, in Moscow the barriers remain open. Winfield unwittingly took this as an invite to pass straight on without a ticket, but as soon as he was almost through, the barriers clamped shut hard around his leg like a Venus fly trap. 'Arrrggghh!' he yelped and pulled himself free, the steel teeth peeling back into their hiding place. He tried again, this time inserting his ticket into the small hole. He passed through cautiously, wincing at the expectant thrust, but the vengeful barrier stayed gracefully open, awaiting its next unsuspecting foreign victim.

The post-Cold War era has led some to suggest that a second, deeper metro system exists; under military jurisdiction and designed for the emergency evacuation of key city personnel in case of a nuclear attack. It is believed that this secret tunnel system connects the Kremlin, the Lubyanka (headquarters of the Federal Security Service) and the Ministry of Defence, as well as other undisclosed installations.

Around lunchtime, we arrived back at Red Square and joined the queue waiting to see the city's most gruesome attraction. When Lenin died in 1924, the Soviet government was besieged by telegrams from all over Russia begging that his body be preserved. So within three days, the corpse was embalmed and a tomb designed, where he would lie in state until a burial date was decided. In six weeks, more than one hundred thousand visitors flocked to see him, and apart from a brief stint during the Second World War in Siberia, where he was hidden in case the Nazis took Moscow, he has been firmly rooted in Moscow's sightseeing list ever since.

Winfield volunteered to wait outside first, since no cameras were allowed. From the exterior, the red granite mausoleum looked shiny and its classical yet timeless architecture gave it the appearance of being brand new. I entered the little pyramid and followed the line of Russian tourists into a dark passage and down a narrow staircase into the inner chamber, atmospheric in the blackness. The corpse itself is housed in a glass cabinet deep in the heart of the construct. I wanted to linger and get a good look, but the queue was shuffled along by sombre soldiers barking orders from the shadows.

One Russian had smuggled in a camera and tried to take a clandestine photograph right in front of me, but as he was about to press the shutter, a fist flew from the darkness and vigorously punched the man's arm. The guard gripped the poor fellow mercilessly by the bicep and shoved him violently towards the exit. I retracted any jealousy that I might have had about the prospect of getting a decent picture.

Outside, back in the bright daylight, I squinted and saw Jon waiting for me. 'Well, what's it like?'

'Looks like a Madame Tussauds' waxwork,' I replied honestly.

'I bet it's plastic,' Jon remarked, as he handed me the camera and went to join the queue to inspect it for himself.

Later we met Marc outside of an impressive shopping complex that forms the northern flank of Red Square; it was five o'clock and already getting dark. The unlikely row of shops that faces the Kremlin are on the site of the old Upper Trading Rows, as they were known, but now they contain designer clothing outlets and boutique stores selling sunglasses and computers. Marc was in high spirits and greeted us enthusiastically.

'I haven't spoken any English in weeks, I'm so glad you could make it!' said the good-looking Berkeley undergraduate, in a refined Californian twang.

'Let's go and see Moscow.' He slapped me on the back and I introduced him to Winfield.

And so off we went, like a trio of real tourists, snapping away happily at the sights and drinking in the splendid combination of onion-like domes and concrete stars; of the high definition between old and new, refined and base.

After gawping at St Basil's and the Kremlin, Marc wanted to show us his personal favourite church. 'It's called St Nicholas of the Weavers,' he said, as we stood before a beautiful white and green exterior with five tall golden crosses glistening beautifully skyward. On entering the nave, we breathed in the fragrant aroma of frankincense and admired the faded icons, some of which appeared badly damaged. 'Years of communist philistin- ism,' lamented Marc, as he led us to the transept.

The church was very busy, and we found ourselves amidst a crowd of mournful locals. They seemed annoyed at our presence and eyed us contemptuously. I soon realised why, when on entering a small enclave next to the postcard stand we stumbled upon a dead body, smartly dressed and lying morbidly on a stone slab. We had inadvertently interrupted a wake. 'I think it's best we leave,' said Marc, a little embarrassed. So, with apologetic nods, we backed away from the grey cadaver in his elegant wool- len suit and headed rapidly for the door. Two corpses in one day were enough for everyone, so we left and went for something to eat.

Over the next three days we saw a lot of the city, thanks to Marc and his boundless knowledge. We walked along the banks of the Moskva and inspected the state museum. We drank vodka in dusky bars and even found an obligatory Irish pub near to the Max Gorky public park. Occasionally we exchanged the poor man's borscht for a decent meal, at Marc's insistence, as he exclaimed sympathy for our spartan eating habits. One day we went to see the Moscow Palace of Culture theatre, a short bus ride south of the river, and Marc pointed out the bullet holes that strafed its cream facade.

'Two years ago, this place hit the headlines in a big way,' Marc said, gazing up at the building like a pensive scholar.

'Yes, I remember hearing something about it. What happened?'

'It was in October 2002. Fifty Chechens took hostage over eight hundred theatre-goers right here. It brought the eyes of the world onto Moscow for a while. Did you hear about the debacle of a rescue mission? It was a complete embarrassment to the Russian government and a tragedy for all the victims. The two-and-a half-day siege finished up with the Russians sending Spetsnaz forces into the theatre and using some sort of chemical gas, which was supposed to knock out the terrorists, but in fact ended up killing over one hundred and thirty of the hostages as well. It was a total screw-up. Using gas like that. Even the doctors who treated the hostages afterwards complained that they were not told of the properties of the secret gas, so they couldn't save many of the victims.'

The episode was part of an unsettled insurgency by Chechen rebels. The first Chechen intervention had resulted in eighty thousand deaths and the second Chechen war, which began in 1999, resulted in a full-scale invasion of the region by Russian troops. By 2000, the Chechen rebel military apparatus was almost dismantled but even so, terrorism was still rife – in fact, it was on the increase. Just four months before I travelled in the region, the former insurgent leader Akhmad Kadyrov was killed by his own followers. They had put a bomb under his VIP seat during a parade, because they felt he had gone soft and betrayed the militarism of the cause. The result was a spate of suicide bombings across western Russia to remind Vladimir Putin that the Chechen problem would not simply go away.

In late September, there was a new wave of fear across Russia. As Winfield and I drank vodka and took photographs of the Kremlin, the Russian security forces were busily engaged in hunting down the most recent perpetrators of yet another siege. This one had happened only a couple of weeks before and was even more horrifying than the theatre siege. Its name will forever go down in Russian history; the school siege of Beslan. As we would soon find out, it was not a good time to contemplate travelling in southern Russia.

Despite the warnings, we needed to carry on south soon if we were to cross into Asia before winter closed the mountain passes, and so we went off in search of the Georgian embassy to try and get our visas. A little office was hidden away down a dingy alley-way in the Arbat district of the city. I implored Jon, not known for his smartness, to wear his best polo shirt, and I put on a clean collar to assist the application. We were admitted by a Georgian official, who from the first instance was exceedingly helpful and ushered us immediately to the front of the queue on account of our being British. A short dark man with round glasses and enormous bushy eyebrows that curled upwards pushed away the indignant Russians and insisted on practising his workable English.

'England very good. I like much. You know we have same flag!' The little man pointed excitedly to the national emblem of St George slaying the dragon and proceeded to highlight our ancient ties and similarities. He disliked the Russians intensely.

'You would not believe these terrible people. So rude,' he said, flicking his fingers dismissively at the window, which overlooked a street below. He led us to a desk where a raven-haired girl asked for our passports and smiled coyly.

'Are you really English?' She leant forward and eyed us thoughtfully. 'I have never met Englishmen before.' She couldn't quite decide if we were telling the truth.

'You don't look like Englishmen. In fact, you look like Georgians. You should shave your beards.' I was struck by her frankness and familiarity, but at the same time quite flattered. Winfield was in his element.

'You are very pretty,' he teased her, 'and very efficient in your work.' He gave a wink, as if to hurry her along in stamping the passports. 'Are all the girls in Georgia as pretty as you?'

'Oh, yes,' she said, quite unashamedly, 'we have the most beautiful women in Europe.'

Winfield's charisma seemed to work as she barely looked at our papers. I had been quite worried, because you are supposed to present a letter of invitation from a Georgian host, or possibly even an in-country travel agent, but we hadn't given it much thought until it was too late and we'd had to rely on the services of a rudimentary online forger to create the necessary documents. In any case she gave us both visas straight away, telling us that although normally it takes five days, since we were English she would 'make special considerations'.

With that we were able to relax, safe in the knowledge that now we could theoretically travel over the Caucasus. As I was comforted by the prospect of travelling through Russia's troubled south, Jon became a little agitated.

'We really need to get a move on. I have to be back at work in a month. I'm not sure how far I'm going to come, you know.'

Spurred on by the threat of Jon's impending employment, we made the decision to leave Moscow the following day. We treated Marc to several vodkas that night in the trendy Propaganda bar near to Kitay-gorod, and woke up to our final day in Moscow with an appalling hangover. Since it happened to be a Saturday, Marc had suggested that we spend the morning at the huge Izmailovsky Saturday market and so we did exactly that; it was a sight to behold.

Like a mixture between a Bavarian Christmas market and a massive jumble sale, the wooden stalls sold great quantities of pretty much everything. Endless junk was mixed with genuine antiques and Soviet-era collectables. Furs, Persian rugs and wool from the Caucasus battled for space with delicate Russian dolls and Second World War postcards. I noticed with interest that anything from the Nazi era – helmets, buckles and badges – all had the swastikas scratched off completely.

I settled for a couple of Lenin postcards (one of which went to Hunter, our first lift to Stansted) and a set of Russian dolls for my mother. It would have been easy to wile away a full day drinking Russian cognac and wincing at the sorrowful dancing bears, but we had a train to catch. We took Marc for a final lunch at a café near to the statue of Marshal Zhukov at Okhotny Ryad and he wished us a hearty *bon voyage*. In an appropriate final scene, a motley crowd of octogenarians rallied outside of the window, pathetically waving immense communist banners ready to march on Red Square. These committed old reds chanted in vain for a return to the good old days, but as we looked on in curious bewilderment, the shrill notes of a ringing mobile phone, belonging to a young man conducting his business on a laptop at the next table, made me think that for all its remnants of a dark communist past, there was no stopping the inexorable tide of change in this strange but alluring country.

We left Moscow as we had entered it, by train. By now any notions of hitchhiking in and out of these glum Soviet sprawls had gone out of the window and we resigned ourselves to paid transport – for now, anyhow, until we were into the wilds. Making our way to Pavlovsky station, we stocked up on essentials before boarding the 14.20 to Volgograd. We settled into the cramped little four-bunk sleeper and pulled out of the station dead on time, leaving behind the sprawling city with its ugly towers and miserable people.

6

Enemy at the Gates

After about five minutes, there was a bang on the cabin door. A young official with narrow, cat-like eyes opened the door and stepped to one side as he directed two more people into our quarters. The first in was a round, cheerful woman wearing an immense fur coat reminiscent of a 1940s Hollywood starlet's, though it looked rather ravaged and worn. She squeezed herself past Jon, who was busy rooting through his rucksack. Behind her came a thin young man with a Mongol appearance, who nodded to each of us solemnly.

'*Dobry den.*' Good afternoon. We nodded back. He quietly climbed the three-runged ladder onto the top bunk and was asleep before the minute was out.

After checking our tickets, the guard scuttled away, hauling shut the metal door behind him.

'Too good to be true, as always,' sighed Jon, lamenting the loss of our short-lived monopoly over the bunks.

'*Otkuda vy?*' The owner of the fur coat squinted at me as she sat down and peered over her small round spectacles that looked as old as she was.

'We're from England,' I replied, hoping that I had grasped the question.

'*Minya zavoot Olga.*' She looked like an Olga. She beamed warmly, and in perfect English continued, 'I am from Novosibirsk, I am Siberian.'

'How do you find this place Russia?' Olga said, looking at Jon.

'Cold,' Winfield replied. I hoped that she would not understand the double entendre.

'Yes, it is rather ...' she smiled, '... and the people are suspicious of foreigners, but don't worry, they mean no harm.'

I had underestimated the Russian sense of depth. Sensing my embarrassment, she broke into a broad grin. Jon tried to address the awkwardness.

'Mind you, we have met some very pleasant people in Moscow.' He lied well.

'Believe me, if you leave the cities you will find very hospitable people. It is like anywhere in the world, cities are soulless; they make people hard and lose their manners. You should visit Siberia. Now there you will find warmth!'

It seemed odd that she talked about Siberia and warmth in the same sentence, but I suppose she was right. So far we had seen only the metropolitan Russia and not given the provincial areas a chance. I imagined how welcome a Russian would feel in London; I guess it amounts to the same.

Olga took out a neat piece of paper from her handbag and wrote on it some of the places that she thought we ought to visit. She copied it into Cyrillic as well, so that we could translate and understand the signposts should we ever get to see any of the places. Stavropol, Elista, Vladikavkaz were all beautiful towns, she assured us. But again she returned to Siberia. 'You MUST visit Lake Baikal,' she implored. 'Please, it is the most beautiful place in all Russia. We call it the Pearl of Siberia.'

'I'd love to,' I apologised, 'but we are travelling to the Caucasus, and won't have time.'

'Now that's a shame. Maybe next time. But listen, just be careful in the south, it isn't safe these days.' With that she hauled her weighty frame onto the bed and quietly began to preen herself in a little hand mirror that she had produced from her bag.

Jon, too, was silent. I noticed how ever since the policeman in St Petersburg had warned us not to go any further south than Moscow, he had seemed on edge. I put it down to nerves. Looking out of the window from the warmth of the cabin, I eyed the stillness and uniformity of the gently undulating countryside. Olga had dozed off on the bunk opposite and I started reading William Dalrymple's *In Xanadu*. Jon was at the one-thousand-page mark in *War and Peace* and was dwelling on his achievement. 'Have you learned anything about Russia from that book?' I enquired. 'Yes. That it's a bloody stupid idea to go anywhere near the Caucasus.'

After the sun had fallen below the golden horizon, we made a foray to the restaurant car, where the food was expensive and bad, and the staff dour.

We played cards for a while, but soon grew tired and decided that the best course of action was to follow the example of Olga and the Mongol and get some sleep, content in the knowledge that we were speeding through the hinterland of European Russia.

I woke early to find the rolling void of yellow corn fields had transformed into true Eurasian steppe. It was clear that Central Asia was nearby. I felt it. In amongst the low wooded escarpments lay vast expanses of prairie, intermingled with rough scrub. The sun rose gradually over the pink-blonde landscape as Olga brushed her hair violently. With less than an hour until we were due to arrive in Volgograd, I kept my eyes fixed on the landscape through the window as the suburbs closed in around us. First the sight of a grey factory with a pillar of smoke belching from a chimney, then the ubiquitous tower blocks, and suddenly, as the centre drew nearer, a vast statue of what appeared to be the Greek Goddess Nike with her sword thrust into the heavens could be seen atop a hill that overlooked the city. Beyond that lay the mighty Volga River. Olga pointed at the immense apparition and proclaimed, 'Mother Russia.' I sensed the pride in her voice. 'Built for the brave boys who died here.'

'What is it?' Jon asked.

'It's our war memorial for the battle of Stalingrad.'

I was excited and insisted that we go and see the monument at the first opportunity. I noticed that piles of rubble lay all around in a way that made me wonder if the city had been fully restored after its near destruction sixty years ago. I imagined the bodies of the thousands of souls who perished in the German siege of the city during the Second World War.

The reason for the debris soon became apparent at the brief glimpse of a party of workmen, digging furiously into a pile of freshly made cement. It wasn't the remains of battle, but the beginnings of a new city. Volgograd was still under construction, and many of its buildings were lacking roofs or were still shrouded in scaffolding. We pulled into the station and thanked Olga for her sound advice. She waddled off the train, laden with suitcases – the only happy Russian we ever met. Our other companion, who hadn't said a word, nodded to us once again and disappeared into the crowd as quickly and mysteriously as he had arrived.

We ambled slowly to the central square, 'the square of fallen fighters', glad to be stretching our legs. The place was immediately recognisable from the pages of the history books and grainy war footage. I tried to imagine the same scene in monochrome, the buildings mere skeletons, a brave soldier pushing forward, ever forward – waiting tragically, nay expectantly, for the death of a comrade so that he could have his chance with a rifle before being shot down himself. One of the million victims of that terrible battle.

Today it was overcast, but the wind had died down to abate the cold. I looked around at the arresting plaza. Amidst the scene was the looming Hotel Volgograd, a huge neoclassical edifice rebuilt in 1955 after its destruction in the war. In fact, all of the buildings are follies. The grand Hotel Intourist, the immense post office, the Greco-Roman Drama Theatre, all carbon copies of their nineteenth-century predecessors. Nothing original remains.

The receptionist said that we could leave our bags with the concierge while we explored the city. She tapped a little brass bell and from across the hallway a very old man in a blue outfit approached us, grinning inanely. He looked grand, like an ancient relic that commanded both awe and pity. Looking at him, I guessed he was over eighty but it was hard to tell. Sharp, intelligent blue eyes pricked out of shrivelled sockets.

'*Guten Tag meine Herren*,' he addressed us formally in fluent German, before picking up our bags with apparent ease and striding off across the lobby. As he disappeared, I wondered where he had learned the language of his enemy. He was certainly old enough to have fought in the war or perhaps he was one of the few descendants of the German settlers that had populated the region in the late nineteenth century.

Outside we set off to find the Volga, the lifeblood of the town, and so we headed south for a few hundred metres, where, almost without warning, the mighty river presented itself.

It is vast. In parts, the river is nearly a mile wide, and on a misty morning it is often impossible to see the far bank. I imagined the advancing German army as the Russians were forced back into the malignant water, all the while fighting tooth and nail for their lives. The Volga today had a black cloud hanging above it and the spitting rain gave the place a sinister feel. A shudder ran down my spine and I sensed that Jon had felt the same. Looking out across the bleak water, I saw a few solitary beings working on their moored boats, which were bobbing with the tide: poor city dwellers eking out a living from these black waves and a few fishermen preparing their nets for a night afloat.

Set back from the river by a wide promenade, the modern city in its varying stages of completion competed for space. But in spite of the grey humdrum, huge tracts of green wasteland seemed to spring up in-between the buildings. In some places, the promenade appeared to blend seamlessly into the river. Concrete would converge with wild grass, as if an apocalyptic battle for control was being waged. Nature was winning on the banks. Weeds sprouted everywhere and I couldn't discern between what was half-built and what was half-demolished. Huge concrete ingots were strewn haphazardly across the quayside, and on the far side of the river, a grey-green cluster of shaggy trees seemed to haul itself out of a sandbank. It was wilderness, all right.

As we wandered along the dismal waterside, I pondered the city's turbulent past. The city of Tsaritsyn was founded in 1589, after the stone fortress that occupied its place on the confluence of the Volga and Tsaritsa Rivers. Because of its favourable location, it soon grew to become an important trading settlement, key to the Tsars' wealth. Like many cities in the south, it was witness to much violence and was twice captured by Cossack rebels in their bid to resist governance from St Petersburg.

In the twentieth century, the city was fought over during the civil war, when the Bolsheviks were attacked by white Russian forces. In 1925, soon after Stalin succeeded Lenin as party leader, he renamed the city after himself, marking the commencement of his infamous personality cult. The dictator, now with a personal interest in the city, encouraged the development of industry in Stalingrad and it soon became a nucleus of tranship-ment and heavy manufacturing.

Due to its importance to the Soviet economy and no doubt because it bore Stalin's name, the city was attacked by the Nazis when they invaded the Soviet Union. In 1942 the city became known around the world for the infamous battle, which saw the Nazis surround and force the Soviets into a tiny pocket on the western banks of the Volga. Stalingrad was besieged for six months before Soviet reserves came and counterattacked, forcing the eventual German withdrawal. The battle apparently saw the greatest casualty figures of any in the history of warfare. (It was roughly on a par with Leningrad, although some historians don't count that as a battle because it was more of a blockade.) Estimates vary between one-and-a-quarter and almost two million dead.

Turning away from the river, we entered one of the more pleasant avenues, where tall poplars made some attempt to conceal the Stalinist apartment blocks and endless construction works. We trundled upriver to find what was called the State Panoramic Museum 'Stalingrad Battle'– recommended as having a good film show of the battle with lots of original footage. It rose from the river in the form of a giant white cylinder, taper-ing slightly in the centre. It looked odd and alien in these bleak surroundings.

'*Ponedelnik* (Monday),' announced the security guard prop-ping up the wall outside, where a small green tank pointed its defunct barrel out across the Volga.

'It's closed,' Jon squinted, trying to understand the Cyrillic sign and the guard's mutterings.

'All this bloody way and it has to be closed, because it's a bloody Monday.' I was disappointed that we wouldn't get to see the exhibits, but our initial disenchantment thinned somewhat as we rounded the museum and took stock of an incredible sight. At the top of a flight of steps that led up to the promenade, we came across the stark Grudinina flour mill, built by German traders in 1903. It was strafed with bullet and shrapnel holes – a bare skeleton and a desolate reminder that the whole city was once in this state of ruin. It was the only original building left in the city and looked like it would collapse at any moment. As the angry clouds converged to hide away the meek Russian sun, the red brick shell of the factory contrasted sharply with the white museum in the background, and the wreck was cast into darkness.

I realised that every building, every sector of the city we were seeing, had played its part in the action. The central train station, for example, where we had arrived bleary-eyed that morning, changed hands thirteen times during the battle.

Many consider Stalingrad as the turning point of the war in Europe. During the winter of 1942, German forces controlled ninety per cent of the city and looked as if they were going to defeat the mighty Soviet army. Taking Stalingrad would have opened the door to the Russian oilfields in the Caucasus and guaranteed a Nazi victory, but after a massive Soviet counter-attack led by the military genius Marshal Zhukov, the Germans found themselves encircled. The battle had incredibly swung in favour of the Soviets and on 31 January 1943, Feld Marshal Friedrich Von Paulus surrendered to Zhukov, destroying forever the German hopes of defeating Russia.

Like its northern counterpart, Stalingrad was also awarded the title of Hero City in 1945, and King George VI of Britain was so impressed that he awarded its citizens the bejewelled 'Sword of Stalingrad' in admiration for their bravery. The link with Britain doesn't end there. Stalingrad was also twinned with the bombed remnants of Coventry shortly after the war in a spirit of post-destruction solidarity.

It began to rain in earnest now, big, fat globules that drenched the concrete and resupplied the weeds in their bitter struggle to reclaim the city; so in an attempt to forestall the spirit of gloomy despondency, we went for a late breakfast in a little café just off Lenin Square, where a little bald man fed us stale croissants. Sometime mid-morning the rain abated and we went on foot in search of the statue of Mother Russia.

We walked the direct route, following the course of some train lines for a couple of miles and up an embankment, passing a series of factories, until the vast statue came into sight in the distance on top of a scraggy hill that was covered in stumpy birch and the occasional Russian olive tree.

'This can't be the way in.'

'You're right.' Nonetheless, there didn't seem to be an official entrance and we found ourselves hopping precariously over the railway tracks and then gradually climbing the heights that reminded me of an enormous Potteries slag heap. There was a kind of path that wound its way through the undergrowth and we made an effort to follow it as best we could. At times, when the path petered out entirely, we found ourselves scrambling amongst the loose shale, trying to keep in sight the tip of the statue's sword – the only thing keeping us from getting lost in the thicket.

Suddenly, although I suppose unsurprisingly, we stumbled upon an old war bunker. It was made of bricks, with a thick concrete top, half-hidden under the long grass. The narrow openings that looked away to the south were edged with a rusted iron frame, but the whole pillbox was otherwise intact.

'Shall we have a look inside?' I looked around, but couldn't seem to find a way in.

'Here it is,' shouted Jon, a few metres away to the rear. I found him gazing down into a hole in the ground. We both clambered into a small, circular hatch about the same size as a manhole cover and followed it down into a narrow tunnel that soon widened into a little room. It was dimly lit from the sunlight that passed through the narrow machine-gun slits. I peered out through the holes and could see the grassy slope tapering away to where a wild hedgerow had grown up around a fence. This would have been the 'killing area' – the zone in-between the defenders' arcs of fire. It was well-placed; this bunker had excellent views down the slopes and although there were some trees sprouting up, they were all saplings and would have been cleared by the defenders in 1942.

The defenders. I wondered about their fate in this particular little trench. How many souls had perished at the hands of the gunner blasting away into the German advance? Or had this belonged to the Germans when the Soviet counter-attack came? This spot had probably changed hands seven or eight times, too, and must have been the scene of so much death and agony.

I tried my hardest to imagine the emotion and fear of those inside – Russian or German – but it was difficult. How can anyone possibly know what went through a man's mind as he pulled the trigger, letting loose an orgy of destruction; tearing lead through the air and cutting to pieces all that stood in their way? Perhaps they felt numb; only the pressure of the trigger and the repetitive clunk-clunk as the bolt rattled back and forth and the satisfying clink as the links dropped into neat little piles with each new assault.

And what about the attackers? What motivates a man to shuffle on towards his own death – to storm a bunker knowing that the defender has every advantage and he has none? Perhaps he was courageous and thought of nothing but duty and sacrifice, the glory of retaking the hill, or simply being seen as brave by his comrades. For some, this is enough, and more important than whether they live or die. Then again, maybe it wasn't about glory, or death, or following orders at all – only being scared about the one thing that above all else eats away at a man's spirit. The one thing that separates him as a man, as a warrior: the urge to not be seen as a coward.

We left the bunker in silence.

Eventually we neared the top of the hill and the foliage came to an abrupt end. Beyond a fence lay a neatly manicured lawn that opened up to present the hilltop monument.

'No, it's definitely not the proper entrance,' said Jon, as we climbed over the barbed-wire fence. I ripped my jeans on the barbs. 'I wonder if there are any landmines still lying about down there?'

Once in the open, the statue loomed large across the field. We had come a bit of a circuitous route and arrived in the grounds of the imposing feature from the rear. Crossing the neat grass, we made our way onto the stone slab footpath that ringed around the massive memorial. The statue itself dominated the heights and I noticed that the enormous female gazes northwards towards Moscow, her sword thrust triumphantly into the heavens mimicking Nike, the Greek goddess of victory.

Nothing can prepare a visitor for its vastness. Dressed in classical robes, she stands tall at eighty-five metres. Jon walked forward to the base as I took some photographs from the path; he appeared to diminish to minuscule proportions as he neared her. I followed, and for some reason felt unduly disappointed at the fact that the whole thing was made of concrete. I don't know why, perhaps because of its magnificence from afar, but I was expecting it to have been hewn – impossibly – from a single piece of rock. I shook away these nonsensical thoughts, took a few paces back and came to the conclusion that despite its vulgar substance, the Colossus of Rhodes could not have been a more impressive sight.

There was a little steel door right at the base of the statue, but it was firmly locked shut. Apparently, a set of stairs winds up the statue's interior, all the way to the top of the head, but on this occasion it was out of bounds, allegedly due to high winds. The real reason, I was told in a hushed voice by the guard, is the continued subsidence of the statue that threatens its very existence after sixty years.

The monument represents the motherland calling her sons and daughters to fight for victory and resist the advancing Germans. It was built between 1959 and 1967 at the height of the Cold War and purposely dwarfs the Statue of Liberty, which is only forty-six metres tall. After walking around the statue, which is on the highest point of the hill, we followed the path eastward towards the rest of the memorial.

Down a set of wide granite steps, flanked on each side by immense poplars, swaying gracefully in the autumn breeze, we made our way down to a winding waterway appropriately named the Serpentine. The soothing display of cascading waterfalls made a pleasant introduction to the Garden of Remembrance, an elliptical arcade surrounded by weeping willows and filled with immense angular statues – bold, muscular, semi-naked soldiers adorned with rifles, grenades and even sickles, all representing the ideal of Soviet warriorhood.

On the bas-reliefs, huge slogans are carved in bold Cyrillic – 'Stand to death' and 'Not a single step back' – that describe the sense of Soviet pride. The last striking echoes of a powerful empire celebrating its victory over the Nazi invaders. Whatever one's thoughts on the Soviet regime, it is hard not be moved and impressed at such a grand tribute to the sacrifices made here. As I was pondering the beauty of the gardens, I heard the flowing sounds of what I thought was classical music. As we neared the cylindrical chamber at one end of the avenue, it became louder and the deep bellowing of a narrative came from within. Outside of the building, which was called 'The Hall of the Warrior Glory' an inscription read:

> *Iron wind was blowing into their faces, but they kept advancing, and again and again the enemy was taken over by a superstitious feeling: were these really humans attacking them? Were they mortal?*

We entered the darkness and as my eyes gradually became accustomed to the dim chamber, I could make out a large amphitheatre, in the centre of which rose a gigantic stone hand, over four metres high, firmly gripping a flaming torch. This was the centrepiece – watched over by a pair of ceremonial guardsmen. A tapering podium winds its way around the theatre, allowing the visitor to get close to the shimmering golden walls. Fresh green wreaths adorned the platform as well as the square plinth on which the hand stood. A perfect circle of sunlight lit the eastern quadrant and I looked up to be instantly blinded by the grey pallor of the sky pouring in from the Pantheon-like hole in the roof.

Inside all along the walls were huge, red basalt slabs carved to look like draping banners, engraved with the names of the thousands of Russians that fell on the hill. I began reading some of the names. After the battle, some thirty-four thousand soldiers were reburied on the hill after a temporary interment in one of the largest-ever mass graves. Among them lay Vasily Chuikov, the general, later Marshal of the Soviet Union, who heroically led the defence of the city and requested that on his death in 1982 he be buried at Stalingrad with his men – the only Soviet Marshal not to be interred at the Kremlin.

Loudspeakers played the mournful sounds of 'Dreams' by Schumann, which added to the solemnity. The honour guard in ceremonial service dress and peaked cap, with their bayonets fixed to their rifles, were proud, tall figures and I couldn't help standing in awe of the majestic scene. These guards were the direct military descendants of the elite 13th Guards Division, who were sent across the Volga into Stalingrad as part of the relief effort. Of the ten thousand soldiers who went in, only three hundred and twenty survived; a ninety-seven-per-cent death rate.

Along the top of the wall, near to the roof, was an inscription in answer to the question posed outside:

Yes, we were just mortal humans, and there are very few of us alive, but all of us have paid our patriotic debt to Mother Russia.

It had become cold outside, but neither of us felt it appropriate to complain and so we took the tram back to the centre of town and returned to the Hotel Volgograd. Inside the hotel lobby, we drank some very cheap Russian beer and some very expensive Scotch whisky and made plans to move on that same night, south towards Stavropol. It started to rain again, heavier than before, but at least it warmed the air a little.

There was nothing to be done but wrestle our backpacks from the friendly porter, who was trying to insist on carrying them all the way to the bus station, and begin to walk. Thoroughly drenched and tired, we found a bus just as night fell.

7

The Long Road South

'How the hell am I supposed to finish *War and Peace* with this racket?' said Jon with a growl. As we settled onto the packed coach, any thoughts of a restful night were immediately dashed. The driver was a fan of techno music and insisted on playing it at full volume for the whole trip. Even the scenery outside could not give us any solace. Vast, brown steppe, punctuated by meagre fields for as far as the eye can see, was no remedy.

Irritable and exhausted, we arrived at Stavropol in the heart of Cossack country as dawn broke over the spartan landscape. This was where Conolly had remarked on the vindictive nature of the inhabitants. As we were to discover – things hadn't changed all that much. As the minibus pulled into the outskirts of the city, we were called to a halt at a roadblock by a square-jawed policeman.

'Get out,' he said, pointing at me and Winfield. Without further indication as to what he wanted, he ordered us to follow him. 'Come, now! Bring your bags.' Instinctively and submissively, we tailed our burly captor to what I guessed to be the police station, a two-minute walk across the street next to a crumbling block of flats.

We were told to wait outside the unmarked guardroom, whilst the corporal went inside to fetch his chief. I looked back to the bus, which was still at the checkpoint. The other passengers were all lolling about outside smoking cigarettes, clearly annoyed at having to wait. Some armed militia men watched over to make sure they didn't wander too far.

'What do you think they want?' asked Jon.

'I don't know, they're probably wondering what two foreigners are doing this far south. They'll probably try to scam us about the registering thing.'

'You!' barked a deep growl from inside the doorway. 'Come here.'

A tall, muscular sergeant in his early thirties appeared from an office and beckoned us to stand side by side in a cell that was bare, apart from a wooden table in the corner. He wore a pair of dark grey suit trousers and a light blue shirt with a Russian tricolour on the arm. There was a pistol jutting menacingly out of a leather holster on his belt. As he stood surveying us, I noticed that his eyes were light green and were too far apart. He reminded me for some reason of a lizard. I told myself that, whatever happens, I mustn't think he looks like a lizard.

'What (*forked tongue flickering*) are you doing in Stavropol?'

'We're travelling.'

The corporal who had brought us in appeared from behind the sergeant and began to search us. He took my wallet and passport and handed them to the lizard.

'Terrorist,' he said, pointing to my green army rucksack. His narrow eyes seemed to push even further apart as he closed in to get a closer look. I tried not to smell his foul breath.

'No,' I said, gently. 'We are tourists.'

'*Nyet!* Terrorists!' he shouted, his face only inches away from mine. He took a sidestep towards Jon and stared at him without saying a word. I was waiting for the expectant lurch of a tongue to pluck out an eyeball.

The corporal unclipped the lid of my rucksack and began to pour its contents onto the filthy concrete floor. He rifled through the pile of clothes and books until he found something that interested him.

'What's this?'

He held up the Koran that I had been studying in preparation for travelling through the Islamic world.

'He's not as stupid as he looks,' muttered Jon.

'Quiet, you.' There was silence for a moment until a dog barked defiantly outside.

'You are Muslims, you are terrorists fighting for Al Qaida. You are Chechens.'

'No, we are tour—'

The sergeant raised a finger, telling me to shut up.

I looked through the solitary window that had rusty mesh wire obscuring the view, but I could still make out movement in the yard where these police, or militia or whoever they were, were sitting around a small TV and drinking vodka. It gave me an idea.

'Search his bag, too.' I pointed at Jon's rucksack, which they hadn't touched yet. Jon frowned angrily.

The lizard, looking scalier than ever, gave me a quizzical look, but then took an evident pleasure in shaking Jon's bag upside down. Socks, underwear, a crumpled pair of jeans and a black fleece all plummeted to the floor, followed by Tolstoy with a loud thud.

'And now look in the side pockets.' I pointed to the bulge.

He patted the bulging side pouch and unzipped it to reveal the ten-year-old single malt that changed the course of the day.

'See, we aren't Muslims. Muslims don't drink whisky.'

The sergeant pondered this. He knew enough about religion to know that his troublesome Islamic neighbours, for all their vices, certainly did not drink whisky – not in public, anyhow.

I took this as my cue to move over to him and grasp the bottle, open it and take a throat-burning gulp of the stuff. It wasn't the breakfast I had hoped for. Jon, clearly not wanting to miss out, did the same and offered the bottle to the now floundering reptile. He broke into a broad grin and took the bottle. 'Nazdravia.' Cheers. He swigged for a full five seconds before slamming it down on the table, wiping his mouth on his sleeve. His green lizard eyes winced as he turned away.

He picked up the passports that were lying on the table and flicked through them lazily.

'English, eh?'

'Yes,' Jon and I replied in unison.

'It's your beards. Only two types of people wear beards here. Those in mourning for the children of Beslan – and Muslims. And I thought that since you weren't Russians, you must be Muslims.'

'Oh.' I suddenly felt very self-conscious of my three-week stubble.

'We don't like Muslims here. Do you know about Beslan?' said the sergeant, clearly roused.

'We heard on the news.'

The Beslan school siege began on 1 September 2004, when a group of terrorists took more than one thousand pupils and their teachers hostage inside the town's main high school. The terrorists were led by the warlord Shamil Basayev and demanded a formal end to the Second Chechen War, which was still technically going on when we arrived, as well as independence for Chechnya and the semi-autonomous Ingushetia region.

Despite assurances that no armed intervention would take place because most of the hostages were children, Russian security forces, local police and armed civilians stormed the building and it turned into a bloodbath. It became a full-scale assault with tanks, rockets and phosphorous grenades. Over three hundred children and their teachers died in the tragedy. Several of the terrorists managed to escape and were still at large, which was probably the cause of our current inquisition.

'Horrible tragedy caused by those Islamic savages. Well, you will see for yourselves soon when you pass through.'

'Pass through? We weren't planning on it,' said Jon, suddenly looking alarmed.

'Maybe not, but that's the only road. Look here,' the lizard smiled.

The sergeant led us next door to his office, where piles of boxes full of his things suggested that he was in the process of either coming or going. The window looked out onto the main road, where our minibus was thankfully still waiting; its expressionless passengers still smoking.

I looked at a regional map that was pinned to the office wall and saw that we would actually have to pass through Beslan on our way south to Vladikavkaz.

'You didn't tell me you were taking me to the scene of a bloody massacre,' said Winfield.

'I didn't know! I thought it would be a simple bus ride.'

'You have come from here,' pointed out our now friendly chameleon. His knotted finger crushed Volgograd in an instant, then followed the thin yellow line south to Elista. 'You came through the Republic of Kalmykia,' he continued and I nodded, pretending to know that we had transited a semi-autonomous federal district, when in reality all that I had been aware of was a series of annoying blockades and the constant thud of the driver's techno addiction.

'Now you are here,' he patted Stavropol gently, then swept another hundred miles south-west, forgetting Pyatigorsk and flicking with an aggressive thump the border town of Vladikavkaz, our ultimate destination. 'And here,' he jerked north, only ten miles straddling our road, '... is Beslan.'

'The road from here is very dangerous. But don't worry, there are many police and army to make sure of your safety.'

'OK,' I said, unsure whether the sergeant's words were reassuring or meant as a warning.

'OK, we're leaving now,' said Jon, already heading towards the door. The sergeant looked indifferent and did nothing to stop us gathering up our kit off the floor, quickly shoving it into our bags and darting for the door of the ramshackle jail as fast as we could without breaking into a run.

'Let's get out of here. What the hell are we doing going to Beslan? It's fucking war down there. You didn't tell me about that.'

'Look, I didn't know,' I said, trying to calm him down. 'We won't even stop. We'll just pass through and get to Georgia as fast as we can.'

Jon muttered some obscenities under his breath. 'Last chance, Lev, otherwise I'm doing one.'

We doubled back to our minibus. Conveniently pulled up alongside it was another − almost identical. It had the words Pyatigorsk–Vladikavkaz scrawled in Cyrillic capitals across a piece of cardboard on the windscreen and was about to leave. Our original driver nodded to the new one and we jumped on, still clutching our rucksacks between our knees. Jon and I sat in silence. He looked out of the window and didn't meet my gaze for some time. I knew he wasn't convinced that this was a good idea, but he hadn't given up yet. I was relieved, though I knew we had still a long way to go.

After Stavropol, the rough road darted south and by now the steppe had transformed into green cultivated fields and agricultural farmland. A few miles to the south, the Caucasus mountains rose steeply out of the plain, and as we passed through the spa town of Pyatigorsk, I caught a glimpse of the snow-capped peaks of Mount Elbrus, Europe's highest mountain, looming like a giant over the plain.

There were roadblocks every few kilometres as we drove through North Ossetia, and at each checkpoint we were unceremoniously ordered off the bus and taken away for questioning. The troubled republic had become the centre of police attention, along with neighbouring Ingushetia and of course Chechnya, in the wake of the Beslan massacre and the recent spate of suicide bombings across the region. Again and again we endured the monotony and humiliation of being separated from our fellow passengers and having our bags searched and passports checked.

'This must be the tenth time today,' growled Jon, evidently close to breaking point, as we were escorted to a makeshift tent on the outskirts of Nalchik. 'Only the ninth, actually,' I corrected him, looking at the score tally I had scrawled in red pen on the inside page of my tattered *Lonely Planet*. I noticed with interest the welcome sign at the side of the road: 'Nalchik, capital of the Republic of Kabardino-Balkaria, Russia's second cleanest city, 2003.'

'Maybe we should stay and have a look around,' I suggested jokingly.

'Sod that,' replied Jon. 'I'm getting to the border and then straight on a boat to Turkey.' I could see that this time he was almost being serious.

It was a genuinely beautiful place. It was green and lush and the mountains were tantalisingly close, but neither of us were in any mood for sightseeing and so we changed cars yet again and carried on the journey, before finally arriving in Beslan around lunchtime the next day, irritable, exhausted and probably a little drunk – having gone through the whisky rigmarole more times than we could remember.

The roadblock at the entrance to the town was the busiest and most militant we had seen so far. 'Here we go again.' Once more we were dragged off the vehicle and ordered to empty our bags. A tall, pockmarked soldier, sporting the gold stars on his collar that indicated he was an officer, made us sit down on a bench at the side of the road, whilst another soldier rummaged through our bags. He discovered the bottle of whisky almost immediately and pulled it out enquiringly. He sifted through the pile of dirty clothes and books, spurred on by his discovery of the liquor, and flicked through the pages of *War and Peace*, his curiosity sparked by the front cover illustration of a charging Cossack. Then he came across my Koran, which he handed to the officer.

'Are you a terrorist?' he asked nonchalantly, as if he was enquiring about the weather.

'No.'

'What do you know about the Chechens' involvement here in Beslan?'

'Absolutely nothing.'

'Why then do you have this Koran?'

'We are scholars,' I exaggerated.

'He must be secret police,' whispered Jon.

'Look, I also have a copy of the Bible.' I produced a rather dog-eared King James hoping that the two holy scripts would cancel each other out.

'No, you are Muslims.' He squinted.

'No, we are not Muslim, we are not terrorists, we are students,' barked Jon.

'Passports,' barked our interrogator back. We handed them over, now used to the routine. He looked at mine first and began thumbing through pages of visas. Iran, Pakistan, India. It didn't look good.

Another bus had come to a halt at the checkpoint and the soldiers were rounding up more locals for questioning. Three swarthy men were ordered to sit down on the bench next to us.

'What's this?' The officer thumbed the purple ink of my Georgian stamp.

Just as I was about to answer, he butted in, 'All Georgians are terrorists.' He eyed us up and down, 'You don't look English, you have Muslim beards.' Then he threw a puzzled glance over to the bottle of scotch sitting half empty on the floor.

'Your turn,' I said to Jon, who rolled his eyes, exasperated.

As frustrating as all of this was, having followed the story of the massacre at Beslan in the press, I could understand why the police and soldiers in this area were so on edge.

'The main problem,' explained Pavlo, a local doctor, sitting next to me on the bench, 'was that, like the theatre siege, there was a lack of coordination by the security forces and fear of action by those on the ground until they had orders from above. It's always the same here in Russia. There's so much bureaucracy. Moscow was saying one thing, but what the situation really needed was a firm hand to react to the developing situation in the field. Instead, no one seemed to know what to do, and the clashing headmen of the various police forces and militia units were more interested in proving their worth to one another than actually rescuing the children.'

Pavlo continued, with a weary, distant look on his face. 'The cordon that was manned by the local police wasn't secure and it was far too close to the buildings – meaning that the terrorists inside could actually fire their rocket launchers into the barricades!' He shook his head. 'Can you believe it? Also, there was no fire-fighting equipment on hand, despite the fact there are several stations nearby, and hardly any ambulances at all for when things got bloody.'

Pavlo sighed. 'And bloody things got, especially when thousands of the damned Opolchentsy turned up. You know what they are? They call themselves the Village Militia, but in reality, they are no more than a very angry mob. And then, of course, there were the desperate parents of the poor children, all bent on blood and armed to the teeth with an arsenal of primitive weapons. You can hardly blame them, but not exactly who you want in your rescue team!'

Pavlo sat shaking his head, as we waited for the soldier to return with our documents. Pavlo was forty-five and worked in a hospital in Elista. He was also travelling south. His dark appearance had singled him out for questioning, but he had grown used to it now. I looked around, and again at Jon, who was smoking some of the guards' cigarettes in exchange for a shot of whisky. Apart from the huge police presence, we didn't see anything to suggest that this was the scene of recent slaughter.

'The school is over there,' Pavlo pointed vaguely to the east, but I couldn't see much except a few grey buildings.

'As for the terrorists themselves,' Pavlo went on in a mix of Russian and pidgin English, 'they must have been rehearsing the attack for months. As soon as they took over the school, they set about booby trapping the whole complex with mines and home-made explosives, surrounding the whole place with trip-wires and grenades.'

He continued, 'They threatened to kill fifty hostages for every one of their own members shot by police, so that there weren't any rescue attempts. They also smashed all the windows, after remembering the way that the army had used poison gas in the Moscow theatre. You know, they even prevented the children from eating or drinking, calling the act a "hunger strike". What monsters.' Pavlo fell into a sad silence.

I remembered reading that in the first two days of the siege, efforts had been made to negotiate with the terrorists and a United Nations Security Council was convened, which demanded the immediate release of all the hostages. The US president George W. Bush offered Putin 'support in any form', which may or may not have enraged the Russian premier to have the matter dealt with internally and as quickly as possible, so as to reduce any further international embarrassment.

The whole of Russia was put on alert and increased security measures were introduced in the cities in a nationwide 'terrorist hunt', because many of the terrorists had managed to flee the scene and escape arrest. It was amazing that anyone at all had escaped, considering the vast numbers of soldiers and police, the extra militia, and manned checkpoints at every village. Everyone seemed determined to catch themselves a terrorist.

With our beards and brown eyes, we were prime suspects. In fact, in the weeks following Beslan, over ten thousand people without proper documentation were arrested, of which Jon and I were but two. Anyone looking remotely foreign was viewed with suspicion. The cosmonaut and 'Hero of the Russian

Federation', Colonel Magomed Tolboyev was beaten up in a street in Moscow because of his Chechen-sounding name. Mob rule reigned in the countryside and Russian nationalism was given a dramatic boost. Anti-Chechen sentiment rocketed and Russia once more went into a state of lockdown.

'At first, we didn't know who the attackers really were,' said Pavlo. 'In fact, when negotiations were taking place, the terrorists insisted on speaking to the authorities in Russian rather than Chechen. They claimed they couldn't understand it. We thought perhaps they were from Ingushetia or Dagestan. Maybe even dissident Georgians.' He looked over his shoulder, as if to check whether anyone was listening.

'Putin downplayed the link with the Chechens, and told everyone it was Muslim fanatics – al-Qaeda and the like. Why? Because he didn't want people to think we couldn't deal with the Chechens, of course. It was announced just last week that amongst the dead attackers were nine Arabs and one black African. Putin said the Saudis were behind it all. And you know what else – they say that two Britons were also killed. Algerians actually, but with British passports.'

Later, stories emerged that a UK citizen named Bouralha was arrested some weeks afterwards, while trying to leave Russia with a bullet hole in his chest. All three were linked to the Finsbury Park Mosque in London.

It was only when the Chechen leader Shamil Basayev issued a statement claiming responsibility for the attack that speculation died down. The likelihood is that Basayev was telling the truth and that it was a Chechen attack, albeit with help and manpower from a group of Arab jihadists that had been operating in the region for the past couple of years. In another twist in the tale, after Basayev's statement, his superior, the Chechen leader Aslan Maskhadov, denied that his forces were involved in the siege, and described the perpetrators of Beslan as 'madmen', driven out of their senses by Russian acts of brutality. He officially condemned the action and all attacks against civilians and called for peace talks between Russia and Chechnya.

Putin responded by putting a ten-million-dollar bounty on both Basayev and Maskhadovs' heads. Basayev was killed two years later, when a truck he was in exploded. The Russians declared it as their victory and the Chechens claimed it was an accident. Maskhadov was killed the following year when Russian agents threw a grenade into his bunker. His body and those of several of his bodyguards were buried in secret in Russia to prevent his grave becoming a shrine of martyrdom.

In the weeks after the Beslan incident, the security levels remained oppressive and reforms in the Kremlin led to the strengthening of the president's powers and those of the security forces. It was in this climate of fear and suspicion that Winfield and I wound our way through the foothills and villages of the North Caucasus.

In addition to a shot of whisky, I offered our latest inquisitor a cigar, which I had been saving for a special occasion. With this, he mellowed and let us go. We got up, said goodbye to Pavlo and went to rejoin our travelling companions on our minibus.

To our disappointment, but rather unsurprisingly, the bus was gone. Its occupants were clearly fed up with waiting for their troublesome cargo and had deserted us. Across the road, the officer looked up from behind his makeshift desk, smirking ever so slightly, amused by our plight.

'Bastards,' shouted Jon vainly down the empty road.

Our captain strutted outside, still puffing away contentedly. He seemed to take on a sudden and unlikely compassion.

'Don't worry, Englishmen, I will find you a new bus.' We looked at him, at once suspicious and doubtful. Soon enough another minibus was called to a halt as the militiaman stepped into the road to search its occupants. We stood to one side, ourselves now a part of the whole theatrical proceedings. The captain bent over and spoke to the driver. After a few minutes and a lot of gesticulating, he waved us to get on the bus.

'This one is going to Vladikavkaz.'

'Finally, let's get out of this hellhole,' sighed Winfield, now exhausted by the whole carry-on. The bus was full of swarthy Georgian men and a few giggling children. We pulled off and drove a mile or so down the road before the bus stopped and the driver turned around. 'Five thousand roubles,' he demanded abruptly. 'What? That's ridiculous – it wasn't that much from Stavropol, and Vladikavkaz is less than ten miles from here. The Russian said you would take us for free.'

He shook his head. 'Not free. Nothing here is free. Pay me five thousand roubles.'

'Bugger off.'

In fact, it was us that had to bugger off, and we left the bus, humiliated and disgruntled by the whole day's affair.

'Let's just walk, it's only a couple of hours,' I mooted.

'Not a chance, I'm not walking ten miles. Besides, I want to give that bloody Russian a piece of my mind.'

Wearily we walked back to the checkpoint in total silence. Winfield had now lost all interest in the trip and although he had given up complaining out loud, he had lost much of his usual imperturbability and wasn't in the mood for light conversation.

The captain was sitting in the concrete bunker and seemed genuinely surprised to see us back.

'What happened?'

I explained that we had been thrown off the bus and he seemed concerned.

'Fucking Georgians!' he bellowed. 'All the same, they'll try to kill you, if you give them a chance,' as he drew a finger across his throat in a deliberate murderous motion.

Pavlo, who was still sitting on the bench looking like a dishevelled refugee, rolled his eyes mockingly.

Half an hour and several shots of whisky later, another bus came to a halt. Once again, the officer spoke to the driver, but this time we insisted on agreeing a price up front. He told us that we must pay one hundred and fifty roubles each, which was a fair rate. He assured us that this one would take us all the way.

'Kavkaz, no problems.' The driver flashed his teeth and gave a strained thumbs-up. We got in and set off, hoping for the best. Luckily there were no more checkpoints to the south of Beslan, and we covered the ten miles without further setback and finally arrived in the ugly little frontier town of Vladikavkaz at six in the evening.

The clouds were low, but high above them the mighty summits of the Caucasus could occasionally be glimpsed jutting through. I smiled at the prospect of leaving Russia and tried to enthuse Jon into following me over the mountains. His reply wasn't encouraging.

'To be honest, I think I've had enough, but let's see what the situation is with getting over the mountain pass and I'll decide based on that.'

I could tell that I had only a couple of days to convince him and things weren't looking all that promising. To make matters worse, we were arrested yet again as we were walking through the dusky streets towards the centre, this time by a fat policeman,

who was sitting in a car seemingly waiting for potential terrorists like ourselves. He ordered us to get into the car and his
second in command, a gaunt youngster, kept his hand firmly on
his pistol handle whilst we complied wearily. He drove us to the
nearby station and once more we were subjected to a full search
and the same routine of questioning. The fat man's trotter-like
hands sifted through our belongings across the floor, as he
rummaged in search of something with which to condemn us.
He found neither the Koran nor the whisky and so quickly
became bored.

Finally, we persuaded him to take us to a hotel and thankfully,
he ordered his sidekick to give us a lift. We found ourselves at
the Hotel Vladikavkaz, a pleasant old building, which seemed
like it would be considerably out of our price range. The other
guests were all very businesslike and I thought I heard a couple
of American accents emanating from some suits at the bar. In
the corner of the lobby, sitting around a small table, were a pair
of serious-looking aid workers.

'We look a bit out of place here, don't we?' I glanced at my
reflection in a huge mirror behind the reception and saw a filthy
vagabond in faux leathers sporting an old army rucksack. 'Eighty
dollars. Special reporter room. With balcony,' said the plain,
forty-year-old woman in passable German.

'We're not journalists,' I explained, 'we're students. Any room
will do. Do you know somewhere cheaper?' I shamelessly
continued my pretence.

'No problem, student discount. We have special student room.
With balcony. Twenty dollars.' We were led up some stairs to
the first floor and shown to the special student room, which I
suspected was rather similar to the special reporter room and
found myself pleasantly surprised.

It was a splendid en suite with a large bath, a television that worked and a balcony overlooking the gushing river below. This was sheer luxury compared with what we were used to and worlds away from the nightmarish past few days.

Jon and I looked at each other. 'We'll take it,' he said, nodding.

At dinner, as we were trying to make heads or tails out of the Cyrillic menu, we were rescued by a pretty Irish woman of around thirty, who invited us to join her. Kathy spoke good Russian and was working in the region for the United Nations Refugee Agency.

'You're doing what?' She stared, disbelieving as we explained our travel plans.

'I think you'll struggle to get over mountains. The highway is a notorious place – it's hardly ever open, either due to the snow or the political situation. I have never been myself, but I'll try to find out if it's possible.'

The Georgian Military Highway crosses the Caucasus mountains, linking Vladikavkaz with Tbilisi, some one hundred and fifty miles to the south. It was built by the Imperial Russian Army in 1799 to assist the conquest of the Caucasus. It follows the traditional invaders' route some two hundred kilometres through the Terek valley and the Darial Gorge, passing the jagged Mount Kazbek and creeping over the high Jvari Pass. It has been the scene of battles both ancient and modern and is littered with the debris of medieval forts and Soviet tanks. It was the same route that Arthur Conolly took in the winter of 1829 on his overland journey, as he tested the way he thought an invading Russian force might reach India.

In the morning, we woke up surprised to find that the whole town was covered in a sheet of white snow, giving it a new glory. The peaks of the mountains rose steeply from the valley and I felt a new excitement taking root in the adventure. Just over these hills lay Georgia, Azerbaijan and the Caspian Sea – the gateway to Asia and the Silk Road was now really in reach. Winter was here, and it added to the sense of urgency that if we wanted to get over the mountains, we would need to act quickly.

After breakfast, we took a walk around the town. Vladikavkaz was founded in 1784 as the base from which to build the highway and launch the Imperial conquest of the south. For many years it was the main Russian military fortress in the region, but now most of the buildings were closed or derelict, and its population appeared glum. For them, the snow brought the onset of months of misery and they had little to be cheery about. Moreover, the town had been a prominent centre of the horrific ethnic cleansing of the 1990s, and more recently, the focus of a series of bombings, assassinations and kidnappings borne out of the sectarian fighting and Chechen insurrection.

As we were ambling about, I noticed the distinctive blue flag of the United Nations fluttering from the roof of a dreary block of flats. I remembered that Kathy said she worked at the mission and suggested that we make a call in and see if she was there; perhaps we would even be able to get an up-to-date report on the situation in the mountains.

We climbed the drab staircase to the fifth floor, where a peeling sign indicated the UN office. I pressed a buzzer. 'Da?'

'We would like to speak to Miss O'Donnell.'

The door opened with a buzz and a clunk and we followed the corridor to the end, where a small sign was emblazoned with the UN logo. We knocked and entered. Inside was a scruffy office, with a great view looking out over the north of the town to the Ossetian plains and beyond towards the sad ruins of

Beslan. I looked around the bureau; there were a few maps on the walls and one room seemed to contain an inordinate amount of radio equipment. In fact, according to the sticker on the door, this diminutive outfit was the broadcasting headquarters of the rather gallantly named 'Radio Free Europe' – a station dedicated to dispersing waves of democracy around the region.

'Hello, *privyet*, is anyone here?' Jon poked around.

'*Da?*' A Russian came out of another door. He had dark, sunken eyes and was wearing a moth-eaten woollen jumper and a pair of stonewashed jeans. There was no sign of Kathy. The man sat down and lit a cigarette and flicked through a semi-pornographic magazine.

'Perhaps you can help us,' Jon addressed the docile individual. He looked up, wholly disinterested.

'*Nyet.*'

'Hang on, I haven't even asked you anything yet.'

'*Nyet.*' He shrugged.

'Oi. We've come for information.'

'*Ny—*'

'Come on,' I interrupted, 'we aren't getting anything out of this imbecile.' I pulled Jon away.

'Let's come back with Kathy later.'

We wandered back across the town disappointed and sat on a bench in the wintry park. A gaggle of geese shuffled towards the river leaving a trail of tiny footprints in the snow. Glistening icicles were beginning to form on the fence and Jon tilted his head back to breathe a column of hot air into the chilly atmosphere, creating a perfect translucent steam cloud. I could tell he wanted to say something.

'If the road is closed, then I'm definitely going home,' he said, after a brief silence. 'I don't want to leave, but I can't afford to get stranded in Georgia, because my job starts in a couple of weeks. Plus, I'm fed up with getting arrested and to be honest I'm not overly keen to get my head cut off by Islamic nut jobs.' He reminded me of Kathy's advice that the region was still very hostile.

'Not only because of the militant Russian forces, don't forget there is also the threat of Chechen and Dagestani guerrillas, North Ossetian separatists, and Ingushetia dissidents, not to mention the multitude of criminal gangs and roving bandits. It's bloody dodgy.'

'Fair enough. I understand,' I replied, trying to conceal my disappointment. Of course, I did understand. Jon had only ever really wanted to come as far as Russia, and I had half-suspected that he only applied for his Georgian visa to humour me. At the end of the day, he had a job and I didn't, and he was looking forward to the bright lights of London. I could understand that. What did I have? The prospect of the next few months living as a vagrant, in the wilds of Asia, alone and unwashed. The realisation hit home.

'I understand,' I nodded slowly, if only for my own benefit.

We went for a drink at the Hotel Imperial, which had a nice lobby and prices to match, while we reflected what was to be done. Kathy sauntered in, looking tired. 'Sorry I missed you, been so busy,' she drawled. I smelt alcohol. I guessed she had better things to do than pander to the whims of a couple of demanding backpackers. As if to apologise, she took us to a 'UN security approved' restaurant. It was plain and the food was dreadful. She avoided my questions about the highway and began talking about how busy she was at work. I resolved to ask her outright.

'Listen, Kathy. Can we cross the highway or not?'

'I thought you weren't serious, I thought you were joking.' She paused to take a gulp of wine, 'To be honest, I think it would be lunacy. But if you insist, I will arrange a meeting with our security advisor.' I was annoyed that she hadn't even tried to find out for us, but agreed to the meeting.

The next day we followed Kathy back to the UN office and trudged back up the stairs to where the same miserable Russian was sitting watching some dreadful local television. He grunted at Kathy.

'Take no notice of Maxim. He's our administrator.'

'And this is Scott, our security advisor.'

Scott turned around from the map he had been studying on the wall.

He was a short, balding Englishman, with a hint of a cockney accent. He wore grey cargo pants and a neatly pressed check shirt. He was a former sergeant in the British army, and the only other English speaker to reside permanently in the town.

'Alright? What do you pair want?' he snarled.

His chin was thrust forwards and he seemed to be looking down his nose at us. He looked a bit like an angry Jack Russell. Before we could answer, he turned his back to us and banged his fist on the wall map. 'Facking Rashans,' he swore loudly, probably for Maxim's benefit. 'Can't do anything with 'em.'

'Well?' he flicked an eye in our direction.

'These two want to go over the highway down to Georgia. They want to know if it's safe?' Kathy intervened on our behalf.

'Safe? Ha!' He screwed his face up and blew out his chest so that he changed from a Jack Russell into a pigeon.

''Course it ain't safe. Anyway, far as I know it's closed. You can have a go if you're daft enough, but you'll get arrested by the Russians for certain.'

'We're used to that.'

I looked at Jon, who was shaking his head in resignation. I was getting obstinate and didn't like Scott's patronising tone.

'Why are you here, anyway? We don't get tourists here. You wouldn't last ten minutes in the mountains,' he said smugly.

This was enough, I was on the verge of telling him that he was a narrow-minded scaremonger, so wrapped up in his little world of inventing security issues to justify his own job title, and that I had hitchhiked across Iraq during the war only last year, and . . .

I checked myself just in time. After all, this guy was only trying to help, and I suppose what he said was true. It *was* a dangerous place to be, despite my own optimism and perhaps naive trust in the human spirit and my own ability to get away with things.

'Right, thanks for your help.' I forced myself to shake his hand, and Kathy's, too, and went with Jon back to the hotel to pack our bags. It was a solemn, silent walk and I already knew what was going to happen. It was hopeless trying to convince him to come any further and I was expecting his reply.

'I'm going home,' said Jon. 'There is a train back to Moscow leaving tonight.' He sounded apologetic. I didn't want to prolong the uncertainty and so tried to make light of the situation.

'It's alright. I hope it's a better experience than the bus. Make sure you stock up on whisky.'

Jon smiled, then quickly put on a serious face.

'Lev, do me one favour.'

'Yes, of course.'

'Avoid the highway. I've got a bad feeling about this one, that's all. Everyone says it's lunacy. I know that bloke was a bit of a prat, but what he says is true. Kathy, too. They all say it's dangerous. Find another way, please.'

We both spent the afternoon making arrangements to move on. For about two hours we fumbled around in silence, neither of us daring to speak to each other. I left him alone for a while and went in search of information on how to get to Georgia. I asked around everywhere – taxi drivers, shopkeepers and at the hotel, but nobody seemed to know. It was a place to be avoided as far as the Russians were concerned. Finally, as I was about to give up in exhaustion, I bumped into Kathy in the hotel lobby.

'I heard a rumour that there might be a boat from the Black Sea port of Sochi that skirts around the coast from Russia into Georgia. It's a long shot, but you could have a go,' she said.

No one in Vladikavkaz seemed to know if it was operational, but it would be worth a shot if I could get there. I figured that now Jon wasn't going to be coming with me, there was less of a rush. In fact, after a bit more digging, it seemed my only hope and so I made my mind up to try and make it to the coast that afternoon. What was the point in hanging around? Looking out onto the street, I noticed that the clouds had now parted to reveal the full splendour of the mountains and underfoot the snow was turning to slush. The Russians, normally miserable, seemed to have a spring in their step. Carrying our backpacks, looking like a fine pair of vagabonds, Jon and I took one final stroll together, towards the train station in the brilliant sunshine.

'Looks like one last warm spell to get you into Asia,' Jon said cheerily. His beard was still quite thin, but he had a great moustache, and he reminded me of a young Errol Flynn. I wasn't angry, or even disappointed with Jon. He had made up his mind and I mine. Somehow it seemed right to go our separate ways: I knew we would remain good friends, whatever, and there were plenty more adventures ahead.

The station was busy, full of passengers hauling goods in and out. Women carried huge nylon bags full of blankets and it reminded me that it would be wise to stock up on provisions. We found a market stall outside selling all manner of food. It kept us occupied whilst we waited for our trains and meant that we didn't need to talk about separating.

'Salami looks good, I think I'll get some.'

It was all very English.

'Actually, I need a new pair of socks.'

We bought our tickets: Winfield back to Moscow, via Krasnodar and over a thousand miles of the central steppe; a laborious three-day journey. And me to the port of Sochi, some three hundred miles to the west, via the town of Novorossiysk. We barely said a word to each other until we reached the platform.

'So, I suppose I'll see you in London?'

'Yes. Catch you later.'

We shook hands briefly. As I turned to walk away to my own platform, Jon smiled, but underneath he looked serious.

'Listen mate, don't get yourself on Al-Jazeera.' Alex's words echoed through my mind as Winfield disappeared into the crowd.

The time was four-thirty p.m. and I set off on the train, chasing the sun, a feeling of emptiness engulfing my mind. I was going west, the wrong direction entirely, but onwards nonetheless. Outside, any semblance of the wintry gloom vanished in the dying radiance that lit the steppe a golden orange, as I left the outskirts of Vladikavkaz behind. Only the indistinct outline of a farmhouse or a little lane broke the infinite sea of bronzed corn fields. Yet despite this natural splendour, came the inevitable gloom at losing a travelling companion and friend. From now on there would be no one to share an evening card game, or complain to about the awful food; no one to watch the bags whilst the other went to answer the call of nature, or to help translate the elusive Cyrillic scrawl. From now on, I would have to watch my own back and put myself at the mercy and kindness of strangers.

I turned my gaze to the crowd inside. Ashen, vacant, sad faces. I wondered if they ever took solace in a setting sun or a brilliant sky. Perhaps they did, but it seemed only ever in silent, melancholic contemplation. An old woman with a lurid headscarf scowled at me whilst munching on some hard bread, a pale young boy with black hair scraped back from his forehead listened to his music player as if in a deep trance. I climbed up to the top bunk and found myself veritably squashed against the ceiling as the fat lady below manoeuvred herself in bed. I wondered if Jon was as uncomfortable as I was.

Novorossiysk appeared into view in the late morning and I spilled out, spirit-like, into the train station feeling cold, dirty, exhausted, foul-tempered and not a little lonely. There was nothing about Novorossiysk to cheer me up. It was a dull place and I immediately became the object of attention for a cluster of bored taxi drivers, who all wanted to drive down the coast to Sochi. By now I was fed up with hitching and thoroughly dejected by public transport and for a moment considered the appealing prospect of arriving in style.

My conscience got the better of me and so instead I began to walk out of the town in the hope of flagging down a lift. I was lucky, a lorry picked me up on the outskirts and trundled slowly southwards, stopping every half an hour or so for a cigarette break until we finally reached the coastal road, where I got my first glimpse of the Black Sea shimmering delightfully in the midday light. It's incredible how the sea can cheer you up.

To the southeast, the snow-capped mountains vied for my attention, and I was suddenly filled with a new sense of exhilaration by the knowledge that soon I would be in a new continent. Soon enough, the high-rise flats, towering hotels, and vibrant *dachas* of the city came into view. In spite of the sprawl, it looked a very green town. Strange, exotic palm trees sprouted from the gardens and lawns of the mansions and the sea front looked almost subtropical. I couldn't believe that it had been snowing the day before. *Jon doesn't know what he's missing*, I thought to myself.

The resort city stretches for ninety miles along the coast and lays claim to being one of the 'longest' cities in the world. Sochi has been colourfully described as the Florida of Russia, with its agreeable climate, pleasant beaches and holiday atmosphere, but it hadn't always had such a Disneyland past. Before the mid-nineteenth century, the 'Russian Riviera' used to belong to Georgia, and formed part of the ancient realm of Circassia, a wild region that was the thorn in Russia's side for centuries. Despite the Georgian Military Highway completing in the last year of the eighteenth century, it would take another sixty years of campaigning before Russian troops had successfully conquered the mountain kingdoms of the Caucasus, and even then, uprisings and insurrections continued throughout the nineteenth and twentieth centuries, up until the present day.

After the Georgian defeat at the end of the Caucasian war in the 1860s, the Tsar subjected the whole coastal region to a scorched-earth policy and forcibly ejected almost all of the original population north of the mountains, resulting in the little known 'Circassian Diaspora'. It was a calculated move to Russify the badlands. Almost two million refugees sought new homes to the south in Turkey. Since 1870, the coastline had been actively resettled by ethnic Russians, Ukrainians, Greeks, Germans and several other more 'desirable' races. Nowadays, it was full of Russian tourists.

After its ethnic changeover, Sochi was established as a fashionable resort area under Stalin, who liked the place so much that he had his favourite *dacha* or holiday home built in the city. The coast soon became dotted with imposing neoclassical buildings, even more so after the nearby resort towns of Yalta and Sevastopol became Ukrainian territory in the 1950s.

Sochi soon emerged as the unofficial summer capital and became increasingly popular with wealthy and influential Russians in the last years of the Soviet regime, until the onset of capitalism allowed overseas travel. In more recent years, Putin had put a lot of investment into the city to attract the Muscovite millionaires and gangsters to spend their money there instead of the brothels of Thailand. I noticed that the beachside McDonalds was filled with the trendy children of wealthy northern families enjoying the October quiet season.

I spent a few hours wandering along the promenade looking for a good spot to sleep. Beaches are always a bad idea, because there is always an amorous couple who have the same idea. The hotels were all exorbitantly priced, even in the low season, and so after considerable mental torment dodging prostitutes and tramps in the park, I settled on a bushy roundabout in the middle of a main road, where I hoped I wouldn't be disturbed.

8

Land of the Golden Fleece

'Where have you been?'

'Moscow,' I said to the ill-tempered babushka at the immigration desk, wanting to keep it simple.

I was feeling refreshed after enjoying a morning swim in the icy cold waters of the Black Sea – much to the amusement of some Russian children watching from the promenade – and looked forward to leaving the hostility of Russia behind.

At the port, the queue had been long and volatile, and the female official from the Russian Border Service took over an hour in examining my passport. She eventually led me through a door away from the main hallway and into a small cell that contained a single plastic chair and an old steel table. There was a clock on the wall that had frozen in time and declared 5.30 in perpetuity. I had been ordered to sit down.

'Why have you not registered?'

'I registered in St Petersburg.'

'What are you doing in Sochi?'

'I'm on holiday.'

'Why is your hair wet?'

'I've been swimming.'

'Where are you going?'

'Georgia.'

She left me alone. It was the kind of wearisome conversation that I had grown used to and I was worried I would miss the boat, but after a short while she came back clutching my passport.

'You may leave.' She opened the door. 'But remember . . .', she took on a stern, almost violent grimace, '. . . the Georgians are terrible people.'

With her rather unlikely advice, I boarded the rickety old, modified fishing boat bound for the port cities of Poti and Batumi.

'Which do you want to go?' asked a dark-faced Georgian manning the gangplank. I expected another banal interrogation.

'I don't really know,' was the honest answer. 'Which is closest to Tbilisi?'

He seemed perplexed and shrugged his shoulders. 'Neither. But Poti is cheapest.' The man smiled; it was the first smile I had encountered in a while.

'OK, that'll do.'

On board, we waited another half an hour for the boat to fill up. The passengers were all Georgian, around sixty of them, mostly stocky, middle-aged men, but there were a couple of young women and a handful of children. The captain signalled our departure with a short blast on the rather feeble horn and we sailed out into the late afternoon haze of the Black Sea.

I squeezed my way past the groups that lay sprawled out inside the cabin and made my way to the stern. It was only ten feet wide, but all of the younger passengers were there, eager to wave goodbye to Russia. I joined them and it wasn't long before I was approached by a tall young man with ginger hair and the shiny nose of a whisky drinker. He looked remarkably Celtic. He studied me for a few seconds.

'*Gamarjoba,*' he smiled.

'*Privyet*,' I replied, not understanding any Georgian. He frowned.

'*Ruski?*'

'*Nyet, Ingielski*,' I replied in rather poor Russian.

'*Inglisieli?*' he said, correcting me. The Ginger seemed confused, but incredibly, he continued in English, 'Hello, my name is Lasha.' I was amazed, this was the first confident English speaker that I had met since meeting Olga on the train to Volgograd.

'Lasha Samushia,' he continued. 'I am a footballer from Poti Kolkheti. Do you like football?'

'Yes, of course,' I exaggerated.

'What is your team? Manchester United or Liverpool?'

'Erm, Port Vale.' I hadn't watched football since I was eleven years old, but thought it loyal to name my old team.

'Hmmm. They're very bad. They lost to Derby last week. Do you think they will get promoted?'

Oh shit, I thought. He knows his stuff. 'Erm, probably not this season.' I was running out of ammunition, but fortunately he changed the subject.

'Are you on a journey?'

'Yes, I suppose I am.'

'I have been on mine. I am returning home, for the first time in many months.'

Lasha told me that he had been living and working in Russia for the past six months, where his ill mother was being treated in a hospital in North Ossetia. 'She will die soon. I will probably never see her again.'

'Where are you going?' he asked with a smile.

I told him I was trying to hitchhike to India.

He looked unimpressed. 'We don't get many tourists. Are you looking forward to my country?'

'Of course,' I said. But in reality, I was quite nervous, expecting another round of arrests and miserable people, but within ten minutes, Lasha had altered my outlook immeasurably.

'You will love my country, I am sure. You will be our honoured guest.' He slapped me on the back with the familiarity of an old friend.

The atmosphere was totally different on the boat than amongst any group of Russians I had met. For a start, these Georgians were smiling. More than that, they were laughing and joking amongst themselves. Lasha was travelling alone, but before long he'd found a girl to whom he could chat.

'Meet my English friend, his name is *Left*.'

I was surprised that Marina, too, spoke very good English. Soon there was a small crowd, all asking where was I from and what I did. Lasha announced proudly that I was his guest in Georgia; moreover, his good friend. I was taken aback at this rather rapid acquaintance, but equally impressed at his swift trust and friendliness. Lasha then asked me if I would like to visit his family home and see his city.

'It would be an honour,' I said, welcoming the prospect of meeting some friendly people. He was evidently genuine, and I relished the thought of actually getting to spend some time with the locals, rather than actively avoiding the suspicion or hostility that I had experienced in Russia.

We made our way back inside, as the cold sea air began to take its toll. The cabin was full. Already the men had begun to smoke and drink and eat. Small groups had formed circles, where they were starting to play card games; others produced veritable picnics on the deck and invited strangers to join them. Lasha approached the oldest man, a stout individual of over sixty, whose leathery skin, stubble and grey eyes could not help giving away a snapshot of former strength and wisdom.

Lasha introduced himself first and then me. The man studied me for a moment with a deadpan expression, before suddenly raising a smile and offering me a glass of vodka. I took it and swallowed the syrupy liquor in one. Lasha slapped me heartily on the back and the old man shook my hand with an iron-like grip. It appeared I had done well and before long we were pirouetting around all of the groups in a similar fashion. We drank plenty of vodka and ate delicious flat bread.

One of the teenagers who had been outside came up to me. He couldn't speak any English, but tried to communicate with his hands enthusiastically. He was short, fat and had one immense eyebrow that went right across his face. He offered a podgy hand that had more fur on it than a bear's paw, which I shook, before the little chap took off a bracelet that he was wearing – a handmade black thing that looked like a small rope – and thrust it into my hand with a huge grin. 'A gift from Georgia,' is what I guessed he said. I thanked him in English, quite embarrassed by his generosity, before remembering to ask Lasha for the Georgian word for thank you. '*Gmadlobt.*'

I was wearing some 'travelling beads' myself, cheap wooden things that I had been forced to buy the year before by a persistent vendor in Cairo, and that had proven useful in convincing Russians that I was a tourist rather than a Chechen. I took them off and gave them to the monobrow. He was positively beaming with pride.

The girl, Marina, came over. She began talking with me and Lasha winked. 'Mari' was a receptionist in Batumi, but had been working in Sochi because the money was better there.

'I love the English language,' she said, 'I am studying it in my own time.'

She had never met anyone from England. In fact, she had never met an English speaker. Nevertheless, her pronunciation was excellent and she asked if I could help her with some vocabulary.

'He will help you if you give him your phone number,' Lasha interjected. I was expecting her to withdraw coyly, but she didn't.

'He will get my phone number when he asks for it,' she smiled sweetly, as Lasha raised his eyebrows and walked away grinning.

Someone turned on a radio and before long the boat had become a very merry party scene, which continued, accompanied by several bottles of vodka, well into the early hours.

I woke up feeling terrible, face down on the wooden slats of the deck. I found that someone had covered me with a woollen blanket. It was light outside and a few of the others were already awake. The noise of crashing waves and the steady undulation came to my attention and I remembered that I was on a boat. I rubbed the sleep out of my eyes and leant over the body that happened to be next to me and then stepped over the others, who seemed to have simply passed out where they lay. I made my way steadily outside of the cabin, trying carefully not to vomit or step on someone's head, to where Lasha was already standing, quite awake and looking sprightly. Although he was only two months older than me, his pale features and carrot hair made him look much more senior.

'*Gamarjoba!*'

'*Gamarjoba*, Lasha,' I replied, squinting into the bright fresh morning air. It hurt.

'Look!' he exclaimed. 'Georgia!'

We had followed the coastline south throughout the night and now, only a few miles distant, lay the town of Poti. I could make out a grey, low-lying port with the pink and white hues of

Arthur Conolly, the early 19th century adventurer and explorer in whose footsteps I followed. Portrait by James Atkinson, *c.* 1840.

Alexander the Great, depicted on a Greek coin from the 6th century, whose conquests laid the foundations for the Silk Road.

The Moroccan explorer Ibn Battuta (1304–1369). Illustration from a book by Jules Verne, 1878.

The famed Italian explorer Marco Polo (1254–1324). Mosaic from the Municipal Palace of Genoa.

Hitchhiking through France. I travelled through ten countries before getting stopped at the Russian border. Hitching was unpredictable and often down to sheer luck, but it was a great way to meet people.

Red Square, Moscow. The beating heart of metropolitan Russia.

Old communists protesting about the recent moves towards capitalism.

The German mill at Volgograd (formerly Stalingrad).

An old Soviet bunker position under the watchful eye of the Mamayev Kurgan ('The Motherland Calls') statue on the site of the battle of Stalingrad.

The mighty Caucasus. These mountains form the dividing line between Europe and Asia.

The boat from Sochi, Russia, to Poti, Georgia, with Lasha Samushia (middle).

Lasha's apartment in Poti, Georgia. It had no running water, gas or electricity.

Khertvisi, Georgia. Once a key site on the Silk Road, and under constant attack from invaders. It is claimed that both Alexander the Great and Genghis Khan took the fortress at some point in their careers.

Vardzia, Georgia. This cave city is still home to hundreds of people.

Tabriz Bazaar. The largest and oldest covered market in the Middle East.

Murals of anti-Western propaganda on the walls of the former US embassy in Tehran, Iran.

Si-o-se-pol Bridge, Esfahan, Iran. A marvel of Safavid architecture.

Friday prayer time in Naqsh-e Jahan Square, Esfahan. A glory of the ancient Silk Road.

Two women in a *chador* and a *hijab*, Esfahan, Iran. A place where cultures and ideas collide. Iran remains a fractured society where a dichotomy of conservative Islam and modernity exists in fragile balance.

the administrative buildings. There was a huge black factory immediately behind the harbour wall and in the distance the outlines of apartment blocks became visible. A breakwater jutted out into the sea, into which the dark waves crashed violently, despite the calm yet overcast skies. As we neared the harbour, I noticed the Georgian flag fluttering over the port authority office. The distinctive red cross on a white background at once made me feel at home, yet at the same time, I remembered that this would be a very different place. Technically, we were in Asia.

Or that's what I thought. I had always assumed that the Caucasus Mountains had formed the border with Europe and Asia, just as the Ural Mountains do in Russia.

'Asia? Please, no,' Lasha implored. 'We are a European country. We are Christians, our heritage is Greek. We are certainly a lot more European than Turkey.'

I thought about this and supposed that he had a point. But where was the line drawn? Georgia, Azerbaijan and Armenia all lie to the south of the Caucasus. To the south of them was Anatolia – Turkish Asia Minor – and Iran, most definitely Asian, and to the east is the Caspian Sea, flanked by Kazakhstan and Turkmenistan, again undeniably Asian. You could see how Azerbaijan ought to be Asian with its Muslim majority and Persian-Turkic heritage. Armenia, like Georgia, is a Christian state and also falls into the Eurasian no-man's-land.

The problem, of course, is caused by the fact that the European and Asian landmass is one and the same. People have been traipsing between the two for as long as man has been traipsing at all, and those places that do not fit conveniently on either have always been the ones torn between the two competing cultures. But speaking with Lasha, he had no doubts as to where his country belonged.

'Let me tell you a bit about my city. Poti has been recorded in history since classical times. It was here that Jason and the Argonauts came to find the famous Golden Fleece.'

'Do people really believe that?'

'Yes, they do. Of course, it has been embellished by myth and legend, but it is based on the truth. You go into any old person's home and you will see a little statue of the *Argo*. They think they are descendants of the Greeks.'

The legend is a popular one in Georgia, and archaeologists have discovered that there is some truth in it – the coastline was being settled by the Greeks as early as the seventh century BC. Meanwhile the lands to the south came under repeated attack from firstly the Persians, the invading armies of Alexander the Great, and finally the Romans. After the collapse of the Roman Empire, Georgia proclaimed itself as an independent kingdom – and this proved to be a golden age, where culture and the sciences boomed. But being sandwiched between East and West, Islam and Christianity was a double-edged sword. Soon the Mongols were marching across the Caucasus and the invasions devastated Georgia's economy, population, and cities. The rise of the Ottoman Turks further sealed the deal.

It wasn't until 1805, when Russia invaded Georgia to repel the Persians, that it became known to the outside world again. Georgia was soon incorporated into the Tsarist dominions and for the first time in centuries was united, albeit at the loss of her autonomy. For a while, things seemed to be on the up, as the country was ruled by a prince who was a poet, novelist and orator. He financed new schools and supported the Georgian national theatre and in doing so revived a sense of independent culture and nationalism.

But then the Russian revolution happened in 1917 and plunged the region into bloody civil war and chaos. In 1921 the Red Army invaded Georgia again and it was to remain under harsh and cruel Soviet rule behind the Iron Curtain for seventy years. Stalin – Georgia's most famous son – killed over a hundred and fifty thousand of his own countrymen in the purges.

In the Second World War, many Georgians and other Caucasian peoples actually fought on the German side, where they formed the Georgian legion, on account of their acute hatred of Russia. As a result of this so-called duplicity, Stalin ordered the mass exile of the Chechens and Muslims to Siberia. As a Georgian himself, he refused to believe that his own countrymen were capable of disloyalty and instead scapegoated these northern Caucasus tribes.

It wasn't until 1991, after the fall of the Soviet Union, that Georgia regained its independence. But not everyone was in favour of unification; some provinces wanted to be self-governing.

By far the most troublesome region was Abkhazia, a semi-autonomous region in the north-west that began a campaign of violence against Georgia almost as soon as the Cold War was over. Government forces were sent in to quell the violence, but the Abkhazians fought back with the help of paramilitaries and covert support from the Russian military. A year later, the Georgians suffered a catastrophic defeat and the entire Georgian population was expelled from the region. Thousands were killed and hundreds of thousands become refugees. Some fled to Russia and others into Georgia proper.

It was to one of these refugee families that Lasha belonged. As we made our way from the port, Lasha told me about his family.

'We had been forced to flee the violence in 1992, when I was just a child, and I miss my homeland.' Lasha's family had been torn apart by the fighting and many were now living north of the mountains inside Russia. Others weren't so lucky.

'I haven't seen my cousins in twelve years, I have no idea if they are dead or alive.'

Tensions between the Caucasus republics and Russia were steadily worsening. The Russian government had now publicly accused Georgia of harbouring Chechen terrorists during the Second Chechen War and, of course, the Beslan massacre hadn't exactly helped. Everyone knew that Georgia's small Muslim population were some of the most fanatical jihadists out there.

There was more friction caused by Georgia's close ties with the United States and a very 'Western' looking policy of alliance. In fact, the US had been sending aid and troops to Georgia for the past two years to train and equip the fledgling Georgian army. Georgia had also stated its ambition to join NATO and the EU, a further snub to the Russians.

To counter this, Russia continued to provide political, economic and military support to Abkhazia and South Ossetia, and stationed its own troops inside these Georgian territories as peace-keepers. The month before I arrived, there had been several clashes in the mountains north of Tbilisi between Georgian forces and roving militias.

'The mountains,' Lasha informed me, 'are still full of bandits.'

Lasha hailed a taxi and we drove through the town to his apartment. I was excited. So far, Russian inhospitality had meant that I had either stayed in cheap hotels or slept rough; this was the first time that I had been invited to stay at a complete stranger's house.

I didn't care that the city looked like a post-apocalyptic Orwellian slum. The roads were in a terrible state, full of holes;

the buildings were crumbling and hadn't been repaired in decades. Piles of rubbish was strewn in the streets and covered the pavements. Cars that hadn't been driven in years were simply abandoned.

Lasha lived on the seventh floor of a concrete block of flats. From the outside, it looked as though some of the rooms had been burned out, as smoke stains darkened the grey facade. A red rust-coloured smear, from years of water leaking from the iron pipes, ran down from some of the windows. It was a miserable hovel and if this had been Russia, I wouldn't have dared go anywhere near it. Lasha put on a brave face and as we climbed the stairs (the lift had long since given up), he apologised for the state of the place.

'We used to have such a beautiful house in Abkhazia. One day, I shall earn enough to move out of here.'

Lasha knocked on a steel door, which was partly obscured by a dripping water pipe that jutted out of the wall on the landing.

I felt a little uncomfortable as his sister answered. They hadn't seen each other in six months and here I was, intruding on their reunion. She looked at me, with her head cocked to one side.

'This is our guest, he will be staying for a few days,' Lasha told her. 'He is from England.'

She smiled warmly and greeted me with a formal curtsy and a coy handshake. She was a few years older than him, with shoulder-length, raven black hair and narrow and piercing eyes. 'I'm Lali,' she said, continuing in English, 'Please come in.'

Lali was an English teacher, and like the girl on the boat, had never met a native English speaker.

'You look different to how I imagined the English people,' she said as she rushed around making her brother and this strange foreigner comfortable.

'You look almost Georgian ... apart from the beard.' I suddenly felt rather scruffy as I sat there in my jeans and parka jacket, acutely conscious of the fact that I hadn't shaved in some weeks. Lasha was wearing a shiny black shirt and trousers with pointy shoes, looking like he was about to audition for a job; she was in a pretty black-and-white striped dress that reached the floor.

'Yes, um, sorry about that – it's just that I am travelling south to Turkey and then to Iran and I will need to blend in.'

'Did you say Turkey? Iran?'

Lali looked aghast at this. 'Why?'

They didn't seem to understand why anyone of apparently sane character would travel willingly to a Muslim country.

'It's very dangerous there, you know.'

I thought about how I could assuage their misgivings and realised that for some people, a truthful explanation would not be satisfactory. How do you explain to a poverty-stricken refugee that you are travelling for no apparent purpose through, to them, incredibly dangerous and inhospitable places? It seemed a little frivolous and indulgent, so I fibbed.

'I'm a journalist. It's my job.'

'Yes, yes, a journalist. I thought so – you look like a newspaper man! Left, the writer of dangerous travels.'

I turned a shade of purple, but this seemed to comfort them somewhat, and allay any fears that I was going to such barbaric and far-off lands out of sheer inquisitiveness. At least by saying that I was working, they could empathise a little, especially Lasha, who had been in economic exile for so much of his life.

'It's a shame, though. I don't think I could do that job. So much travelling in dangerous places, and away from your family all the time,' said Lasha with genuine concern.

Now I felt like a total fraud, playing on the sympathy of these honest folk. But they didn't think I was mad anymore, which was the alternative.

The three of us talked for some time. Lasha told me about his experiences as a footballer and Lali went into more detail about their family's struggle. Not only was she a teacher, but quite a poet, and produced a child's school notebook full of English poetry that she had written.

> *Someday this People will manage to reach out*
> *To a more benevolent fate*
> *But just now*
> *At the very edge of death*
> *In this gloomy canyon*
> *Where it's dark and damp*
> *This People, who have not yet settled*
> *Their life*
> *Are squirming painfully in the body of the world.*

'It is called "The Seeds of Fire",' said Lali, with a shy smile.

It was a pleasant day of twenty degrees and reminded me of the weather back home on a warm September night. As we ambled around the city, Lasha was energetic in pointing out every detail that an aspiring journalist might require for his studies, and as we proceeded to inspect bronze busts of town notaries, I began to regret my falsified profession. He was also quick to apologise for anything that was not particularly new, or in his eyes worthy, and would shake his ginger head.

Inside the town market, a bustling food hall full of fresh produce, he enthusiastically pointed out a crate of apples that had the European Union's blue flag stamped across the wooden outer. He grasped me by the arm and pointed at it with an unusual vigour.

'Look, these have EU standard!' he beamed proudly. 'Soon we will become part of the EU, and then nobody will call us Asian again.'

On one stall, I noticed something incongruous – a huge ceramic plate with an ornate painting of an English country scene. Being from the Potteries, I asked to see it. The elderly shopkeeper nodded wistfully, as though I was asking to root through his garbage bin.

'Is this one EU?' enquired Lasha.

'Not quite.'

It was a nineteenth-century piece of Wedgwood fine bone china, worth a small fortune. How it got here to be used as a holder for plastic baubles will forever remain a mystery. I placed the precious bowl delicately down on the wooden table, sighed, and continued the tour with my new Georgian family.

Lasha was quite the homecoming hero. As we wandered about the town he was treated like a prince, people everywhere flocked to shake his hand and ask him about his Russian sojourn. He introduced me to literally hundreds of people that after-noon. In every encounter, he was personal and graceful – explaining to them with outright delight about his guest, 'a real Englishman'.

'Come, newspaper man, there are more people I want you to meet.'

Lasha knew people in all levels of society. Young children playing in the street came to kick a football in his direction, so that they could boast they had played with a professional. He was very popular with all of the women at the university. Old men on street corners called him over and spoke to him like a long-lost son, though I did not know what had become of his own father.

Scarcely a car went by that didn't give a toot or a wave, nor did a single person fail to stop or cross the street to welcome back this champion of the city. We called on many houses, including several of his elderly relatives, and by the end of the day I felt that I had met the entire population of Poti.

We went back to Lasha's flat for a candlelit meal (since there was no electricity), then I freshened up as much as possible (there was no running water, either) and we went out for another round of evening visits. It was strange to wander the dark alleyways that, although pitch black, were bustling with people. There were no street lights and the only illumination that came from the windows was the flicker of a candle or the red glow of a cigarette. Yet even out of the shadows, strange faces would appear from nowhere; huge grinning teeth and bristling moustaches.

'*Gamarjoba, Gamarjoba!*' would come the cry, and another hand would be thrust out of the blackness wanting to rally with Lasha's coveted palm. Perhaps it was his unique red hair and Celtic features that set him apart and gave him an almost phantom-like appearance. What a pair we must have made – an English-looking Georgian and a Georgian-looking Englishman.

We ended the night inside his neighbour's room within the apartment block, where an old man taught me to play backgammon. The air was filled with cigarette smoke and if you stood up you could barely see across the room. The vodka flowed freely, though, and I dished out the last of the scotch and it was three in the morning before Lasha and I settled down to sleep on the floor of the living room. It was a cosy arrangement, but one out of necessity. Lali occupied the only bedroom.

As I settled down to a drunken slumber and listened to the gentle patting of rain on the windowsill, I felt grateful for having a roof over my head. Moreover, I felt grateful that I wasn't born in Georgia. The standard of living in Poti was low. Few people had electricity or gas, almost none had running water. Whole families lived in single rooms that served many purposes. Even televisions were scarce, so the people had to make their own entertainment. It was curiously Victorian; there were some books and a few instruments, and families gathered around a piano and sang happy folk songs that reminded them of better times.

Still, I didn't hear anyone complain. The smiles were genuine and hospitality unequalled. I had been plied with coffee, wine and vodka. Sweets and cake were brought out, even though they were a luxury and had probably been saved for a special occasion. Like simple poor folk around the world, they stuck together as families and looked after not only each other, but anyone passing through who happened to be in need.

In the morning, we visited the language institute, which Lali told me was part of the university where she taught. It was full of incredibly handsome women. They were vivacious creatures; not afraid to stare and giggle at the sight of a strange Westerner and it wasn't long before some of them approached me.

Girl 1: 'Hello, my name is Lulu.'

LW: 'Hello, I'm Lev.'

Girl 1: 'Are you married?'

LW (somewhat embarrassed): 'No.'

Girl 1: 'Here is my phone number. Maybe we can get married.'

LW (very embarrassed): 'Maybe. Not just yet.'

Girl 1 exits, smiling.

Girl 2: 'You don't like Lulu?'

LW: 'She seems very nice.'

Girl 2 (interrupting): 'Maybe you want to marry me instead . . .?'

'I want to marry that one, one day,' Lasha proclaimed, as he waved to a beautiful woman who was leaning provocatively against the entrance to the library.

'Well, why not, you are very popular here. And she is very beautiful,' I said truthfully.

'Yes, but where would I live? I would have to send my sister away.'

It was true. I had always assumed marriage to be a choice, something that would inevitably happen when you found someone to love, but it doesn't always happen like that. Lasha simply couldn't afford to be married.

'Maybe one day,' he sighed.

Caucasian girls have long been admired for their exquisite good looks. The famed Circassians of the North Caucasus gave rise to the nineteenth-century legend of the 'Circassian beauty'. Several early European travellers commented on the celebrated beauty of these girls. Lord Byron praises them in *Don Juan*: 'Beauty's brightest colours ... all the hues of heaven'. And Voltaire observes: 'The Circassians are poor, and their daughters are beautiful, and indeed it is in them they chiefly trade.'

Circassian beauty brought its own problems. Females from the region had for centuries been objects of desire for lustful Turkish Sultans, and the acquisition of a Caucasian slave girl became a status symbol of some significance. During the days of the Ottoman Empire, Circassian girls formed the upper echelons of the imperial harem. Actually, the term Circassian was strictly speaking inaccurate, since Circassia was limited to the small coastal region on the present site of Sochi; however, after the population was evicted during the diasporas, there was a lot of intermarrying with Georgians to the south, and anyway, the Turks weren't fussy. Mark Twain lamented that the traffic in Circassian slave girls was still going on as late as 1869.

Word of this beauty soon got back to Europe and it wasn't long before the ladies of London and Paris wanted to know the Circassian secret. Entrepreneurs and showmen were quick to capitalise, and as early as 1782, there were advertisements offering concoctions such as the 'bloom of Circassia'; a potion made of vegetable extract that claimed to be the source of the famed race's loveliness.

The franchise expanded. Circassian lotion, Circassian eye-water, and Circassian hair dye all hit the market as best sellers within a few years. This popularity and the growth of an interest in Orientalism, combined with the issue of slavery, provided sufficient notoriety for an American circus master to display a 'Circassian beauty' at the American Museum in 1865. The girl, Zalumma Agra, was a tall young woman with a fantastic 'Afro' hairstyle, an exact forerunner of the 1970s fashion, whom he dressed in colourful contemporary garments. In actual fact, the girl bore no resemblance to a real Circassian, and it has been suggested that she was a local gypsy woman. Nevertheless, the show was a huge success and captivated the Western imagination.

By the mid-nineteenth century, Circassians were being heralded as the purest form of the white race and this idea became central to the disturbing trend of racial theory. The German anthropologist Johann Friedrich Blumenbach was the first to coin the term 'Caucasian race' in 1800, based solely on the assumption that the tribes of the Caucasus, most notably

Georgians, 'produce the most beautiful race'. It was his interpretation that was to give rise to later pseudo-scientific studies, including the terrible racial theories of the nineteen thirties that were part of the basis of Nazism.

That is how one of the biggest myths of the past two hundred years came to be: all the result of a marketing campaign for beauty products.

In the evening, we visited Lasha's uncle George, who lived in a nice detached bungalow, its garden overgrown with bushes. He was a small man, crinkled by the sun and wind, with greying hair and a wonderful drooping moustache. We sat down to eat *khachapuri* – a kind of bread stuffed with cheese – and *lobio*, which reminded me of chilli beans. At the table were his wife, a plump and jolly lady with shiny cheeks, as well as his son and two daughters.

After the meal, George raised a toast to me and I replied with one to Georgian hospitality. He seemed pleased.

Following that, a toast was raised every few minutes: to Lasha's return, to the good health of the sons, to the hopes of marriage to his daughters, and so on until the jug of vodka was finished. Everyone was quite drunk (except the two girls) and the youngest daughter, who can only have been twelve, then began to play the piano with incredible skill. She began with Beethoven and moved with ease into Georgian folk songs and fluidly into the latest pop music. George clapped with fervent praise and we all joined in.

Suddenly, the eldest son stood up and began to dance; Lasha joined him, and mid-whirl grabbed me by the arm and flung me into the commotion. The table was moved and soon every-one was dancing around the small living room in unabashed merriment. More vodka and more dancing continued well into the night. I felt immensely privileged that these total strangers had invited me into their lives to be a part of a poor but intensely happy existence, if only for a short while.

I came away laden with gifts, including an ornamental plastic statue, which George assured me was an exact replica of the famed *Argo* that came in search of the Golden Fleece. It looked, however, suspiciously like a Venetian canal boat.

9

Cross Roads

I was sad to be leaving Lasha and Lali, but promised to write to them from the capital. Lali filled my rucksack with all kinds of food: small cakes and bread, wine and sweets. Before I left, we ate a filling breakfast and raised a final toast. I was by now accustomed to downing vodka at eight in the morning and threw it back without wincing.

Lasha walked with me to the bus station and tried to insist on paying for my ticket to Tbilisi. I naturally refused and instead bought him a beer, to thank him for his incredible kindness. I told him that one day I would like to return. But as the shaky old bus pulled out of the station and sped eastwards, I felt a tinge of regret that I would never be able to fully repay the debt that I owed these humble people.

The bus wound away from the coast and followed the Colchis valley inland. The mountains, which had previously been distant pimples on the far horizon, grew nearer on both sides; the Caucasus massif to the north and the lesser Caucasus to the south. The landscape was transformed into a barren scrubland as we snaked upwards. Abandoned houses and decrepit factories littered the arid moorland. Dust began to fill the air, and the Black Sea with its humid coastline became a distant memory. I would not see the coast again for another five thousand miles.

With Europe behind me, I felt an immense sense of

excitement at the thought of the unknown road ahead. We passed by a roadside shack selling what looked like dumplings, and flies swarmed unopposed around the rough flatbread. An old man with a weathered face was asleep under the shade of the wooden canopy, and nearby a small brown bear was chained to a post, looking miserable. It had sad eyes that seemed to stare deep into my consciousness, as if it knew I was a foreigner, and the only one that took notice. I got back on the bus and that bear didn't take its eyes off me, even as we pulled away and trundled on up the mountain.

Further up the road, in the shadow of a huge cliff, a hotel stood half built. The roof was open and iron girders poked from the breeze blocks into the clear sky. A neon sign announced its name: The Silk Road hotel. I felt, strangely, a wave of satisfaction come over me, perhaps because I had made it this far, and had finally caught up with the elusive trail that had caught my imagination so many years ago.

The Silk Road: it was the backbone of world trade for hundreds of years, and yet now there is barely a trace of it. This was the same path of the great Persian invasions, and later, those of the Mongol hordes. Its trail led to Central Asia and to Afghanistan and beyond that, India and China. Its followers, with their great caravans of camels laden with great treasures, traversed some of the highest mountains on earth to acquire the silk of the Far East and spices of the subcontinent.

Marco Polo trekked this way in the fourteenth century to pay homage to Kublai Khan, and the Mughal warrior, Babur, used the same route to conquer India a century later. It is famed in the history of civilisation as the link between East and West, of Occident and Orient. But now, after the days of empire have long since passed, it is a mere dusty track, passing through endless deserts and high mountain passes. The roads have disappeared under centuries of sand. All that remains are the names.

It was almost nightfall by the time that we pulled into the dusty brown suburbs of Tbilisi. As I had come to expect, the scene was dominated by ugly, pale tower blocks dating from the Soviet occupation. We drove through the dusky streets to the bus station near to the river. The powerful green waters of the Kura river were named by travelling Europeans after the Persian King, Cyrus the Great. The Georgians, however, refusing to name their national river after a long-forgotten invader, call it the Mtkvari, meaning 'good water'. As I peered down into its eddies from the clifftop (an unusual sight in the middle of a city), a pretty Georgian woman, who stood a few metres away, playfully tossed a twig over the edge and it disappeared before I could see it hit the water.

'The water here is very famous, you know.'

Gulisa introduced herself in English as a local travel agent. Her long black hair fell down the back of a grey jacket.

'How did you know I was English?' I asked, startled by the way she had addressed me.

'I didn't, but I could tell you were a foreigner, and all foreigners speak English.' She smiled brilliantly. I couldn't tell if she was naive or just teasing me.

'Tell me more,' I said, captivated by a pair of emerald eyes. She brushed her hair from a mesmerising brow.

'Well, according to an old Georgian legend, Tbilisi was covered by a thick pine forest until fifteen hundred years ago. There was nothing here but wolves and roaming barbarians. But then one day, our king, the great Gorgasali, was out hunting in these woods with a falcon. The king's bird of prey caught a pheasant during the hunt and in the process of the fight, both creatures fell into a nearby hot spring and drowned in the sizzling pool. Now, most people would be cursing their luck at this point, but not King Gorgasali. He was so impressed by the quality and heat of the water that he cleared the forests and founded a city on the site. That's how Tbilisi was started. The name Tbilisi comes from the old Georgian word meaning warm.'

I wanted to ask her more, maybe even see if she wanted to go for a drink, but with that she disappeared, walking off into the night like a ghostly apparition.

It was late, but I was frustrated and didn't feel like sleeping, so I wandered down Rustaveli Avenue to try and shake off this renewed sense of traveller's loneliness that goes hand in hand with shattered hopes. The main shopping street was lined with tall sycamore trees, which gave it a grand, almost Parisian air. It was lit with twinkling neon signs advertising the latest in women's fashion and mobile phones. It looked like Christmas had come early here, but as I walked it was like a ghost town. There was barely another soul in sight and everything was closed. Even the road was empty, no one was driving. Perhaps it was a Sunday. There was no way of telling. I went back to the hotel to have a shower. It was the first since Vladikavkaz. As I got undressed, I smelt myself and winced. No wonder Gulisa had done a runner.

The next morning, I returned to Rustaveli to find it barely busier than the night before, but at least I had the opportunity to see the Georgians about their daily business.

I found the historic centre of the town and was cheered up a little by its historical quaintness. The narrow, cobbled side streets were lined with scruffy shops selling religious icons, little wooden crosses, silver pendants and everywhere, the image of St George dealing death to the dragon. The haunting smell of frankincense lingered in the air like a thick soup. There were trinkets and books and candles. Provincial nuns scurried around buying up holy water, looking terrified of the crowds. The Orthodox priests sat in pairs on benches all sporting magnificent black and pepper beards.

Wherever I went there were churches; the unique style of the little cross cupolas made them look like they belonged in a traditional English village and gave the city a sense of identity that I had sorely missed in southern Russia. Looking up, I noticed the older buildings painted in pastel shades of yellow and blue. They stood out as precious relics that had somehow survived the Soviet onslaught. Neoclassicism mixed freely with baroque and patchwork shanty. The wooden balconies that seemed to be everywhere often had intricate carvings and designs that reminded me of their Moorish equivalents in Tangiers and Seville. The bridge that spanned the Mtkvari led me up the steep hill to the looming Metekhi Church, which balances precariously on a cliff overlooking the river.

A good place, I thought, to sit and write up my journal, so I found a table in a pleasant café where I heard the unmistakable twang of an American accent from a nearby seat.

'. . . it's just so gaw-geous.'

'Bet'ya'll won't eat some of this Geo-orgayn food. It's got some *real* crazy names.'

'Damn, give me a soda.'

'What do you mean, *what's* a soda?'

I was horrified. There were six or seven of these podgy sightseers wearing baseball caps and matching T-shirts. Could it even be a tour group? I didn't wait to find out. A sudden sense of loathing came over me like a black cloud. I find it difficult to describe in hindsight, but it was such an overpowering, all-encompassing feeling of spite, that I needed to leave immediately. I bounded back to the hotel with a sick sense of revulsion that only made me even more nauseous at the thought that maybe, just maybe, I, too, was a tourist.

What right did I have to pass judgement? What made me any different? I fought hard to reconcile what it was that I despised so much. But no matter how hard I tried, I couldn't figure out why I found them so distasteful. Traveller's snobbery, perhaps, or selfish aestheticism? The same desire to be away from normality and 'civilisation', whatever that may be, that drove men like Conolly to travel the overland trail. These tourists had spoiled my splendid isolation and possession of space on the Silk Road.

On the way, I passed by a monstrous building overlooking the river that claimed to be the Hotel Iveria. A relic of the Cold War, it stood abandoned and derelict, yet it dominated the heart of the city like a giant, decaying monolith. The outside of the multicoloured facade looked like a giant container ship full of gaudy metal isolation units and I realised that these were balconies. They had been bastardised beyond recognition, with corrugated iron, plywood and tarpaulin. Rags and unclaimed washing fluttered apocalyptically from the railings. It was as if the Georgian architectural tradition of deep wooden balconies had somehow grafted itself onto this modernist skyscraper to create this revolting hybrid.

I asked a teenager, who was sitting outside, what had become of the place. I wanted to regain a sense of perspective.

'It used to be a luxury hotel,' he yawned. 'The best in the city ... but then the government put all the refugees in it.'

It turned out that what was once the most famous and iconic hotel in Tbilisi, a five-star showcase of Soviet architecture, had for a while housed over a thousand Abkhazian exiles. The Georgian government had put the refugees in the Iveria as a desperate temporary measure after the 1992 conflict, but a lack of funds or assistance in rehousing meant that they had been there now for over a decade. There was no water or electricity and the inhabitants had been forced to occupy the balconies due to overcrowding. They burned carpets for fuel and cooked on little fires inside the rooms.

Only two months before, however, in August, the government had made the decision to bulldoze the building and had ejected the refugees. Now it was an empty shell ready for destruction, a melancholic symbol of Georgia's troubled recent past. The Abkhazians had been moved on yet again.

'Where are they now?' I asked the boy.

'Who knows?' he said with a shrug.

I yearned for the countryside and so the next day, riddled with a deep feeling of hypocrisy, I treated myself to a punishingly long walk to the bus station. It was bustling with Georgian travellers, like me, all apparently bent on escaping the capital. I shoved my way through the crowds in a vain attempt to find an information desk. The whole plaza was buzzing with activity. Hundreds of taxis were either lined up, coming or going. In their midst was a throng of commerce; swarthy people selling sweets, loaves and packets of crisps. There seemed to be no centre of mass, or any way of telling where the cars were going.

'Ask him,' someone said, pointing to a sinister man in a long woollen overcoat.

'Not me,' he grimaced.

'Ask him.'

'Over there.'

'No, there.'

I bounced from one minibus to another. These Marshrutkas were invariably old, broken and crammed to the rafters.

I didn't even know where I wanted to go, except that I was well and truly fed up with cities. I had a vague plan of probing into Armenia or Azerbaijan, but I had heard that both countries' borders with Iran were closed, so that was out of the question. The only other route would be through Turkey, but even this was unreliable. Nobody could tell me which of the borders were open. ('Why would you want to go to Turkey?')

Shoving my way through the crowds, I eventually found a list of destinations, chalked on a wooden board next to the stinking public toilets. The Georgian script did little to ease my choice and I found my eyes wandering to a tatty poster that was pinned to the wall. It showed a huge cliff filled with tiny pockmarks that resembled caves and a close-up shot of some ancient Christian frescoes that depicted angels and kings. In the corner of the poster was a very rough map of the country with a red dot close to the Turkish border.

'Where is that?' I asked a toothless man, who was smoking two cigarettes at the same time.

'Vardzia,' he spluttered.

'I want to go there.'

I was ushered quickly into a battered, ten-seater minibus that had seen far better days. It took half an hour to fill up, by which time I was squashed against the back seat with my rucksack on my knee.

As my co-travellers all squeezed into the bus, scowling at me for having such a big rucksack, the driver led a chorus of 'Kalaki, kalaki, kalaki.'

He turned around and I could just make out a crinkled face chirping like a mad man.

'Kalaki, kalaki, kalaki.' He sounded like a zoo keeper talking to one of the birds of prey. He thrust a hand out and demanded payment. 'Five lari.' (About three dollars.)

'To Vardzia? Is that all?' I was impressed, since it was several hours' drive away.

'No to Akhalkalaki. We don't go to Vardzia.'

'But the man said ...' I tried to point out of the window, futilely searching for the double smoker.

'There is a junction in the road. Vardzia is twenty kilometres further on.'

'I'll walk from there.'

'Are you crazy?' He frowned and shook his head. 'It's *twenty* kilometres.'

I decided to risk it, confident that I would be able to hitch from the junction and so we set off shortly after five p.m., heading due west into the red glimmer of the dying sun.

At first the road meandered through the foothills and forests of central Georgia, but soon climbed up and over steep ridges and back down into deep ravines. Sometimes we would break left and head south and then twist abruptly north again, as if the track was winding senselessly away into oblivion. As the sun cowered behind the black peaks of the lesser Caucasus, we descended once again into a wide valley and passed dark fields and darker villages. The road was never level for more than a few miles. Up and down, left and right, we jolted onwards. Five hours later, just as I was dozing off, nestling my face into the rough creases of my canvas rucksack, the minibus came to an abrupt halt.

'Vardzia,' said the driver, shaking his head.

I looked out of the window and saw nothing except a silhou-etted barren landscape of loose escarpments and distant forests. The passenger next to me, an old woman with enormous hips, prodded me.

'Come to Akhalkalaki and you can carry on tomorrow,' the driver implored, as I squeezed past the other passengers. But I was in no mood for another town and politely declined.

'I'll be fine, thanks.'

I was sure that I would be able to hitch; there was no reason to think otherwise and I had been lucky so far. But by now it was completely dark and I noticed as I got out of the bus that the road had deteriorated into little more than a dusty dirt track.

'Be careful of the bandits,' said the driver, with the shrug of someone washing his hands of a troublesome burden. I smiled at him and waved. I wasn't worried. Georgian hospitality had been nothing short of impeccable so far and I felt sure that this remote hillside would not be any different. He looked at me with a mix of pity and bewilderment.

'Oh, and don't forget the wolves.'

The bus sped away into the moonless night and I was left alone.

I looked up into the blackness and a droplet of rain fell onto my cheek. I thought suddenly that perhaps I should have stayed on the bus after all. I fumbled around for a minute or two trying to adjust my eyes to the darkness, whilst looking for the track that led off to the right. It seemed to be nothing but gravel descending sharply off down the hill into a valley.

I could vaguely make out the silhouettes of some cliffs to my left and some trees that fell sharply away to the right. The only sound was the crashing of water in a river somewhere below. I tried to remember whether my torch had any batteries, or in fact, had I even brought a torch? I stumbled down the track and realised that I wasn't going very far tonight. The best option would be to bed down for the evening and carry on at first light, when I would be able to follow the path, so I continued a little farther down the hill, following the sound of the water to where the road flattened out a little. Even though it was dark, I could see some shapes. To my surprise I could just discern the outline of a wall, a huge sheer wall above me at the top of the cliff. It could only be a castle.

I thought for a moment about trying to scale the cliff and sleep on the walls – as I had done so many times already – but realised that there was no way I would find a way to the top in the darkness. No, all I could do was find a place to sleep and wait till the morning. I damned my own impatience.

Further along the path, right next to the river, I came across what appeared to be a makeshift waiting shelter; it looked a bit like a bus shelter. There was a thin wooden plank with a corrugated iron roof propped up by some timber joists. Perfect. I got out my sleeping bag, laid it out on the bench and began to settle down, listening to the continuous crashing of the river and the chirping of crickets. Sleep came easily.

I woke up with a start. Where was I? What time was it? I looked at my watch and then squinted into the blackness. It was still only eleven-thirty; I had been asleep for just over an hour. Then I realised that something must have woken me up. I sat up and strained to hear, opening my mouth and closing my eyes to enable complete audible perception, as I had learnt in the Officer Training Corps with Winfield. I heard the patter of footsteps getting closer. A whisper. A cough. Then a gravel-like voice deep in conversation with somebody else.

I slipped silently out of the sleeping bag to free my legs, in case

I needed to move quickly. Then I froze. Thoughts of bandits and separatist guerrillas raced through my head. Maybe if I sat still, they wouldn't see me. The voices grew nearer and I could now make out the figures of three men. One was holding something long. Was it a gun or only a stick? Another looked drunk, as he seemed to be stumbling. The other two dragged him along violently. They were level with me now and I kept still, hoping not to be seen.

'Oi!' the biggest man shouted directly at me.

I had been spotted. The three men suddenly crowded around me before I had time to stand up. The one with the stick barked something incomprehensible. I sat up straight and gave a bold '*Gamarjoba*,' hello, unable to remember the phrase for 'I don't speak Georgian.'

They squinted, unsure what to make of me.

'*Gamarjoba*,' I repeated, louder this time, feigning indignance. 'Do you speak English?'

There was no reply. So I tried again in German – the only other language I could muster, '*Keiner Sakartvelo. Sprechen sie Deutsch?*' which I hoped would roughly translate into, 'No Georgian. Do you speak German?'

The biggest of the men, an immense shadow from what I could make out, stepped forward to get a closer look at me. As his face neared mine, I clenched my fist in case I needed to whack him. I thought back to the last time I had been disturbed sleeping on a bench; in Poland, where I woke up to find a gang of youths robbing me of my bag and shoes. Suddenly he bared his teeth and broke into a friendly smile.

'*Gamarjoba Deutscher.*' He took a step back and motioned for me to follow. '*Kommt*,' he ordered. I guessed he must speak a little German after all. His voice sounded kind and so I quickly packed away my sleeping bag and followed him warily.

The drunk man meanwhile was leaning perilously on the third and they both poked a hand in my direction which I shook, trying to maintain an air of dignity. My new guide bade them goodnight with a brutal shove towards the river bank and led me along the path towards a flickering light in the distance. As we entered what seemed to be a small village, I attempted some conversation with my awful German.

'What is the name of the village?'

'Khertvisi.'

'Is it nice?' I didn't really know what to say to my new host.

There was no comment.

We passed through a wooden gate and into a farmyard. An enormous Caucasian sheepdog barked viciously and I heard the whinnying of a horse nearby. A couple of chickens ruffled their feathers, annoyed at having been disturbed from their sleep.

I was glad when he lit a candle as we entered the front door, so that I could inspect my strange host in earnest, and I have no doubt he must have felt the same. His face was a generous one with wrinkles around his eyes and cheeks from a life of smiling. His chest was as big as a barrel and he had the gnarled hands of a farmer. That he was a rough brute was beyond doubt, but at least he was a friendly one.

I was relieved that he didn't seem bent on killing me, and I had to trust my instincts that he didn't have any equally foul designs. His smile was instantly infectious and I decided to give him the benefit of the doubt.

Gocha wasn't as old as he looked. I guessed that he was no more than thirty-five, but his deep, weathered features could have been those of a fifty-year-old.

'Sit down,' he said with a fatherly tone. I wondered at my luck as he went to the larder to retrieve some cheese, fresh bread and a jug of homemade vodka.

'Drink?'

He began to pour the clear liquid before I had even responded.

It turned out that the big-hearted brute was not only a farmer but also, it seemed, an amateur historian and budding artist. He pointed out some of his rough paintings and I noticed a bookshelf full of dusty classics. He was eager to talk and although we didn't have much common language apart from a smattering of German and Russian, we sat and spoke for over two hours. They say don't talk politics with strangers, but he was straight to it, and the conversation (or rather a combination of wild gesticulation, Russo-Germanic spluttering and imaginative sketching) revolved around a spinning collaboration of current affairs, geography and medieval history.

'So, *mein Deutscher*.' He disregarded my protests at being English, before continuing, 'Do you like Hitler?'

'No, not really.'

Frowning, he said, 'But why not? He was a very misunderstood man.' Gocha pulled a book from its place on the immense casing. It was a fragile-looking German text from the thirties all about phrenology and the hierarchy of the races.

'Some interesting ideas, no?' said Gocha, as he offered me another glass of vodka. I hesitated momentarily, not sure of the wisdom of drinking with a self-professed Nazi. Fortunately, the conversation turned to other things, as I explained for the third time that I was English, not German.

'English, ah well, why didn't you say so?' He didn't seem to mind that he had forfeited the axis for the allies, though, as he gave me a big thumbs-up.

'England, Wales, Scotland, and, how you say . . .? Cornwall?'

'Cornwall? What? You mean Northern Ireland?' I was as surprised by his knowledge of the British Isles as by the slight inaccuracy in the history of the union.

'No, Cornwall. Very independent country. You know Artur?' (Another vodka.)

'Artur? Author? What!' (Head spinning.)

'William, Harry, Philip, Queen ... (Thumbs-up) ... Artur.'

'King Arthur?'

'Yes, very brave man, from Cornwall, no?'

By now, all notion of sense had gone out of the window. The fact that Gocha thought that King Arthur was a living member of the royal family, residing happily in Tintagel Castle (presumably waiting for the next opportunity to fight the Germans), summed up the atmosphere perfectly. But there was no stopping Gocha, he was in the middle of drawing a sketch of Richard the Lionheart (makes sign of the cross), then came a rather butch stick man with long hair and a big moustache: 'Genghis Khan.' (Thumbs down.)

'Understandably.'

A wiry stick man with a face resembling that of a goose.

'Vladimir Putin.' (Thumbs down again.)

'Sure.'

A wiry stick man in a suit with a face resembling that of a baboon.

'George Bush.' (Thumbs up.)

I must have looked surprised, because Gocha assured me that he was a big fan of the American president – possibly because the US had been sending a lot of military aid to Georgia in recent months. And then, in a final statement of authority, he swept his hand across a map, beginning with the Caspian Sea and backhanding everything to the right, sweeping it all into the Pacific. He drew a crescent and stared me in the eyes.

'Musselmen very bad. Evil people. Turkey is very close to here, and so is Iran. Both full of fanatics – crazy Muslims who cut your throat for no reason.' This time it wasn't thumbs up or down, only a very specific finger sliding slowly and menacingly across his neck. He looked serious.

And then, as if he suddenly felt rude for dominating the conversation, he broke into his previous smile.

'So *mein Englischman*, where are you going next?'

'Turkey. Then Iran.'

I went to bed feeling like the history of Western civilisation had been turned on its head – and perhaps a little drunk.

The next day, with a thumping head, I woke up to the sounds of a group of male voices downstairs. I entered the kitchen and Gocha slapped me on the back and sat me down at the dining table. Three others were present, one of whom I recognised as the drunkard from the night before. Before them on the table was breakfast, a loaf of bread and a large ceramic jug filled to the brim with mulberry vodka. After five minutes of pleasantries and much handshaking, the glasses were distributed and the ceremony began. It continued well into the afternoon. They tossed back quarter pints of the stuff; solemnly at first and then with swelling abandon. Now and then one of them would roll a joint of cannabis, withdraw to the wicker armchair in the corner of the room and smoke himself to unconsciousness, only to awaken an hour later with fresh thirst and vigour. At the completion of one jug, Gocha would disappear out of the kitchen and across the farmyard to a wooden barn, presumably also his distillery, and return with a new one.

There was nothing to do but drink. Trying to leave was futile once it had begun – these men were professionals; hardened farmers who had been up and working since five a.m. and unconstrained by the distractions of the outside world (none of them had ever left the village, save to purchase horses from a nearby town) for whom this foul, sickly syrup was their life-blood, and to turn it down was tantamount to rejecting a culture, a way of life. But after five hours, I began to lose hope. There was no end in sight. It is bad enough to drink vodka all day under any circumstances, but this homebrew had a peculiar vileness about it and to attempt a litre of the substance before lunch can bring on a general failure of constitution.

I took advantage of a hashish break to escape. I went back to the castle that I had seen the previous evening and explored its ruins in an inebriated state. My imagination was running amok. I wish I had known at the time that this was the great Khertvisi castle – perhaps the oldest in Georgia. Historians have dated its foundations back to the second century BC, although local legend says that Alexander the Great passed through even earlier, razing whatever was originally there to the ground. The current walls, though, are about seven hundred years old, rebuilt after the Mongol invasion left the place in ruins.

Nowadays it is in ruins once again, and I was free to climb about its vast stone towers and admire the view down the sheer cliff to the Mtkvari, where I had contemplated sleeping the night before. With a swirling mind I imagined the Greeks, Mongols and Cossacks, and maybe even Arthur Conolly himself, standing on the battlements of the castle, surveying the wild lands below. They'd all been here in their own times: thousands of years of fighting, war, and no doubt drinking had happened on this very spot.

Castles and drunkenness do not mix well. I stumbled and almost twisted my ankle and spent some time sitting pathetically on a pile of rocks. It wasn't until after an hour of rummaging around the fallen masonry that I felt sober enough to walk back to the village, where I found Gocha waiting with a battered car. Despite the fact that he had been indulging in a morning of drink and drugs, unlike me, he looked surprisingly sober.

'Botso will take you to Vardzia. He is travelling down the valley today. You should go if you want to see the caves, it's a good place to get some fresh air, his will be the only car today, maybe even this week.' I went to get my bag from inside the farm building, thinking this was my opportunity to make it to the border, but as I was doing so, Gocha intervened as if he read my thoughts.

'You will be coming back.'

'But I want to carry on to Turkey, the border is that way.' I pointed down the valley.

'No, that border is closed. You need to go west to Türkgözü, it's the only way.'

Well now I was stuck with two choices: visit Vardzia and stay another night, or head straight to the border. I thought for a moment. Although I wasn't feeling much like any more archaeology, well, I had come this far and so resigned myself to another day of backtracking.

'I'm not in any rush. I'll be back tonight,' I told Gocha. At this rate, I would have doubled my mileage and travelled about as much in a westerly direction as that to the east in the Caucasus.

Gocha said that he would kill some chickens for supper and waved me off, still with a joint in his mouth. My new companion Botso didn't say a word for the whole journey, he only grinned inanely and seemed to delight in driving like a maniac, thinking that it impressed me. He was clearly still half-cut. We followed the path that hugged the cliff all the way along the river. It was a beautiful, timeless valley filled with orchards and swing bridges that spanned this tributary of the great Kura.

For most of the way, though, I was concentrating only on looking to my left, into the cliff face, so as to avoid the sheer drop to my right as we hurtled over the bumpy road. Luckily there were no other cars, because in parts the road was barely wide enough for one. I was glad to arrive at Vardzia a terrifying forty-five minutes later and let the old fool carry on.

From the car park, the caves present themselves as a sheer cliff, like a sliced-open beehive, small holes in the rock face. It was hard to imagine that this had once been a thriving population centre, full of monks and medieval scholars. There was no one else to be seen. I wandered up to the caves and looked around. It used to be a hideout for Christian monks, when the rampaging Mongols came crashing over the mountains. Hundreds of years ago, thousands of people lived here, hidden from view in one of the most enigmatic tunnel systems anywhere in Asia – they were invisible to the outside world until an earthquake ripped apart the mountain and exposed their subterranean existence. The whole rock facade fell away and the monks moved on. All except one, it seemed. An old man in black robes, with a long white beard, appeared around a corner.

'*Gamarjoba*,' I said, waving.

The monk just stared at me.

'Hello,' I said, again, in English.

'Where are you from?' he said, without a glimmer of a smile.

'Britain,' I told him.

'Oh,' he said, muttering. 'I thought you were Iranian.'

'Why?'

'You look like one,' he said. 'And we don't like the Persians.'
'Why not?'

'Because they came here in the sixteenth century and raided the monastery. They stole everything and destroyed all the icons. There's barely anything left now, apart from a few frescoes that were lucky enough to survive when the smoke and soot from the fires covered them up, so that the Muslims didn't scratch them off.'

With that the old monk wandered off into a cavern and that was all I saw of him. I carried on exploring the maze of tunnels and rock-hewn steps. From the top, near to the monastery, I spent a couple of hours sketching the view and the sun was bright and warm. Far below, the river trickled between the boulders and the distant villages seemed unreal. Perhaps it was the morning vodka, still flowing in my veins, or maybe the blissful ambiance of a warm October afternoon. Whatever it was, I found myself dropping off into a dozy slumber.

By the time I woke, it was already late afternoon. I looked up and noticed that the sun had moved behind the cliff and although it was still balmy, I was concealed in the shade of the mountain. I saw an eagle soaring at a great height, or perhaps it was a buzzard, gliding effortlessly before vanishing behind the shadow of a steep gorge.

It was time to think about getting back. The place was deserted and I looked at the track that led back to Gocha's village, some fifteen miles distant, and realised that I hadn't seen a single car drive past all day.

I began to walk. The way was beautiful and the valley was silent apart from the occasional magpies squawking at one another. The afternoon sun gave the brown hills a golden brilliance and its warmth filled me with idyllic contentment. I walked past a small farmhouse, where I was saluted with a friendly *Gamarjoba* by local villagers. As I passed by the gate, one of them unwrapped a cloth pouch to reveal some shiny fresh apples. He smiled and handed one to me.

I arrived back at Gocha's house shortly after dark, exhausted, but glad to have completed the walk. He was nowhere to be found and the horse was gone, too, so I assumed that he was out in the fields. I let myself in and read until he got back. True to his word, he had slaughtered a fat chicken and made a fantastic stew accompanied by fried potatoes. Another of his neighbours visited and between us we finished off another bottle of vodka. For another twenty-four hours the binge continued.

The following day I felt it was time to move on and couldn't face another all-day drinking session, so I woke up at seven. Gocha, however, had already gone to work, and although I would have liked to have thanked him in person, I knew that if I waited till he got back then I'd be in for another endless binge. So I left a note simply saying *Gmadlobt* (thank you), which I did my best to copy into the strange Georgian alphabet. But as I opened the front door, I realised that escape wasn't going to be as easy as I thought. The dog was off the chain and rushed straight at me, his snarling teeth flashing through a foam of slobber. The great white and shaggy beast didn't want me to leave, it seemed, so I slammed the door shut and realised that I had only one option.

I made my way back up the stairs to my room, opened the window and climbed out onto the ledge. From there I made a precarious jump from the first floor onto the roof of the garage. The sheepdog was going berserk now, sensing my imminent departure. The only way down off the roof was to fling myself onto the dividing fence and onto the neighbour's kitchen roof. There, hoping that I hadn't upset whoever was doing the dishes, I shimmied down the drainpipe and into their garden and ran as fast as I could, leapfrogging their hedge and back onto the gravel road.

Fortunately, the dog couldn't escape and had to be content with growling as I made off up the road, past the castle to the track junction where the bus had left me three days before. If I carried on at this rate, I thought, I'd never make it to India.

10

Musaafir

Türkgözü was as remote and unearthly as Gocha had warned me. The brown hills stretched as far as I could see, except in the small oasis of tall poplars that served to hide away the nearby village. The frontier itself consisted of a few ramshackle, concrete customs buildings, and a dilapidated old metal gate that was painted a gaudy lime-green. On the Turkish side, some attempt had been made to differentiate the place from a desolate scrapheap by constructing a bright red truck shelter, but even that looked incongruous and disturbing. Gocha was right – nobody ever did come this way, except a few hairy lorry drivers.

The border guard, a fat, cheerful policeman, seemed pleased to see me. For some reason I had expected the usual visa problems, or perhaps some hassle for bakshish, but the Turkish official was so helpful that he said I needn't bother getting a new visa, since I had been to Turkey the previous year and he thought it would 'probably still be valid'.

'Great,' I thought for a second, 'that's saved me twenty quid,' but then I realised it wouldn't be worth the risk if I wanted to enter Iran without any problems.

'If it's okay with you, I'll take a visa.'

He shrugged and rummaged in his drawer for a stamp and duly pounded my passport.

I waited for him to deprive me of some exorbitant entry fee, but instead he simply asked me if I had any cigarettes. Luck would have it that I had bought some for occasions such as this and he was happy enough with this token gift. 'Welcome to Turkey, Ingeez.'

At the truck stop, I came across a solitary blue lorry. Its driver was sitting in the cab, leisurely reading a newspaper. A column of cigarette smoke wafted out of the open window like a translucent beanstalk crawling towards the sky. I approached him warily, always careful not to get my hopes up. Since I didn't speak a word of Turkish, I hazarded an English greeting, 'Hello, are you going to Erzurum? Can I get a lift?'

The driver lowered his newspaper to reveal a swarthy, wrinkled face with several days of stubble protruding from a lean chin. He took a last draw, slowly removed the cigarette from his mouth, and flicked it out onto the pavement before his gaze met mine.

'Yes, mate, jump in.'

Ischa had been driving lorries around Europe for ten years and had been to Britain several times. His uncle lived in the UK and his brother owned a kebab shop in London.

'Welcome to Turkey, mate. Small world, eh? First time?'

It wasn't my first time. I had come through Turkey a year earlier after travelling through Iraq with my friend Alex Coutselous and had been pleasantly surprised with a warm reception in the south-eastern Kurdish areas. As we drove, Ischa talked about his job and of driving around Europe, and he told me about his family, who were living in an apartment on the outskirts of Ankara. He pointed at a photograph that was pinned to the dashboard. It showed him wearing a cream suit next to his wife, a beautiful young woman with pale skin and fiery eyes.

Three children, two boys and a little girl, stood obediently straight. It reminded me of those old Victorian photographs you see, where the children are bolt upright in their Sunday best.

The lorry ascended into the mountains and it wasn't long before the meandering road that snaked through the barren rocks became engulfed in a sea of white snow. Mist enveloped the hills, as we hauled over the bleak passes of Akdag and Narman. Soon, though, we had begun the descent through the Tek valley and the snow gave way once again to desolate shale and then, further down, the undulating plains of the Horasan. I had finally arrived in Asia proper and the realm of Islam spread out before me.

Behind us the mountains loomed large, their peaks still shrouded in an unrelenting cloud. Ahead, a few brick huts and a lone shepherd were the only distractions in the otherwise barren moorland landscape. Then, suddenly, as if to alleviate the starkness, in the middle distance several hundred cattle could be seen crossing the road, creating an immense dust cloud in the now rolling scrub. It was a scene that reminded me it was somewhere near here that Alexander the Great paused briefly to address his men, before crossing into Persia in hot pursuit of Bessus and beginning his long campaign into Central Asia. Eastern Turkey has a history of foreign invaders. The Mongol hordes came this way, too, galloping on their way to conquer an unsuspecting Europe in the summer of 1241 after subduing the Caucasus.

I was on the main trail of the Silk Road now, where the path from Istanbul – or Constantinople, as it was then – converges with the Caucasus route that I had followed in the footsteps of Arthur Conolly. Somewhere out to the east the convergence would be complete, when the southern routes to the Levant and Baghdad, through Syria and Iraq, all met on the plains of Persia.

Several hours passed as we drove along; the sun began to bow down and relent in its domination over the hills. A profusion of reds and crimson took hold of the wilderness on either side and the shadows became long to our rear. We began to chase the sun again, now heading west towards Erzurum. Ischa, who had been quiet until now, seemed to come alive in the late afternoon brilliance. He began to talk with increasing enthusiasm about his homeland, about his dream for Turkey to enter the European Union, and lamenting the exorbitant cost of potatoes in the market square.

He drove very fast, and on the empty highway there was no reason to do otherwise. Occasionally we passed by a small village and the humble minaret of a small mosque. A few men sat around plastic tables playing draughts in exactly the same way they did in Georgia. The only hint that I was in a Muslim country was the sporadic sight of a woman wearing the *hijab*, the traditional veil that covers the head and chest as a symbol of modesty. I offered Ischa one of the sweets from a bag that Lali had given me.

'No thanks, mate.'

'Not hungry?' I asked, more to make conversation than anything.

'Oh, I'm bloody starving, thanks, but it's Ramadan, in't it, mate.'

'Oh,' I spluttered, half-wondering if I should spit out the toffee, and suddenly feeling very self-conscious. Instead, I tried to swallow the sticky mass in one.

'Sorry, I forgot.'

'Don't worry, mate, I sometimes forget, too,' consoled Ischa.

Ramadan. Little did I know that the Islamic holy fast had begun only that day, and for the next month I would have to abide by local custom and refrain from any eating, drinking and 'immodest behaviour' from dawn until dusk.

'But don't worry, mate,' he continued.

'Sorry?'

'There's more to Ramadan than just fasting. Everyone thinks it's only about fasting, but it's not, mate, I tell you. Ramadan's when us Muslims seek forgiveness for our sins and pray for guidance in our future lives. In't it, mate.'

'I see.'

'Sorry, I must be boring you.'

'No, not at all, I'm fascinated.' I really was. 'And I really should learn about it where I am going. Please carry on.'

'Well, in Ramadan we're supposed to offer more than just prayer; we are expected to not do all sorts of everyday evils and purify ourselves through self-restraint and good deeds. You know what I mean?'

I could tell that Ischa was devout and knowledgeable about his religion. He wasn't preaching, simply explaining, and I found it enthralling.

'Ramadan changes every year according to the lunar calendar, and it goes back to the time of year that the first verses of the holy Qur'an were said to have been revealed to the Prophet Mohammed, peace be upon him. But of course, to the outsider,' he politely avoided use of the disagreeable *infidel*, 'the most obvious aspect of Ramadan is fasting. More to it than that, though – you see, mate?'

He went on, 'Every day during the month, we get up before dawn to eat the first meal of the day. Can't eat or drink anything until after the fourth prayer of the day at sunset, *Maghrib*. Only then can we eat and drink until the abstinence begins all over again in the morning.'

I tried to imagine how difficult it must be.

'Ramadan, mate, is a time of reflecting and worshipping God,' Ischa continued, as if in a trance, carefully reciting what he had learned from the mullahs. 'It teaches us patience, modesty and spirituality. We try to put more effort into following the teachings of Islam and seek a raised awareness of closeness to God. Fasting, you know, takes the heart away from worldly activities, its purpose being to cleanse the inner soul and free it from harm. More than that, it also allows us to practise self-discipline, self-control, sacrifice, and empathy for those who are less fortunate; it helps us be more generous and give to charity.'

'It sounds like very hard work.'

'It is, but don't worry, mate, you're exempt.'

'Because I'm a foreigner?'

'No, mate, not just that, because you are a traveller. Travellers – *musaafir* – are excused fasting, but they are expected to make up the days they miss afterwards.'

'Naturally,' says I.

'However, to be considered a proper traveller, you must travel more than forty miles per day to qualify.' He winked.

I didn't ask whether whisking along at ninety miles an hour in a lorry was quite what the faith had in mind.

Eventually the lights of Erzurum could be seen in the distance, as the sun dipped below the mountains to the west. The city was in darkness now, only the snowy peaks reflected the last of the day's light, and with it the end of today's fast for my driver. The junction where Ischa dropped me off was a couple of miles from the town and he offered to take me all of the way in, but since he still had a long way to drive, I told him that I was happy to walk.

'Thanks now, *musaafir*, I'm off to break the fast. Take care, mate!'

It was completely dark when I reached the centre of the town, and since I was only planning on staying for one night, I searched for somewhere to sleep rough. I found a grassy park off the main street and began settling down on a bench, when a group of three teenagers approached noisily. I prepared myself for another round of questioning, but found my inquisitors were nothing more than harmless boys.

'Mister. Where you from?'

'Ingeez. Very nice country. David Beckham. Man-ches-taar.' (Thumbs up.)

I had heard it all before, and I was thinking of a suitable way to bring the conversation to a close, when one of the boys made a very good point, 'Very cold at night, mister. Minus degrees. Very cold. Also, many wolves. Come with. My uncle has hotel. Very cheap. Much discount . . .'

I hadn't thought much about the cold. I had forgotten that Erzurum was seventeen hundred metres high and although it was still mild in the late evening, temperatures would plummet in the early hours. My thin sleeping bag would be useless.

'Alright, take me there.'

I let myself be led away, consoling myself that whilst I could probably handle the chill, I didn't fancy my chances with a scavenging wolf.

'Is it far?'

'Very far, take taxi. Very good taxi. I know – my brother have taxi.'

'No, I want to walk.'

'Walk. Yes, walk. Very close. No problem, Mister Ingeez.'

I looked at my guides. The eldest, a boy of fifteen, led the way. He wore a smart, shiny purple shirt and black trousers, perfectly creased. In the darkness, I could make out the foreshadowing of a wispy down on his upper lip. He looked like he was on his way to a 1950s dance hall. The younger two were scruffier, and hadn't yet inherited the cosmopolitan style of their brother. The youngest wore a tatty blue, fake football shirt. It had two stripes instead of three. It brought back childhood memories of family holidays in the Mediterranean, where swarthy merchants openly flogged their counterfeit wares, swearing on their mothers' lives that the goods were real.

I followed the boys to a crumbling hovel that wasn't very far at all.

'Welcome to hotel Sivas.'

'Uncle' beamed as he rose from a plastic stool, from which he had been watching a Turkish TV talent show, where the contestants seemed to be all dressed in Lycra and were beating each other over the head with giant rubber sticks.

'Ingeez. Very good,' came the well-rehearsed line. 'David Beckham!'

I shamefully acquiesced and forced a smile. 'Very good.'

'I give you special price.'

'I'm sure you will.'

With a sinking heart, I followed him up a nearly vertical flight of stairs past the reception desk. We continued down a narrow, brilliantly lit passage, the boys bringing up the rear to cut off my retreat. The doors on either side were open, and I could see into the rooms. The occupants all seemed to be fat men, gazing at the dripping ceilings, semi-clothed. Everywhere, like a lingering haze, was the unforgettable smell of oriental plumbing.

'Double room for Mister Ingeez,' said the proprietor, flinging open a door at the far end. It was like a scene from a Hitchcock horror movie. A forty-watt bulb flickered intermittently, illuminating for a second at a time a miasma of huge black flies, circling overhead, no doubt excited at the prospect of new prey. The walls were olive green and something foul was growing near the window. The bed was repellent, shaped like a large bowl. Underneath it was a stack of magazines that looked like they were the sole support of the mattress. In the corner, there was a washbasin containing a clipping of small black hairs and a tap, which dripped ominously. As I neared it, the sounds of the downstairs television seemed to reverberate through the pipes.

'Three dollars for you, mister.'

'Two, and not a penny more,' I said.

I closed the door and gave the boys a tip of the remaining dollar and confined myself to the cell. In spite of the wailing pipes, I slept soundly.

I didn't stay in Erzurum for long. I was in a hurry to get to Iran. It was somewhere new and exciting; I longed for the desert and the wail of the *muezzin*, the call to prayer, two of the things I missed about the Middle East; so after a breakfast of onion soup accompanied by some questionable yoghurt, I hurried out onto the main road and flagged down a bus to Doğubeyazıt, the place where the desert begins.

The road carved its way through the mountains of Aras and slithered over the rugged volcanic flats. Scores of nomadic tartars, descendants of the first Silk Road traders, drove cattle into the distance. After Eleşkirt even the houses began to blend into the geography, as stone and concrete became replaced with mud adobe. The little gardens and walls that divided the brown scrub into feudal fields became fewer as the road darted eastwards and wilderness gradually prevailed. Grassland succumbed to empty scrub, and then rock and then sand. It was the sign of a new continent; a new phase in my journey. I had reached the gateway to Persia.

11

Axis of Evil

Looming large in the distance, just outside of Doğubeyazıt, lies the snow-capped twin peaks of Mount Ararat. It was mid-afternoon and I was relieved to be finally at the remote frontier town in the shadow of its peak. At over five thousand metres high, the mountain stands alone, rising inexplicably from the Armenian plain as if it were being sucked into the atmosphere. The sky was perfectly clear and I stared in wonder at the immense spectacle through the hazy glass of the Dolmus van.

'You know it is the final resting place of the ark of Noah?' said a young Kurdish man proudly on the seat in front, turning round to indicate his mountain.

'Yes, so I'd read.' I remembered seeing coloured illustrations in my Sunday school lessons of how the ark had landed on the 'mountains of Ararat' after the great flood.

'Scientists have found much evidence,' continued my speculative guide. His name was Omar. 'Much wood, many nails.'

'Where, right at the top?' I pondered, looking up at the snowy summit.

'No, it's all buried now. It is a volcano, covered in lava,' he replied in an authoritative tone. 'But I am sure it is there. We will find out in our lifetimes. I am sure.'

It's a nice idea. After all, Ararat is the highest peak in the area and since it isn't part of a mountain range, in the event of a huge flood it would have been the only area of dry land for over a hundred kilometres, so it could have made an obvious stopping point. But one thing puzzled me – how on earth did all the animals get down off the slopes? It is rather high and rather steep. I said as much to my new acquaintance.

'Well, take the elephants for example. They went over the Alps, didn't they?'

'Oh, you mean Hannibal?'

'Exactly. Stranger things have happened.'

As I was trying to imagine a procession of elephants trooping down the mountainside, the bus came to a halt.

'We're here,' said Omar, the young Kurd, as we pulled over in the outskirts of the dusty town. 'Remember,' he pointed back to the mountain, 'God works in mysterious ways.'

It was hot outside and I felt like stripping down to my T-shirt, but checked myself at the last minute, remembering that it was Ramadan. I thought of the recent spate of kidnappings and decided that this was no place to be cultivating the bias of Muslims, whom I assumed would universally decry Western immodesty.

I sighed away the thought as I unloaded my rucksack from the boot of the bus and felt a stream of sweat run down my back, where, for a brief moment, my drenched shirt came unstuck from my skin. I noticed a small building across the road. Outside, little red parasols advertising Coca Cola, and bleached by the blistering sun, jutted out from white plastic picnic tables. A fat man, who was sweating more than me, was leaning idly against the doorway in a sleeveless vest, smoking a cigarette and directing a young boy to serve tea to old Turks at the same time. So much for Ramadan.

It was outside the tea stand that I met Wim. He was the first fellow backpacker that I had spoken to since leaving Estonia, except Jon Winfield. There had been none in Russia with whom Jon or I had the chance to meet, and I hadn't encountered any at all in Georgia. The American tourists didn't count.

Wim must have noticed me jump off the bus and he waved at me enthusiastically.

'Hi, are you looking for a bus to Iran?' said the scruffy man in his mid-twenties.

'Yes, as a matter of fact I am.'

It is natural that if you travel with a friend, then you automatically become insular and don't tend to go out of your way to meet other travellers. When travelling alone, though, there is normally an instant bond, a collective feeling of sticking together and looking after one other. Meeting Wim was no different to meeting the hundreds of other travellers that had, for a short time, been the closest and most important people to me.

Travellers, out of necessity, must rely on other people. Certainly, in those places that are not visited so frequently by tourists, a traveller must have faith in the kindness of strangers. A traveller must depend on the advice and hospitality of locals. But when you meet someone else in the same circumstances, it is quite right to become attached to them. After meeting for the very first time, and, often for only a few minutes, travellers must trust these total strangers with their rucksack, their money, and sometimes with their life. Such are the rules of the road.

Wim was a kind of professional traveller; the sort that somehow, year after year, finds the money, and the energy, to spend several months on the road, quite alone. His matted blond hair was long and curly underneath a faded baseball cap, and his magnificent beard was some weeks old. Wim had set off from his native Belgium a couple of months ago and was on the same trail as me. He had also travelled across Russia, but came to arrive in this remote part of Turkey by way of Central Asia, and had reached Georgia by crossing the Caspian Sea from east to west and traversing Azerbaijan.

We shared a lift to the Iranian border at Gürbulak, some thirty-four kilometres to the east. The crossing was a fairly desolate place in amongst some brown sandy hills. As we passed through Turkish immigration, a huge picture of a solemn Ataturk wearing a dark suit and cream tie seemed to wish me goodbye; it was almost as if he was wishing me good luck, too. The grey eyes seemed to echo Gocha's warning: *Iran is full of religious fanatics – crazed Muslims who will cut your throat for no reason.*

On the far side of no-man's-land, the Iranian customs building was a place to enter with caution. I had heard all sorts of stories about Iranian official brutality and even if I wasn't convinced that I would have my throat slit, I was expecting at the very least a sound interrogation, if not a full strip search. The place itself was empty, apart from two smartly dressed immigration officials in khaki stood behind a bare desk. 'Follow me,' said Wim confidently. 'I have been to Iran before.'

'What,' asked the young official in perfect English as he held up my passport, 'are you coming to Iran for?'

Here we go, I thought, anticipating the next questions in my mind. *Are you spies? Do you have any alcohol? Are you Israeli?* All the questions I had been asked the year before when I entered Turkey from Iraq.

'We're tourists,' smiled Wim casually. 'We are here to visit your beautiful land.'

'Well,' said the guard politely. 'Have a nice trip. You are welcome to my country.'

I could hardly believe my ears. That was it. The guards had barely looked at our bags; in fact, they were almost embarrassed and apologetic that they even opened them in customs. Of course, I had already made sure that there was nothing incriminating in my possession. The whisky was gone and I had placed the Koran conveniently near the top of the pack.

'Bloody hell, that was easy,' I exclaimed, as we walked down the hill towards the exit gate of the wire enclosure, suddenly cheery that Iran wasn't as bad as I had expected.

'Oh yes, they're very friendly here. They really love tourists.'

I looked up at the entrance gate that led to the main road. 'Welcome to the Islamic Republic of Iran', read a sign written in both Farsi and English, straddling the dual images of Khomeini and Khamenei; fathers of the revolution, surrounded by the red, white and green of the Iranian tricolour, an omnipresent reminder that, despite the fact they might welcome tourists, Iran was a despotic theocracy.

Beyond the fence, the road led down a narrow sandy gorge, which then levelled out beyond the cliffs into the western Azerbaijan plain. There were several taxis waiting in the shade of a concrete building that advertised itself as the 'Bazargan tourist agency'. Nor were these the old beaten up Ladas or Marshrutkas I had come to expect; they were brand-new Toyotas shining in a polished yellow. The tourist agency, however, wasn't in such good condition – probably through severe underuse – and the inside looked completely vacant.

'Come on, we won't find any information in there.' Wim bounded off in the direction of the taxis.

'Where do you want to go?' He turned towards me as the gaggle of eager touts converged on the pair of us.

My sole points of reference were Dalrymple's *In Xanadu* and Byron's *The Road to Oxiana* and so in deference to the pair of them, I hastily declared, 'Tabriz. The gateway to Persia.'

'Sounds fine to me. I don't really have a plan until I get to Tehran. Shall we travel together?'

I didn't see why not. After all, here was an interesting fellow traveller who had experience in Iran and could speak a few words of Farsi, the main language of the country, and I liked the way he said *he didn't have a plan*. There was a touch of serendipity about it.

'I told you they love tourists,' said Wim, chuckling away, as a pair of taxi drivers argued over which one would drive us the three hundred and fifty kilometres. Eventually the biggest of them claimed victory, which was seemingly as a sole result of his ability to wave his arms in a more spectacular manner than the other.

'How much?' I must have looked shocked when he told me the price.

'Five dollars!' I was about to burst out laughing at the ridiculously low price, but before I could, the sweaty taxi driver suddenly looked sheepish.

'OK, four.'

Wim looked at me disapprovingly. 'What? It's too much?'

'No, of course not, I just wasn't expecting it to be so cheap.'

Wim laughed. 'I bet the locals only pay two.'

He carried on, 'They've got so much oil here, fuel's so cheap, I don't think it's taxed either. You know you can take a bus across the whole country for twenty bucks?'

The driver strapped our bags onto the roof of the taxi and we set off to the east. The land was sterile and barren, it was proper desert now. Sitting in the taxi, I was able to take in something of the scenery and state of the people. The land was how I had imagined, a vast desolate tract, populated by the occasional village with rocket-like minarets jutting from the roofs of the mosques. It wasn't all that different from Eastern Turkey or Northern Iraq, except one thing stood out. The cleanliness of the place.

As we passed through the small towns of Maku and Margan, I noticed how spotless and orderly things were. The villages were impeccably tidy, the roads were excellent and there seemed to be an almost manicured perfection to the infrastructure. It was unlike anywhere I had seen in the Middle East.

'Look at how they dress,' remarked Wim. 'No – how do you say – dishcloths here.' He was right. Almost all the men we saw were wearing smart suits and black shoes.

'Nobody is wearing ties, though, I wonder why?' said Wim, as if reading my mind.

'It started in 1979,' interrupted the taxi driver, who until now hadn't said anything. 'The Islamic revolution said that ties were decadent and un-Islamic symbols of our Western oppressors.'

'I see.'

'Load of old rubbish, though,' he continued chirpily. 'Just the mullahs trying to control the state. We all wore ties before the revolution.'

We sped into the sprawl of Tabriz shortly before sundown, but the driver didn't seem to slow down in spite of the busy traffic. Despite the urban sprawl and ugly modern buildings, even Tabriz appeared quite sanitary compared with what I was expecting.

'Very nice town, eh?' He pointed at a passing carpet shop with both hands. We swerved a little and Wim looked at me in a state of nervousness. We were heading directly for an oncoming taxi that was zooming as fast as we were, but luckily passed safely on the wrong side of the road.

'Hmmm, yes, very nice. Anywhere here will do.'

We found a plain little hotel on the Kheyabun-e Emam Khomeini. It was a typically grand name that was otherwise known as the high street. Around the town, I noticed how fancy coloured bulbs adorned the bountiful trees on the otherwise dark avenues, which gave the place an almost festive feel. Despite being exhausted and hungry from the bumpy ride, nevertheless we waited until nightfall in due compliance with Ramadan and then went in search of a *kebabi*.

'Welcome to Persia, man,' said David – a French hippy with a huge blond beard and the look of a seasoned dope smoker. He was finishing up a kebab himself as we walked in. David was on his third jaunt to Iran, where he came to meditate and 'get away from Americans'. His accomplice, a dark squat man called Pierre, simply smiled and took long drags on cigarettes in slow succession. With them was a well-dressed and clean-shaven twenty-year-old Afghan called Hamid, who said he was in the 'import-export' business. The three of them sat around a plastic table covered in the remains of lamb and chicken skewers.

'Very welcome, sirs. Very welcome indeed. Please come and join Mr Daveeed and Mr Pie– Pie–'

'*Pierre*, Hamid, *Pierre*,' said Pierre, clearly used to the Afghan's plight with the French accent. Hamid lowered his head in shame.

'Just arrived?' asked David, in an arrogant drawl that only the French can achieve with such perfection.

'Yes.'

I ordered some *chai* and a lamb kebab.

'Ze carpets here aren't what zey used to be,' said David suddenly, in a pensive manner.

'No?' I asked, sensing that this was going to be a one-sided conversation.

'No, man. Ze good ones are ze old ones, but they're so expensive now. All ze new ones are terrible.'

'It's my third time in ziz country,' he continued. 'I used to like it, but now ze police always follow me. Zey think I want to sell drugs.'

'Oh. Do you?'

'No, man. I don't sell drugs. I just smoke zem.'

'Of course.'

'Back in France, I used to grow hemp. Did you know hemp has over five thousand uses?'

I didn't.

'Yeah. It's all politics, man. Ze governments hate zis plant – zey want to exterminate it because zey are afraid of it. You can use hemp to make clothes, ze seeds have natural antibiotics, it helps with hyperventilation. Henry Ford even made a car that ran on hemp fuel.'

'Really?' I wasn't so convinced.

'You know, hemp could replace plastic.'

David was getting wearisome now and his sentences began to clash with increasing contradiction. He gazed, somewhat vacantly, at a faded poster of the Imam Ali that was pinned to the cream-coloured plastered wall. Hamid had heard it all before, but was keen to please his patron and attempted to display his comprehension by nodding enthusiastically. Wim looked bored and stole a glance in my direction, indicating with a flick of his head towards the door that we should leave. We munched down the kebabs and I drank my *chai* in one gulp.

'See you around, man,' said David with a lazy nod. Pierre grinned inanely and Hamid stood up, giving us a servile bow.

'That one is wilier than he looks,' said Wim, as we walked out onto the street.

'Which one, the Frenchman?'

'No, the Afghan. All that bowing and yes sir, no sir. The Afghans only do that if there's something in it for them.'

'Drugs by the looks of things,' I said.

'Exactly. It wouldn't surprise me if he was a dealer.'

'Isn't it dangerous for them to be so stoned in the street, though? I mean, Iran has got a reputation for coming down pretty hard on that kind of behaviour.'

'Yes. They're idiots. If they get caught by the morality police, they'd be locked up for life.'

Back at the hotel, the night watchman had fallen asleep across the doorway, causing us to leap delicately over his exposed belly and avoid contact with his tremendous whiskers.

Tabriz is the gateway to Persia. Iran's fourth largest city, it is generally unknown to travellers unless they approach by land heading to or from the west. Historically, it has been claimed that near to Tabriz, in the plains below the Sahand mountain, was the site of the biblical Garden of Eden. In the morning, though, a blue haze hung low and it was difficult to discern the lemon-coloured foothills described by Robert Byron in his famous pre-war journey, *The Road to Oxiana*. Try as I might, I couldn't associate the place of Adam's temptation with this industrial sprawl.

I looked out across the city from the window of the hotel to see a skyline spoilt by ugly factories and high-rise flats. Most of the ancient mosques and monuments have long since been destroyed by the frequent earthquakes that have plagued its history. But still, I was excited to be there. I was finally on the main drag of the traditional Silk Road. In its heyday, virtually all of the goods coming from China and India passed through the bazaars of Tabriz on their overland journey to the markets of Constantinople and Venice. It was where the northern and southern routes converged after avoiding the great Karakum desert, before splitting again to wind westward through Anatolia or south to Baghdad and the Levant.

Despite its drab exterior, one part of the town remained as it had for centuries. The bazaar still stands. It is one of the oldest covered markets in the region and allegedly the largest in the world. Wim and I set off exploring the several miles of tunnel-like alleyways with their distinct red-brick vaults, each subdivided into separate 'districts' selling distinct types of wares. We fought through the rows of shops near to the outskirts of the bazaar, which sold modern electronic imports and cheap plastic bangles, to reach the more traditional goods in the dark interior.

It didn't seem to have changed much since Ibn Battutah, the famous Moroccan traveller, visited in 1347.

I entered the city by a gate called the Baghdad Gate, and we came to an immense bazaar. One of the finest I have seen the world over.

And he should know, having travelled in virtually every country in the known civilised – and not so civilised – world.

Every trade is grouped separately in it. I passed through the jewellers' bazaar, and my eyes were dazzled by the variety of precious stones that I beheld . . . the women were buying them in such large quantities and trying to outdo one another. As a result of this, I witnessed a riot – may

God preserve us from such! We went on into the ambergris and musk market, and there witnessed another riot like it, or worse . . .

Battutah stayed for only one night, because he was in a hurry to reach Baghdad, but he was impressed with the town, which had a population of almost a quarter of a million – a massive city in the Middle Ages. I couldn't help thinking, though, that now it had a very provincial feel about the place and, like the illustrious Moroccan, I decided that a couple of days was enough. Before we left the bazaar, we decided it would only be right to go and see the 'carpet district', still famous throughout the Muslim world for the quality of its rugs.

Despite the massive crowds, I wasn't a bit surprised when we bumped into the odd threesome we had met the night before, sitting inside a carpet shop on top of a gigantic pile of Persia's finest floor coverings. After all, travellers do tend to have the same mindset.

'There are over one million carpet weavers in Iran,' Hamid boasted. 'The finest in the world,' he added, 'except, of course, Afghanistan. Herat is best, Tabriz comes second. All very, very good.'

'Rubbish,' interrupted David. 'Zey are all rubbish now. None of zem are ze genuine article.'

David seemed to take pleasure in insulting Hamid, for whom I began to feel sorry.

'I think the Persian *kilim* is the best,' Wim broke in. This brought a smile back to Hamid's face.

'Yes, yes, very good kilim. Made by the desert nomads.'

'What is the difference?' I asked rather naively.

'A *kilim* is a small rug, it's a kind of carpet usually associated with the rough weave of the nomadic tribes.'

'You want to buy one?' Hamid jumped at the chance to make a commission.

'No thanks, I think maybe if I visit Afghanistan, I'll buy one then.'

Hamid didn't know quite what to say. His commercial streak wanted to try and persuade me, but his national pride held fast and he congratulated me on my decision.

'A wise choice,' Hamid nodded solemnly.

'Do you know where we can get tickets to Tehran? We're leaving tomorrow,' interrupted Wim.

'Come, I take you to a man who know everything.' Hamid seemed glad to have an excuse to take his leave of the two Frenchmen and led us from the narrow passages, with their claustrophobic tunnels and warrens, outside into the comparative calm of the central square. We were led inside a modern office building that declared itself as the tourist agency. A tall, smartly dressed man in his early fifties, with a huge bald forehead and small menacing eyes, beckoned us into his office.

'I am Nasser,' he said, offering a limp handshake. He waved us to a ragged sofa next to a wooden bookshelf stuffed with colourful guidebooks and maps of Iran.

Nasser claimed to be fluent in eight languages.

'Tea?' he grinned, offering us a freshly brewed sweet tea in tiny glasses. 'How can I help?'

Hamid had now scuttled out of the room, and as I glanced at the faded posters showing photographs of Bam and Shiraz, I suspected that we had been brought here so that we might buy a tour – a fate even worse than being encouraged to buy an oversized carpet. Before we could answer, Nasser had already begun the polite preliminaries.

'Where are you from?'

'Eng—'

'England. Yes, I can always guess,' he butted in quickly.

'And you are from Holland.' He offered Wim a sugar cube from a small bowl.

'Belgium, actually.'

'Of course, of course.'

'And you are in Iran for the first time? No, you look like very big travellers, probably here many times. All travellers visit Nasser. Look at my pictures.'

Beyond his impressive glistening dome, I craned my neck to the far wall of the office, which was covered in badly printed photographs of our host with an array of Westerners, mainly chirpy looking women.

'Everybody knows Nasser,' said Nasser.

'I am very trustworthy man,' he continued, with the weasel-like craftiness of a double-glazing salesman. I took an immediate dislike to him. Anyone who says that is in all likelihood utterly untrustworthy.

'So, I am told you want to go to Tehran?'

'Actually, I think we . . .' I was about to make the executive decision to buy the tickets from somewhere else, but Nasser must have sensed my apprehension.

'Wait,' he said, offering more tea. 'My friend. I get you half-price bus tickets to Tehran.'

Now normally I would have brushed away the sales patter, but both Wim and I were about as budget conscious as you can get, and I decided to let him finish.

'My cousin is big man at bus station. He will make you special deal, because you are my friends.'

'There's always a cousin or an uncle involved somewhere,' Wim whispered, as Nasser fumbled for his phone. I smiled to myself as we both resigned ourselves to the inevitable. It takes a strong will to fend off oriental charm – especially when it involves business. And it always involves business.

We helped ourselves to another *chai*.

'Ten minutes and tickets arrive.' Nasser grinned again, displaying an obnoxious rack of yellow distorted teeth.

'So how do you like our new Iran? It is much improved, don't you think?'

I wondered for a moment what he meant. Was he talking about the revolution?

'Things are very good now,' he explained. 'We have a very liberal government, the country is very progressive. Look,' he pointed out of the window that overlooked the high street.

'See how informal the women's clothes are. Nowadays the girls are wearing very nice, colourful hijab, not too restrictive. And see the men, everybody is now wearing short sleeves.'

I peered out of the window to see his romantic vision of liberality and instantly began to question my own sanity. I remembered reading in a book about the hippy trail a description of Iran in the early 1970s, which described it as a breath of fresh air after Turkey, full of girls in short skirts and camp men driving Cadillacs.

But now, of course, there was none of that. Lost were the loose hijabs and bare forearms among a sea of black *chadors*: the tent-like robes that cover an entire woman's body except the eyes. Almost all the men had buttoned-up, long-sleeved shirts. *No, Nasser, there is a long way to go yet*, I couldn't help concluding, but decided to keep the thought to myself. Hamid reappeared clutching a package under his arm, smiling like a child who had just returned from a successful foray. He whispered, loud enough for all to hear, 'It's a photograph of me and my girlfriend.'

He was clearly expecting us to be extremely impressed.

'She very nice. Very sexy. Much boom boom,' he winked at Wim.

'I'm sure.'

I was beginning to see a commonality in many of the Iranians, who were keen to show how liberal their country was supposed to be, but only in private. Outside the veneer of public piousness and Islamic conservatism, it was as strong as ever, perhaps more so. The chador reigned supreme in the over-forties and the women kept a deferential few paces behind their husbands. The younger women were cautious and the men frustrated. But whenever I spoke in private to any young man, it was clear that you simply can't stop young people doing what young people do and the human instinct will find a way to thrive.

I found it interesting to see how the hypocrisy governed with absolute clarity here. There was a way that you *should* behave, which was binding and universal, but then there was another way – the reality – in which individuals actually carried on their daily lives, and in it contained the beliefs, the desires and the taboos of this subdued people. Iranians did smoke, they did drink alcohol, even during Ramadan, and they did have sex (a lot) outside of marriage.

But for the traveller, there is a more wearisome side to this duplicity. Because of our transient nature, and a combination of ephemeral familiarity, brief confidence and probably an element of envy of Western freedom, it often means that local hosts, guides like Hamid, frequently expose their most revolting confessions. Hamid's adolescent tales of pornography collections and underage girlfriends were only the tip of the iceberg.

I thanked Nasser for his help and we left him to his petty delusions, gazing out of the window to an Iran that hadn't existed for twenty-five years and probably wouldn't for another generation. Back inside the bazaar, I wanted to change some traveller's cheques and so, amongst the bustle of young entrepreneurs, Hamid found us a man touting outside of the bank. The hustler looked like a comic-book pickpocket and couldn't have appeared shiftier if he had tried. I took out a fifty-dollar cheque and showed it to him. He looked around, as if to check if anyone was watching.

'No! Traveller's cheques are not allowed here. We will get arrested for these. Very illegal here.' The man then began to chastise Hamid in Persian for bringing us to him. Hamid looked rueful and apologetic. It seemed he couldn't do anything right.

'Don't worry, Hamid,' said Wim as the dealer disappeared into the crowd. But I was suddenly worried. A lack of foresight now meant that I had a grand total of forty dollars in cash and since there were no machines that accepted Western cards in Iran, they would have to last me until I got to somewhere more congenial, and that probably meant Pakistan – some two thousand miles away. In the meantime, I would have to tighten my belt. I wasn't about to start begging just yet.

'I know a place that might interest you,' said Hamid at last, as we walked back towards the bazaar, impatient that we should find something to like about his adopted home.

Fifty kilometres outside of Tabriz lies a small village called Kandovan. The taxi sped through the desert to the small settlement, which appeared to rise out of the rocky hillside like a huge termite mound.

'Isn't it amazing?' pointed Hamid out of the window. 'These people live like cavemen.' He began to chuckle at his own humour.

But although the houses were carved out of the solid volcanic rock, forming natural conical mounds that pointed into the clear desert sky like witches' hats, there was a distinct air of civilisation and dignity about the place. Unlike the touristic Cappadocia in Turkey, or the uninhabited Vardzia in Georgia, this was a fully functioning village with several ancient Iranian families living inside the hollow mounds.

The troglodyte population didn't seem to mind us trespassing in their gardens or amongst their tiny houses and were probably quite used to visitors. I watched as a frail old woman emerged from her hole to shake down a carpet outside. Above her, two small children, a boy and a girl, were perched happily like a pair of finches on the next cone up. I smiled and waved to them and they waved back, but as soon as I took out my camera, they vanished, scurrying away back into their rock.

I climbed up to the highest point, following the little lanes, and sat on a stone that looked back down over the village. At the bottom, which was flat, the taxi was still waiting next to a stream and another one turned up, despatching a group of Iranian tourists, probably a wealthy family from Tehran or Esfahan. They didn't climb up to the top, instead posing for each other's photos before filling up plastic water bottles from the stream.

'Hamid, why are the people collecting this water?' I asked when I climbed back down to the road.

'Because they are very strange.'

'No,' interrupted the driver, who just so happened to be Nasser's brother. 'Ignore this ignorant Afghan. Come.'

With scant regard for Ramadan, the driver insisted that we ingested some of the stream water.

'It is a very famous mineral water. People come from all over Iran to take it home. It cures many diseases of the stomach.' He picked up a small round pebble from the sandy bank.

'How do you say when you have a rock inside?'

'I think he means kidney stones,' said Wim.

'People have been living among these rocks for eight hundred years and the mineral water has been attracting sick *musaafir* for just as long.'

Apart from the telegraph poles that brought modern communications, I don't suppose things had changed all that much during that time.

The next day, Wim and I left for Tehran, hitching a ride in a minibus.

'Where are you from?' asked Nazir, the landlord of the unfortunately named Sham hotel, near to Imam Khomeini Square.

'I am from England and he is from Belgium,' I replied.

'Belgium. Belgium?' Nazir looked thoughtful. 'Where is Belgium? USA?'

'No, it's in Europe, quite near to England.'

'Yes. Bel-a-jum.' He peered over the counter, as if inspecting us for some tropical illness.

'Ingeez. Are you married?'

'No,' I replied.

'I am very sorry.' He shook his head apologetically.

'It's quite all right, I am far too young,' I said, wondering why he was so concerned about my marital status.

'Never too young!' He banged his fist on the counter with a sudden authority. 'You should find a wife as soon as you can. There is nothing better than a good wife.'

'But how would I travel if I was married?' I thought I'd play along.

'Why would you want to?' He cocked his head in a quizzical fashion. 'And anyway, you could always lock her up.'

Imam Khomeini Square is Tehran's central square, but in reality it is little more than a huge, busy roundabout surrounded by several hundred little stalls selling exhaust pipes and brake cables and used car batteries. Hundreds of taxis competed for right of way and the noise of the horns was deafening. It wasn't exactly the romantic scene from *One Thousand and One Nights* that I had imagined.

After a sleep, though, I decided to give the city a chance and risked crossing the road to explore the downtown area. I had expected Tehran to be a smog-ridden, third-world mess like Cairo, but it was a relief to discover a rather pleasant city. Yes, the traffic was chaotic and crossing the road was a perilous undertaking, but amidst the normal bustle that you come to expect in the Middle East, the people were smart and the streets were clean. More so than in Tabriz, the women seemed at ease; I noticed far fewer full-body chadors and most of the young women wore only a loose scarf barely covering their head. Many of the girls wore fancy gold earrings and glossy lipstick, whilst the men here did wear short sleeves and had long, styled hair.

This was more like the vision of reform that Nasser dreamt of. It was beginning here in Tehran, the fledgling signs of individualism and freedom that may one day spread to the provinces like Tabriz. I wanted to see more and find out if this liberalism was ready to break out of its infancy and return Iran to the twenty-first century.

President Mohammad Khatami came to power as a democratically elected president in 1997 and was quickly hailed by the international community as a reformist and liberal. He received an unprecedented seventy per cent of the vote and was re-elected in 2001. Not since 1979 had Iran been so free and progressive. His reformist agenda gained him popularity with the young and liberals, but inevitably brought clashes against the conservative Islamists and the mullahs who held the real power.

In 2004, when I passed through, Khatami's popularity had already peaked and many of his supporters had grown disillusioned with his failure to win over the traditionalists. Nevertheless, the public – especially the young – had come to appreciate his common sense and wanted him to continue the reforms that had been so promising. Khatami's foreign policy was pleasingly conciliatory, after years of vocal criticism and lack of any dialogue with the US and Israel. There were even talks of lifting the sanctions and Iran returning to the diplomatic table in world affairs.

But in a twisted matter of fate, things suddenly took a downturn a year later when, due to an administrative oversight, Khatami was seated next to the Israeli President Moshe Katsav during the funeral of Pope John Paul II. Katsav boasted irresponsibly that the pair had shaken hands and indulged in chitchat. This meant that the sixteen-year silence between the two countries had technically been broken, but of course this infuriated the Iranian conservatives, who accused Khatami of being a traitor to the revolution for officially recognising Israel. Despite denying the incident, he lost the next election.

Khatami's term in office was a window of opportunity. People had started to become more liberal, and in reality, the hijabs were falling further back from the fringe line, but less than a year after I left, soon after the hand-shaking incident, the infamous Mahmoud Ahmadinejad was elected and any notion of reform was thrown firmly out of the window, as traditionalists took hold once again and the militant anti-Western flag burners returned to the streets.

I walked to the former US embassy in a pleasant avenue near the city centre. It had found international fame in 1979, when it became the scene of a hostage crisis unlike any other. A group of students from the nearby university assaulted the mission and took fifty-four of its staff hostage for 444 days, with the support of Ayatollah Khomeini, who had recently usurped the Iranian monarch. It was a protest against the USA, which was harbouring the exiled Shah. They demanded his return, so that he could be tried and imprisoned in the brand-new revolutionary state. Of course, the USA, which had supported the Shah during his reign, refused.

After failed attempts to negotiate a release, the US military attempted a rescue operation – code-named 'Operation Eagle's Claw'. It was a total disaster that resulted in the deaths of eight American servicemen and one Iranian civilian. The two countries eventually signed a release agreement in January 1981 and the hostages were formally freed into US custody, but the two countries had been diplomatic enemies ever since.

I walked around the perimeter wall of the infamous setting – this was where the revolution rocketed, and with it, the source of much of the world's current political instability. The embassy is now affectionately known as 'the den of espionage'. The external walls have been colourfully daubed in anti-US propaganda and strange murals depicting romantic images of the revolutionaries: young, bearded intellectuals in 1970s collars, staring into the twenty-first century. Alongside, on the crumbling brickwork, was a huge painted AK-47 – the modern terrorist's weapon of choice. Perhaps the most haunting of all was a fresco of the Statue of Liberty sporting a dastardly skull in place of a head. A burning star-spangled banner formed the backdrop.

The building has since been used as a training base of the Iranian Revolutionary Guard – and to house a museum and a bookshop. Behind the menacing murals, rusty barbed-wire, and broken bottles that topped the walls, there was no way of telling what function it really served nowadays.

I made my way to the park, a beautiful, leafy oasis of calm filled with all kinds of well-tended shrubs and trees, where I met up with Wim, who had been conducting a rather risky experiment. He had been travelling around all morning on Tehran's buses, in an attempt to engage in a conversation with an Iranian lady.

Buses, he told me, were the best place to get close to girls without warranting attention.

'Of course, you can't just walk up to a girl in the street or a shop, or they say you'll end up getting locked up. The buses are divided into the front and back halves and the opposing sexes are expected to separate themselves accordingly,' he explained, shuffling some twigs around to make a diagram of the bus.

'If, however, you happen to find yourself in the middle of the bus,' he jabbed the stick bus violently, 'then it just might be possible to speak to one. They're beautiful, you know.'

'I know,' I said. 'I've seen them.'

Wim had been given the idea by someone he had met the last time he was in Iran, who had boasted that he had spoken to a beautiful Iranian girl by using this method and she had secretly slipped him her telephone number.

'He actually met her as well! They were having an affair for weeks.'

'Well, any phone numbers?' I was intrigued to find out if he'd had any success.

'No way. The middle of every bus is so popular with men and women that it's impossible to get a place there.'

Like a pair of clandestine spies, we ate our lunch, careful not to let anyone see. In all probability, no one would have cared that a couple of Westerners were flouting the fast, but we thought it courteous to try and hide our impiety. I looked around. Next to a beautiful lake, several couples sat next to each other, stealing furtive glances. One or two even dared to hold hands.

'It's an odd place isn't it, Iran?' Wim said, munching on his falafel. In the distance the impressive, spear shaped outline of the semi-complete Milad tower – expected to be one of the largest buildings in the world – rose upwards, as if to remind visitors that Iran was a nation to contend with.

'Here we are, in the twenty-first century, and there is a modern, wealthy country with a theocratic government. You know, it's the first since the fall of the Dalai Lama's government in Tibet in 1957. But I've never heard of any trouble with morality police or the Revolutionary Guard. I've certainly never had any problems.'

Wim took another bite of his sandwich, using his spare hand to brush away a curly lock of blond hair.

'I think they are just confused – they are a proud people and have come to the point where they really want change. They want democracy and they want all of the things that come with it. But until they stop pretending to hate the West, there's no way change will come. You can't have both. It'll only come when the young people have the courage to rise up against the mullahs.'

The next afternoon we went our separate ways. Wim was heading north to Rasht to see if it was possible to go skiing in the Alborz mountains, and I went south to Esfahan.

12

A Pilgrimage

'Farengi welcome' announced the flickering neon sign above the door of the Shiraz hostel in Esfahan. *Farengi* is one of those odd misnomers that have taken hold as a result of some ancient slang. It comes from a mispronunciation of the medieval name *Frank* and dates back to the time of the crusades, when the Germanic Frankish kings were dominant figures in European politics – they gave their name to both France and Frankfurt. When the crusaders invaded the Near East, the local Muslims decided they all looked and sounded the same and forevermore, Europeans became known collectively as the Franks. The name spread throughout the Islamic world, and to this day it is the common term used for white Europeans everywhere from Bosnia to Malaysia in all its regional variations, *franj, afraji, ferenghi, barang, farang.*

It was still six in the morning and despite feeling cold, dirty and exhausted, I had walked the five kilometres from the bus station to the city centre in an effort to clear my head after a long, sleepless night on the bus. I marched through the streets in a trance-like state, weary and barely conscious of the city closing in around me. There wasn't a soul in sight and my eyes remained focused on the cracked pavement that unfolded in front of me, until I happened to glance up and see that stuttering invitation.

The door was closed and after banging solidly for over a minute, I gave up. The Persians weren't early risers, especially during Ramadan. I was too tired to walk any further, so I curled up on a bench outside, wrapped in my coat to ward off the morning dew.

I woke to the sound of giggling. Two elderly Iranian women dressed in full chador had sat on the end of the bench and they were keeping a watchful eye on a little girl, who was playing by herself. I sat up with a jolt, momentarily embarrassed, and attempted a dignified smile to the closest lady. She just stared at me with grey, vacant eyes. Looking at my watch, it was quarter past nine, and people had begun to fill the streets. A few old men hobbled around and the shopkeepers were dragging out their wares. A cat screeched angrily as a bucket of dirty water was ejected from the shadows of a garage.

By now the hotel was open and I asked for a room at the reception desk. The manager, a round forty-year-old, who had the look of an Italian waiter, showed me to a dormitory and even said that he would change my traveller's cheques for the painful commission of twenty per cent. I had no choice but to agree and handed over fifty dollars.

I spent a small part of my winnings in a little tea house next door, where a few less pious Iranians were ignoring Ramadan with some vigour. With a stomach full of flatbread and honey, I set off feeling cheerful to a nearby park and watched some men playing chess, then walked down to the Naqsh-e Jahan Square, known colloquially, like all the others in Iran, as the Imam square. The vast quadrant – as big as five football pitches, was surrounded by symmetrical pointed arches with white awnings. Each arch contained an entranceway to a shop.

Immediately noticeable was a magnificent turquoise and cream tiled dome to the east, which was perfectly reflected in the water of the still pool in the centre of the square. The pool, which glistened in the sunshine, was surrounded by neat little lawns, flowers and well-tended shrubs. Opposite the dome of the Masjed-e Sheikh Lotfollah mosque, there is another prominent building, the Ali Qapu Palace, with a balcony that overlooks the pools, but it looked like it was undergoing restoration and was covered in scaffolding. Nevertheless I walked around, impressed. Not only were the immense vaults beautiful, intricate and massive, but I was taken in by the prevailing peace and tranquillity.

Most of the square was paved and at certain times of day no motor vehicles were allowed inside, and this was one of those times; the only sounds were the jingling of bells from the horse-drawn carriages and the soothing resonance of the gardener's hose watering the grass and shrubs. As I crossed the walkway to observe the serenity, the water fountains in the central pond came on for a while and livened up the scene. I wondered if it was so quiet because of Ramadan and went to ask one of the several hundred carpet sellers that sat outside the stalls under the agreeable shade of the awnings.

'No, my friend. Esfahan is always this peaceful,' said Morteza, a thin young man with a big smile and deep piercing eyes. He was wearing stonewashed Levi jeans and a trendy yellow shirt, with the sleeves rolled up to his elbows. His black hair was parted in the middle and fell in greasy curls to the bottom of his ears. He was clean-shaven, but with a beard he would have borne a striking resemblance to one of those typical Persian bas reliefs showing the head of Darius.

'Close your eyes and imagine you are in a beautiful country

park, you would never think you are in the centre of the city.' He offered me a seat on a pile of red carpets, which I suspected were reserved for paying customers.

'It wasn't always like this, though,' he said. 'There is an old Persian proverb, *Esfahān nesf-e jahān ast*; it means 'Esfahan is half of the world'. My scholarly shopkeeper explained, 'It was once one of the largest metropolises in the world and also one of the most important. We had parks, baths, libraries and beautiful mosques, and even the *farengi* travellers came to visit our great city.'

Located right in the centre of Iran, it flourished for some seven hundred years after the tenth century and was a cultural melting pot and a crossroads for trade, a key stop on the Silk Road. With its strategic and commercial importance, it didn't surprise me that the city was often subject to invasions.

In 1387, the people of Esfahan surrendered to the Mongol warlord Timur. Despite his reputation as a bloodthirsty conqueror, he only imposed a very heavy taxation. Even Timur could be merciful. Or at least, that is what the Esfahanis thought.

One day the residents became so fed up with the punitive taxes that an angry mob decided to kill some of the Mongol tax collectors. It was a mistake. Timur's trademark retribution was swift and vengeful: his army quickly massacred the entire population, killing a reported seventy thousand citizens. One eyewitness counted twenty-eight towers made from their decapitated heads.

The city saw even more bloodshed at the end of its golden era. The Safavids, who had given Esfahan its elevated status and civilised reputation, were defeated in 1722 by Afghan invaders under the leadership of the feared Shah Mahmud, who left the city in ruins and decimated the Persian Empire once and for all. With the growth of European authority and the expansion of the British and Russian spheres of influence, combined with the declining importance of the Silk Road, Iran – almost instantly – disappeared from the world stage until some two hundred and fifty years later with the events of 1979.

But despite its bloody history, as I stood in the Imam square, I tried to imagine the plaza as it would have appeared five hundred years ago in its bustling heyday; full of Chinese silk merchants and Indian spice traders. I'd heard rumours that the city is also one of the centres of Iran's controversial nuclear sites. Supposedly, somewhere deep underground, raw uranium was secretly being converted into Uranium hexafluoride, and hardened lead bunkers were in the process of being constructed to protect the site – ostensibly from nuclear accidents – but also as insurance against long-range Israeli missiles. It wasn't a subject I was going to bring up with my carpet seller, though.

As Morteza regaled me with stories of the beauty of nomadic women and the delicacy of their rugs, I watched solitary old men fiddle contentedly with their prayer beads, while a few couples chatted discreetly nearby. Next to the pools, with their fountains, groups of schoolgirls in chadors sketched the Masjed-e Imam, also called the Shah Mosque, in little black notebooks, while a pair of teenage girls dipped their feet in the cool water, exposing for a second their bare ankles. Now and again the muezzin called the faithful to prayer.

'Are you not going to pray?' I asked the twenty-two-year-old, as a congregation gathered inside the mosque on the far side of the mall.

'Pray?'

'Yes, it's afternoon prayer time, isn't it? I should leave you to pray.' I made to get up out of respect.

'Please, sit down. I pray sometimes, but three times is too much. I don't think God needs us to pray three times a day,' Morteza said with a smile.

'Not even in Ramadan?' I teased.

'Ramadan is a waste of time. Twelve hours with no food is too much. Can you imagine?'

'I've done it a few days now and I agree it's not very pleasant, but I thought it's what all proper Muslims do to cleanse their soul?' I was slightly surprised with the ease at which my new friend relinquished his religion.

'Proper Muslims? Bah!' Morteza flicked his wrist in a dismissive manner.

'I don't care about these proper Muslims. I am a good person, I think, but it doesn't mean I should punish myself. I worry sometimes about the way my religion has been twisted. Being a Muslim comes from the heart. It is about making peace with God and yourself, it doesn't matter when you eat and what you wear.'

As dusk approached, I strolled down to the river past rows of designer shops on a street that wouldn't look out of place in Paris or London. Big window panes with huge stickers advertised gold jewellery, diamond rings, sexy lingerie, mobiles phones and big-name handbags. A branded poster with a heavily edited picture of a black footballer was juxtaposed next to another with the omnipresent face of Ayatollah Khomenei. I crossed the Si-o-se Pol Bridge, which spans the Zayandeh River, to watch the sun set over the mountains, its thirty-three arches producing the same grand reflection in the river for over four hundred years.

As the sky reddened and the crowds gathered to break their fast, people rushed back and forth to buy their flat bread from street vendors. Families spread their picnic blankets on the grassy banks of the river in hungry anticipation of sunset. The last flicker of red converged with the distant horizon and I couldn't tell whether it was clouds or mountains that had swallowed up the sun. The wail of the muezzin began from the top of the minaret of the Imam Mosque, followed half a second later by two or three more nearby and then every mosque in the city followed suit, until the whole night sky seemed to be adrift with the enchanting echo of the *Salat al-Maghrib*. If ever there was a place that evoked Arabian nights, it was here in Esfahan.

The hostel was now full of other *farengis*, many of whom were also travelling overland to India. I sat at the only available table and glanced over at a European man, Scandinavian I guessed, wearing a white Arab-style *djellaba* and an Egyptian prayer cap, sitting in the corner of the courtyard. He was smoking hashish. I overheard him introduce himself as 'the joker' to a stout German girl and explain to her how he was a Middle East expert, having spent six months 'living as a local' in Cairo.

I diverted my attention to a pair a few metres away with unmistakable antipodean accents. By the sounds of it, one was a Kiwi and the other an Aussie – both, of course, lived in London. I invited myself over to join them and we decided to go for a kebab. Matt and Brett had just arrived and were on a whistle-stop, two-week holiday in Iran and Turkmenistan. They were nearing the end of their trip now, but they'd had an interesting time in the strange neighbouring republic.

'Did you know that the dictator – Turkmenbashi – has a big

gold statue of himself in the central square of Ashgabat that rotates with the sun?' exclaimed Matt, in a strangely reverent tone. 'He even renamed the days of the week after his family members.'

'And did you know that the women are so beautiful that he has put a tax on exporting them out of the country? Now you have to pay ten thousand dollars if you want to marry a Turkmani woman and take her home,' said Brett.

Their stories reminded me a little of the eccentric anecdotes that came back from Central Asia with travellers of all genera-tions – the wild tales of dog-headed men that Herodotus spun to the Greeks, and the legends of mermaids as recounted by Marco Polo and Ibn Battutah. In the nineteenth century, European soldiers and travellers were returning home with fantastic chronicles of the barbarian practices of Bactria, Transoxiana and the mystical mountain kingdoms of the Himalayas. Even the Victorian Great Gamers weren't averse to a bit of hyperbole. Conolly took great delight in writing about the savage customs of native tribes he met on the way to India. It seemed that not much had changed in that respect.

What comes as a surprise is the distinct lack of written accounts from our own times. The 1930s were full of more real-istic accounts of travel in the region from the likes of Evelyn Waugh and Robert Byron and even the 1950s had the amusing stories of Eric Newby and Norman Lewis. But the much-vaunted path known as the hippy trail, traversed during the 1960s and 1970s, is almost entirely undocumented.

Sitting in the open courtyard of the hostel, surrounded by hemp-wearing Western travellers openly smoking cannabis and telling each other stories from 'the road', was my first taste of that trail. On the communal bookshelf, where travellers were encouraged to 'book swap', I exchanged William Dalrymple's *In Xanadu* with a reassuringly thin title called *A Season in Heaven*. It was a collection of vignettes from old hippies who had done the overland route some forty years ago. Some had probably stayed in the same hostel that I was in now.

The hippy trail is a generic term used to describe the movements of several thousand Westerners from the mid-1960s until 1979, who abandoned for a short while the trappings of Western culture, setting off from the capitals of Europe on the long road east to India or Nepal, or even Australia. Some hitchhiked, others drove in ancient Volkswagen campervans or Land Rovers, or even converted fire engines and school buses. Not everyone made it all of the way. Many died *en route*, others were arrested (mainly for drugs), but equally, many others stayed in their chosen lands for several years, never quite returning to 'normality'.

Encouraged by the likes of the Beatles, India became an essential destination on the journey, where thousands of youngsters ignored the examples of their parents and adopted Islam, Buddhism or Hinduism. It was the age of flower power and hallucinogenic drugs in a time of counter-culture and social revolution. Never before had so many people been drawn to a particular place out of something other than necessity. In one way, it was a cultural movement, in the most pure form of the word – but to others it was nothing more than the beginning of mass tourism in Asia.

It seems that for all its talk of being a spiritual journey in search of inner fulfilment, the reality was as much a drug- and hedonism-fuelled holiday as the current backpacker trends. I don't know if I was being cynical, or if the same waves of hypocrisy that came over me in Tbilisi were taking hold again, but I suddenly felt disillusioned. Even here in the heart of the Islamic world, at the crossroads of ancient civilisations, in-between the deserts of the Middle East and the mountains of Central Asia, all I wanted to do was escape from the crowds. The crowds, indeed. There were perhaps seven other people in the hostel. Maybe another fifteen travellers in the whole city. Possibly a hundred tourists in the whole of Iran. I consoled myself with the notion that more people sit on the Spanish Steps in Rome at any one time!

But the stories of Turkmenistan from Brett and Matt aroused in me a niggling feeling of jealousy and I began to plot my escape.

In the morning, I left the hostel as early as possible, wanting to make best use of the day. I returned to the square and sketched the Masjed-e Sheikh Lotfollah, disturbed only by the gardener, who occasionally tried to spray me with his hose. I read a few pages of the Koran and then, thinking it would be apt, I wandered over to the Masjed-e Imam and watched as the locals walked freely in and out. I felt unreasonably nervous. Normally I would have happily entered the mosque, as I had done several times across the Islamic world, but this was Iran and I didn't know if I would be welcome.

I remembered watching scenes of jubilation on the television after 9/11 on the streets of Tehran and thoughts of belligerent mullahs ranting against the Western *infidel* ran through my mind. I pictured myself getting arrested by the Revolutionary

Guard and being treated to fifty lashes in public. *Imagine the humiliation.* But then I got a grip of myself. *This is a mosque. It is a house of God, all are welcome.* As I attempted to build up the courage to slip past the guards, I noticed my reflection in the polished marble of the walls and saw a bearded and tanned young man, who could pass as a local anywhere in the Middle East. *I look like an Iranian, don't let all those Russian arrests go to waste.*

I spied my chance and slipped past the armed guards, who I supposed were there to keep out terrorists and schismatic lunatics. Inside I was swept into the inner courtyard and followed the crowd to a chamber of ablutions where, like the others, I washed myself, feeling rather self-conscious.

An arched portico led to an outside courtyard, where another fountain gave the place an airy, natural serenity. Men sat idly on the granite slabs and relaxed. Some were prone, flat out asleep, quite unconcerned about everyone else's comings and goings. There was a real atmosphere of peace and relaxation and also one of community. I had forgotten how sociable Islam is. Religion is everything. Unlike Christianity, which can complement a secular society in a distant, almost aloof manner, it would be unthinkable in Islam. Submission to Allah is more than going to the mosque and following a set of rules, it is what brings families together. It brings friends together, to talk and relax and eat.

In an open room with a huge red carpet, a group of over a hundred men prayed together, standing with their fingertips touching their temples as if in a state of trance. Then, taking the lead of the mullah, they fell to their knees and bowed until their foreheads touched the weave of the rug. As if somehow controlled by one body they rose to their knees, still with their eyes closed, and then stood up before repeating the whole process. It was an inspiring sight. On the far side of the court-yard I entered the doorway that led to the great dome. A group of children had been shown the acoustic capabilities of the architectural wonder and were busy stamping their feet in the centre of the room, waiting eagerly for the haunting echo to reverberate. I looked up and was immediately dazzled by the intricate tile work that had adorned the beautiful ceiling for centuries.

Morteza was still sitting outside of his carpet shop when I left the spectacular arched entryway. After the calm of the mosque, I was keen for some conversation and went over to sit down.

'How did you like our church? Like Notre-Dame, or St Peter's, no?'

'It's wonderful.'

'Yes. Now that you are feeling without sin, why don't we have a drink?' He gave a conspiratorial wink.

'You're a very bad Muslim, Morteza.'

He grinned like a schoolboy and led me into his shop, locking the door behind him and drawing a sheet across the window.

'Sit.' He pointed to a vast pile of rugs and I manoeuvred myself into a cross-legged position, mindful of the Muslim custom of never showing the soles of one's feet to another person – not that Morteza would have given a hoot. The room was dark and musty and every inch was filled with all kinds of carpets. With a devilish smile, he pulled a bottle of Johnnie Walker whisky out of a bag that was hidden under a table.

'Isn't alcohol illegal in Iran?' I asked, as he poured the golden liquid into two tea glasses. I half-expected a team of armed Revolutionary Guards to burst in at any moment.

'Everything is illegal here. It doesn't mean we don't do it.'

He spent his time lamenting how bad the situation was in Iran; how the lack of tourists and money had affected the economy and how individual freedom had been curtailed. He complained about the influence of the mullahs and how ridiculous Iran looked in the eyes of the international community. More than anything, though, he complained about women's dress codes. He assured me that given the chance, both the males and females would throw away the chador and the long sleeves and walk around naked 'like we did in the West'. I wasn't so sure.

As we drank the whisky and ate some of his 'special Ramadan food', there was a knock on the door. I immediately hid the glass behind me and put the plate behind a carpet, expecting Morteza to do the same, but he just laughed.

'Don't worry, it's only my brother Hameed. He's coming for lunch.'

An older man with a kind smile and generous face entered, wearing the traditional long white shirt known as a *kameez*. He didn't look at all like Morteza and I suspected that brother was meant in its broadest, most oriental usage.

'*Salaam*,' he bowed.

'*Wa alaikum as-salaam*,' I replied.

'Oh, don't give him any of that Saudi nonsense,' said Morteza. 'That's Arabic bullshit. Just say *salaam* and that's it.'

Hameed helped himself to some flat bread and began joking with Morteza about his sexuality.

'You know these Persian men are all the same. They like young boys.' Hameed prodded the youngster with a stick used to hang carpets.

'I thought you were brothers? Aren't you Persian?' I asked, confused.

'Persian? Hah.' Hameed feigned indignance. 'I am Lorestani. A Nomad and proud. I am no Persian.'

Hameed told me that his wives made carpets and that was where Morteza and many of the other shopkeepers got their products from. Hameed was the middle man.

After a while I left the pair to their illicit feed and crossed the river to Jolfa – the leafy Armenian Quarter. It was mid-afternoon and another beautiful day. I enjoyed the walk and thought about the confused state of religion and theocracy in Iran and how the young people rebelled against it, yet at the same time accepted the status quo. I decided to visit another group of people, more outsiders, who had played an important part in Iranian history.

It might surprise a lot of people to know that there is a small but dedicated Jewish and Christian population in Iran. I knew I had arrived in Jolfa when I spotted the multitude of little crosses protruding from the domes of the quiet riverside district. The biggest church is referred to as the Vank (cathedral in Armenian). Its actual name is the Holy Savior Cathedral. Whatever people call it, the building doesn't look like a cathedral at all – from the outside it looks exactly like a mosque, with a plain domed sanctuary in the Persian style. In the courtyard is the only external visible reminder that the building is Christian at all – a large, free-standing belfry adorned with a gold cross.

Across the courtyard I found a library and its custodian, an Armenian priest in full black regalia. He told me that it contained several edicts dating back to Shah Abbas's reign, prohibiting Persian interference in the affairs of Armenian immigrants.

'We have lived here for over four hundred years after being

expelled from the Ottoman Empire. Come inside and see the frescoes,' he said.

I followed the priest into the transept and stood in awe of the ornate paintings that covered every inch of the cathedral's interior. He pointed out the scenes of the Creation and an immense depiction of heaven and hell, where grotesque winged devils fought with horn-blowing angels over the souls of men. On another wall were several representations of the torture of St Gregory, founder of the Armenian Church.

Persecution it seems, is synonymous to the Armenians. Next door was a room that contained a museum dedicated to the Armenian massacres of 1915 at the hands of the Ottoman Turks. Televisions played grainy film footage of the executions and piles of dead. It is said that over one million Armenians were killed in that one horrific year.

The Armenians that had settled in Iran had been allowed to keep their faith over the decades, and even after the Islamic revolution, they were allowed to keep their churches and practise Christianity. But the priest was still afraid about the future.

'We thought the revolution would be short-lived. But it is still alive twenty-five years on and there is no end in sight.'

'But I thought that things were looking promising with Khatami?'

'He is transient, but the real power still lies with the Imams and the supreme council.'

'So, reform isn't coming?'

'Not until the young people revolt, it isn't. This place needs a new revolution, one to force it back to reality and the modern age.'

The priest sighed. 'But then again, if that were to happen, I fear that there would be even less tolerance for religion – of whatever faith – and maybe us Armenians would then be under the even greater threat of secularism.'

On Friday, I went to observe the prayers in the square. By midday the roads leading to it were filled completely with shiny motorbikes, and the square was packed with thousands of men and women all congregating in front of the Shah Mosque – women on the left and men on the right. The mosque itself was already full. I managed to squeeze in at the back, just in time for the prayers to begin. The mullah began to chant and sing with the voice of a choir boy.

Prayers lasted for an hour, and the weekly crowd bowed and reacted with even more automated devotion than the daily faithful. Standing, kneeling, bowing.

'*Al Allah Il Allah. Muhammad rasull Allah.*' (There is no god but God and Muhammad is his prophet.)

The recital was almost deafening and the boom of *Allahu Akbar* (Allah is the Greatest) resonated around the normally quiet courtyard. After a while, the mullah, whose voice was given to the crowds outside by an electronic amplifier, began the sermon. I tried to listen for familiar words, but the echo of the microphone and his boyish accent made it difficult to understand. But some of it was unmistakable.

America . . . Imperialism . . . terrorism . . . jihad . . . peace . . . war . . . Britain . . . Afghanistan. But what did it all mean? I fought through the crowds to try to get to the front, to see if I could reach Morteza's shop so that he could translate, but I was barred by several hundred black chadors, squatting and standing like so many sombre tents. This was the female zone and unless I wanted a public lynching, I had better stay away. I waited for the mullah to finish, frustrated that I hadn't understood. As his monologue reached a crescendo, he was cheered by the crowd, either through zealous adherence or else they were glad that it was over, and with as much hustle and bustle as it had begun, the crowds dispersed.

Chadors scuttled about, holding hands, searching for their husbands. Husbands clambered over five thousand motorbikes trying to find the right one, and when all was complete, whole families rode off piled five high on the bikes through the great archway into the bazaars and the square was left in peace once again. All that remained were the litter attendants clearing away the piles of rubbish that made the place look as though it had been the site of a pop festival, rather than weekly prayers.

In the evening, I found myself talking about the revolution over dinner with Brett, Matt, the Joker (who, it transpired, was Danish) and a Turk called Quentsch. It wasn't that their company was poor, or even that I was suffering from a bout of traveller's snobbery (of which I have been guilty), but I was getting increasingly restless. They weren't interested in the revolution. They weren't interested in history much, either. They only cared about *doing* things. In the way that you might *do* the laundry, or *do* the conga; they *did* the mosques and *did* the churches, as if they were household chores or some strange ritualistic dance. They were here like generations of travellers before them, to tick off the sights as if they were an obligatory hassle.

Only Joker didn't play this game. He was far too versed in the traveller versus tourist rhetoric to be accused of being the latter, but somehow to me he was even worse. He sat in the hostel all day, barely moving from his table, where he smoked marijuana and *charas*, a very pure and more potent form of hashish from the Himalayan mountains. He didn't see the sights or speak to the people, because they meant nothing to him. It was quite ironic that travelling, to him, meant being stationary. I felt detached.

Iran aroused in me a mixture of emotions. In some ways, I found its culture fascinating and its mystique alluring. Its people were friendly, but they were also very suspicious, often hypocritical and scared. The cities varied between sterile and dull and tranquil, but if I was brutally honest, I was getting tired of it all. I found myself longing for the wilderness of the mountains and in them, the unabashed self-confidence of the hill people. I wanted to leave behind the hypocrisy of the other travellers and be on my own: to live in my own hypocrisy. I needed to find my own road. As I gazed at the dog-eared map of Central Asia that was pinned to the notice board by the door, I suddenly felt myself drawn to the mountains – dark brown curls that flecked the paper like a trail of mystery.

I had reached a decision point in the journey. Like Arthur Conolly, I would have to decide which route to take from here. All the overland travellers were going, or had come from, the south; by way of the Balochistan and the southern deserts of Pakistan. Although it was a vast, empty wilderness (Alexander came back from his conquest of the Sind this way and lost much of his army to the sand), there was at least a decent paved road and the border was usually open. It was the safest route, and the quickest – William Dalrymple travelled from Saveh to Lahore in only a couple of days. The alternative was the most direct, but potentially hazardous, path, following the ancient camel road across the desert to Mashad and traversing the mountains of Afghanistan. In a moment of reckless pride, I chose the latter. The next day I was on a bus heading northeast through the desert to one of Islam's holiest cities.

'*Salaam*. Kind sir, Reza Ali at your most humble service. Welcome to Iran. Peace be upon you, may it also be upon your family. May your sons be well, and may you have many more. I pray that your flock is in good health and that your business may prosper. I cannot speak English, but we most certainly will have the most interesting and fulfilling conversation. Please, kind sir, do me the honour of asking of me anything.'

I really wasn't in the mood. I'd not slept properly in days, sweating it out in the hostel in Esfahan, and so all I wanted to do was get my head down on the bus. But my hopes were dashed when Reza Ali, resident of Mashad, sat down next to me.

'What, sir,' Reza Ali continued regardless, with an energetic smile, 'is your country?'

'England.' I tried my best to be enthusiastic.

'England,' he echoed. 'It was once a great and noble country. What, sir, is your profession?'

'*Musaafir*.' Traveller. I was used to reciting the word now, although it met with mixed reactions.

'*Musaafir*, a poor and humble profession.' Reza Ali gave a dramatic, solemn look of sympathy. 'And, kind sir, what is your religion?'

'Christian.'

'Christian. May you be forgiven.' Reza Ali was grinning once again. 'But,' he continued, 'we all believe in the same God, so I am sure Allah will have mercy.'

'Thanks, I'm glad.'

'We travel together to Mashad. It is the land of my fathers and of my name. Reza was the eighth Imam and he is buried in my city. Do you like Musselmen?'

I explained that as far as I was concerned I had always been treated kindly by Muslims, and I wouldn't be travelling in Iran if I had any particular dislike to his religion.

'Yes, we are the best,' Reza nodded confidently. 'But only the Shia. The Sunni are not so good.'

The lecture continued for an hour, by the end of which I knew the names of each of the twelve Imams and their personal histories. Eventually, though, I gave up being polite and pretended to be asleep.

After fifteen hours, the bus arrived. I was very tired and very irritated. Reza Ali invited me to visit him and gave me his business card. I thanked him and ran away as quickly as I could. The bus station at Mashad was heaving and I pushed and shoved my way through the crowds, with the distinctive sense of anger and frustration that accompanies a sleepless night and a lack of food. To make matters worse, I was held up at the exit by an officious policeman, who demanded to see my passport and wanted to check my bags. I was in no mood for an interrogation and acted in the exact opposite way that you should in such circumstances. I snapped.

'No. You may not see my passport, you may not search my bag. Piss off,' I snarled.

The young policeman thought about this for a while and then pointed to his car, as if to tell me that I would be taken away and arrested.

'Go on then, do it. It wouldn't be the first time. I'm a *musaafir*, a bloody pilgrim. I've come to visit the holy city of Mashad and you want to arrest me?' By now my blood was boiling with irrational anger.

To this, the poor copper blushed and apologised. I stomped out of the station, but was still in such a rage that even the ubiquitous throng of taxi drivers avoided my glare. I didn't know where I was going, so I just walked. I gritted my teeth as my heavy rucksack chaffed at my shoulders and I tried to embrace the pain. I marched even harder, oblivious to my surroundings. *Damn this place, damn these people.* It may have been the bus journey, or the fact that I hadn't eaten in ages, but I was so fed up that I decided there and then to leave Iran immediately.

I found the Afghan Embassy in a pleasant shady avenue in an upmarket district of the city, away from the bustle of the bazaars and the constant blaring of horns. Only the red, green and black flag of the infamous country dangling half-heartedly from a post gave away its location. After only a moment's hesitation, I approached the entranceway and pressed the buzzer of the nondescript gate and was admitted into the waiting room by a man in a grey suit and flip-flops.

'*Salaam,*' said a rotund Afghan in a deep, gravelly voice. He held his hand against his heart for a moment before shaking my hand. It was a routine gesture, an automatic symbol of warmth that was no more genuine than a polite 'How are you?' in English. But that symbolic gesture suddenly calmed me down, it cheered me up and gave me an impulsive and simple feeling of happiness.

'*Wa alaikum as-salaam,*' I replied and did the same.

'You are welcome,' said the Afghan, who was wearing a baggy

pair of *salwar* trousers and a short kameez, with a dusty suit jacket on top that looked clumsy but well worn.

'Come, you are our honoured guest.' He took me to the front of the queue and introduced me to the clerk at the consular section. Despite my protests, everyone insisted that I be dealt with first.

'Usually,' said the clerk, 'a visa takes a week, maybe two.' He paused, waiting for my inevitable look of disappointment. 'But for you, it will be ready tomorrow. And give my thanks to your country, the people of Afghanistan are very grateful.'

'Thank you,' I replied, feeling suddenly humbled and embarrassed at my earlier outburst.

It wasn't what I had expected at all. The Afghans actually wanted me to visit their war-torn country. I had expected suspicion and a severe questioning, but I had rarely felt so welcome. This was it: this would be the zenith of my adventure. I suddenly felt very excited and decided to give Iran one last go. In a final act of curiosity for my stay, I decided to visit the holy shrine.

Mashhad is a place of graves. Twelve hundred years ago, the greatest of the Abbasid caliphs and hero of *One Thousand and One Nights*, Harun al-Rashid, passed through a small village called Sanabad on his way to quell a rebellion that had begun in the distant lands to the north of the Oxus. The great warrior didn't die in battle, although he fell ill of dysentery on the way and his men buried him there.

He was interred under the Palace of Humayd ibn Qahtaba, a governor of Khorasan, on the site of the present Mashhad. Ten years later, by a stroke of misfortune, Ali al-Reza (the original one – not my bus mate), the eighth Shi'ite Imam and seventh direct descendent of the prophet Mohammed, was allegedly poisoned in the same city. His murderer was Harun's son, the caliph al-Ma'mun.

Al-Ma'mun desired power and fame, but he wasn't willing to incur the wrath of the many followers of the eighth Imam, who was known as al-Ridha, meaning 'the contented'. So, in an effort to avert suspicion, he decided to bury the Imam next to his father.

Unfortunately for al-Ma'mun, everyone knew of his plot and his treason backfired. The site of the Imam's tomb became known as 'The Place of Martyrdom of al-Ridha' or Mashhad al-Ridha. By the end of the century, a dome had been constructed and the place had become a major pilgrimage centre. A town sprouted around the shrine over the next few hundred years and its importance grew, especially during the Mongol raids, when thousands of refugees from the rural areas fled towards the city, increasing its population and prestige.

When the famous Moroccan traveller Ibn Battutah visited in 1333, he described the town as 'large, with abundant fruit trees, streams and mills.' He continued, 'It has a great dome of elegant construction which surmounts the noble mausoleum, the walls being decorated with coloured tiles.'

Shah Abbas the Great, the same king that had encouraged culture and prosperity across Persia and had established his capital at Esfahan, wanted to promote Mashhad as a site of pilgrimage to equal the great Sunni shrines in Saudi Arabia. In a much-publicised stunt, he is reported to have walked there from Esfahan; a distance of almost six hundred miles. Shia Muslims from around the known world visited the Shrine – spurred on, no doubt, by the popular rumour spread by Abbas that one pilgrimage to Mashhad was worth seventy thousand pilgrimages to Mecca.

After a night in one of the filthiest hotels I had ever stayed in, right on the central square and sandwiched between a butcher's shop and a fishmonger, I set off to investigate the holy shrine on my own miniature pilgrimage. I walked across the city through streams of taxis and buses, and arrived at the immense complex, the greatest concentration of holy places in all of Islam.

At the outer wall, a great tide of people was converging on the gates. Amongst them, amidst the black-turbaned preachers and bearded mullahs, flowed the whole spectrum of Shia Islam: Persians in collarless shirts and shiny jackets, Pakistanis in beige salwars, Afghans with white skullcaps and grey turbans, Bahrainis, Iraqis, Lebanese. I hesitated for a moment. I had been warned that the shrine was strictly out of bounds to non-Muslims. I imagined shouts of 'Infidel!' and of being bundled out of the place by belligerent custodians, or worse, being pummelled by an outraged mob.

I was nervous, but tried to feel emboldened by Robert Byron, who entered here in disguise in 1933 and by Richard Burton, who made the famous pilgrimage to Mecca in 1853. I thought once again of Arthur Conolly, who blazed a trail by coming here dressed as an Hindustani spice trader under the clever pseudonym of Khan Ali. I remembered, too, how easily I had blended in at Esfahan and I glanced around to see if I was attracting the glares of the Muslims surrounding me.

Nobody seemed interested. I felt confident that my generic Middle-Eastern attire of check shirt, beige flannel trousers and plastic belt served to let me assimilate, Lawrence-like, as a devout Iranian or maybe a Turk. My beard was thicker now, although I was worried that my hair might be too long and look impious.

Nevertheless, it was now or never. I adopted the tactic of picking out an unsuspecting guide, someone of my own age, and followed his every move at a distance of ten paces, like I had done in the Russian *banya* a month or so before. I hoped that in this way, I could adopt the poise of coolness.

Entering the ugly, concrete external compound – it looks like the entrance to a football stadium and is the shrine's most recent addition, built blast-proof to protect against lorry bombs – you pass through to the first courtyard. It is enormous. The crowds all aimed for a massive archway, where the guards were all armed, strangely enough, not with guns but with pink feather dusters. They seemed to be used to whack impertinent young ladies politely across the head if their headscarf fell back beyond respectable levels.

I passed by the gates gingerly. A feather duster was rapidly lowered, barring my way. I froze. Had I been exposed as a fraud already?

'*Salaam alaikum.*' The guard motioned for me to raise my hands, and I did so, still expecting the worst. '*Wa alaikum as-salaam,*' I replied as he patted me down gently and checked my pockets before ushering me onward into the slipstream of worshippers and into the mosque. I felt a wave of relief as I continued – eyes straight ahead – into the bright marble of the *Enqelab* court.

The mosque is impressive from the outside with its symmetrical minarets and beautifully tiled blue and golden roofs. Inside each of the courts and their respective *musallahs*, or prayer halls, is a glorious array of pink bricks and porcelain tiles. The arcades were lined with crystal mirrors and vaults of brilliant white and deep crimson whilst outside, along the edges of the courtyards, were marble fountains for the combined purpose of glory and ablution.

I took off my dusty sandals and walked down one of the corridors towards the inner sanctum. In an enclave were gathered a hundred or so men listening intently to a mullah preaching a sermon. I moved about at will, almost forgetting where I was. The ethnic melting pot in which I was now floating served to protect me and my identity. Blank faces shifted around like phantoms, their features all different, yet somehow the same. I imagined myself as one of them and let myself be guided by the ebb and tide of the masses.

In one courtyard, several hundred men bowed together in the act of *salat* – prayer, chanting in symphony with their eyes closed and hands cupped towards heaven. In another, a great crowd of women were rocking back and forth whilst silently reading from the Koran, mesmerised by the word of God. In little carpeted rooms that looked like chapels or libraries, yet more simply lay around or slept, exhausted by their faithful endeavours.

It was impossible to guess at how many thousands were worshipping here, and as the afternoon wore on, more and more packed into the chambers. Then suddenly there was the wail of the muezzin and the shouts of the imams. The pilgrims broke into a groaning roar, as they aligned themselves onto colourful prayer mats on every piece of available space. Moving anywhere was almost unfeasible, but I fought alongside several hundreds of others for the opportunity to see what I had come here for; the centre of the Goharshad Mosque; the holy shrine of Imam Reza – and the tomb itself.

It wasn't hard to find, as I mingled in with the steady stream of devotees, passing yet more feather dusters. I felt a strange sense of guilt as I neared the entrance and wondered whether I should be crossing such a venerable threshold. But then it was too late. I was sucked inside and there was no turning back, even if I had wanted to. I was crushed in the immense crowds, all sweeping to the interior of the chamber. Everywhere chandeliers illuminated with a dim glow the sheen of gold and crystals that filled every inch of the walls. There were groans and cries from inside the seething mass of bobbing heads.

I tried to see what lay ahead, but found myself with only fleeting visions of the huge gilded casket. On the far side, an equally pressing crowd gathered – this one of the women, and even more violently intent on touching the august grave. We were separated from the female hordes by thick panels of glass, but through it I could make out the writhing multitude in their black chadors, looking like a throng of a million witches. The stream was moving faster now, as we entered the whirlpool surrounding the tomb. I felt claustrophobic and needed to breathe, so I pushed to the outside and looked up to gulp some air. Staring down were a million crystals and the flashing of gold from a thousand chandeliers. It was like being on the inside of a diamond and in a momentary rush of fervour, I pushed back into the crowd to get close to the grave.

I was squeezed for a second against it – a large silver box, which every one of these devoted pilgrims had come to see, and if possible touch. Clawing hands tore amongst each other and faces were pressed against breasts in the strain. I thought for a moment that this hysteria would carry the whole room away into oblivion, but after a second it was over – I was carried away into the slipstream and a fresh batch pushed forward. I staggered outside into the courtyard and sat for a while in the shade and then out, at last, onto the road and safety.

Satisfied that I had done my bit in following in the footsteps of Burton and Conolly *et al.*, I was happy to concede it was time to leave Iran. After tramping back across the noisy streets to the tranquil oasis of the Afghan Embassy, a polite clerk handed me back my passport. I opened it with mounting excitement and the sight of a huge stamp that took up a whole page sent a shiver down my spine. I had thirty days to look forward to in the newly formed Transitional Government of the Islamic Republic of Afghanistan.

A minibus led a gang of Iranian traders and Afghan carpet sellers far out into the desert to the frontier town of Taybad. I joined them in a state of feverish excitement at the prospect of a new border, but because it was late we would have to stay at a desert hotel. A solitary building – an old *caravanserai* or roadside inn – that had once housed weary merchants and *musaafir* for centuries but now, with cheap decor and twentieth-century lighting, looked like a rundown Arizona motel. There were no spices or silk being traded here; only a few shifty Iranian businessmen in shiny suits and a rogue hotelier were present to greet me.

In my rucksack I had thirty dollars to my name and in my wallet there were a few Iranian rials, amounting to about three bucks. It was all I had left. The rogue eyed me with suspicion as I pleaded poverty, but eventually let me have a room for my meagre stash of rials. I couldn't afford to pay for food, figuring that I should keep the dollars as emergency cash in Afghanistan, and so, in a new low to my dignity, I waited for the other customers to finish their meals and scraped the leftovers onto a plate like a hungry dog.

Perhaps I hadn't given Iran enough time, or maybe my disguise was too good, or perhaps there was some vital flaw in my understanding of the place. Either way, I was glad to be leaving and looked forward to the next phase of my journey. I longed for the mountains and rawness that I had heard so much about over that border. I wanted to see for myself the savagery of the Hindu Kush – that infamous land which has scuppered even the most determined armies and adventurers. I went to bed and slept soundly until the distant sound of the muezzin woke me up in the early hours to begin my journey across Afghanistan.

Part 3

13

Caravanserai

I entered the immigration office through a low door, which, by its tiny size, encouraged all who entered to show their respect and bow before their host. It was almost completely dark inside, and dust filled the thin streaks of sunlight that filtered through the sheepskin drape. A grinning warrior appeared out of the shadows and took stock of the pale Englishman in front of him; I stood there in a creased blue shirt and dirty beige trousers, with a ragged army rucksack on my back.

'*Salaam alaikum*,' I said to the guard, a big man with tremendous whiskers and a curved nose that reminded me of an eagle's beak. He wore a khaki waistcoat over a salwar kameez, the long cotton blouse and baggy pyjama-like trousers favoured by men across Afghanistan and Pakistan. On his head was a *pakul*, a pancake-shaped brown woollen cap that was almost identical to the headdress worn by Alexander's Macedonians over two thousand years ago.

'*Wa alaikum as-salaam*,' he replied to my greeting, 'and peace be upon you', his right hand raised over his breast indicating harmony and friendship. The other hand firmly gripped a rusty old Lee Enfield rifle, a relic from the last time the British invaded Afghanistan. He looked at my passport with a muddled glance and seemed impressed that I had a visa. But he was more bewildered at my photograph and suddenly broke into fits of laughter.

Without bothering to stamp it he handed it back. '*Salaam*,' he bowed with another hand on his heart, still chuckling.

As I exited into the bright sunlight of the courtyard, a crowd had appeared. I sensed the gaze of a hundred Afghan eyes and suddenly felt very alone.

The crowd just stared. They stood there with expressionless faces. Turban-clad tribesmen and dirty shoeless children loitered and a few soldiers who were sitting in the shade with their AK-47s slung over their shoulders came to get a glimpse of the *farengi*. There was nothing to do except stick out my chest, adopt a stern look and head straight through the middle of them, *salaaming* where appropriate. Further on up the road, crowds of tribesmen were jostling to pass through another gate. Shepherds with herds of goats blocked the track and three colourful lorries, covered in shiny pieces of metal and painted in gaudy shades of red, gold and green, were parked at the side of the road.

I had arrived inside one of the most war-torn countries on earth, but today the scene was peaceful – at least for the time being. As I heaved my rucksack higher onto my shoulders, I suddenly felt very self-conscious and vulnerable. I wondered if I was being naive. *I am wearing beige trousers and a blue shirt with a green military rucksack. What the hell am I doing on my own in Afghanistan?*

Because of political problems and the fighting, Colin Thubron and Rory Stewart were both forced to abandon their Afghan forays and return at later dates to complete this particular section of the overland trip. In 1985, due to the Russian occupation, William Dalrymple had avoided Afghanistan altogether and taken the route south through Balochistan. Who did I think I was simply to turn up and expect to hitch through the Hindu Kush?

I looked up and stared at the desert all around. The brown wasteland continued to the horizon, where it rose faintly to disclose the faraway mountains in a pink haze. There were some white Toyota cars, old ones, with all manner of stuff tied to their roofs. It seemed like some of them were acting as taxis, so I cautiously accepted a ride with a friendly young Afghan wearing a white skullcap and a khaki kameez and we drove off towards Herat.

Abdullah spoke no English and I struggled to communicate with only a little Farsi. Nevertheless, he smiled harmlessly and pointed out villages, shouting out their names as we passed. Koh San, Tir Pol, Rowzanak. The buildings were made entirely of mud. The high-walled adobe compounds concealed entire villages. Only mysterious domes occasionally protruded from inside these domestic fortresses. Sometimes we passed by clifftop citadels and I let myself daydream that these were the very same castles encountered by Alexander the Great and Genghis Khan and a multitude of other optimistic conquerors. But, of course, it was impossible to tell. Mud ages well. Often it doesn't age at all, but sometimes after a freak rain storm it simply disappears and not a trace is left.

Solitary shepherds guided their flocks to the meagre vegetation that every so often sprouted out of the barren sand and rock. A Soviet tank, burned out long ago, lay at the side of the road as a stark reminder that this was, and effectively still is, a country at war with itself.

Arthur Conolly wrote in his journal of his entry into Afghanistan under the supervision of the Afghan army in September 1831:

Sixteen miles to Teerpool. The country was plain and the road ran nearly parallel to the Herirood ... we passed through the deserted town of

Kousan ... only three years before the town had been forsaken on account of the constant inroads of the Toorkmans ... the roofs of the houses had mostly fallen in, but in some of the gardens the fruit trees had not been destroyed, and they flourished among the ruins. The contrast touched even some of our party: 'Haif ust,' they said. 'It is a pity.'

Little, it seems, had changed, apart from the fact that the latest occupying forces were Americans and British, rather than marauding Turkomans. Further along, a lorry – as beautifully and ridiculously decorated as the first I had seen – lay over-turned with its cargo of unmarked cardboard boxes spilled across the road. It could have been the result of bad driving, or maybe the consequences of a landmine. No one in the car seemed to pay the slightest notice.

Old men squatted together at the roadside, seemingly in the middle of nowhere. Next to one such group was a man's body. We drove past slowly and Abdullah peered out of the window inquisitively. The head was covered by a blanket – presumably dead. The old men were laughing, apparently unconcerned as to the fate of their former colleague, or perhaps he was an enemy. This was a place where death was commonplace. I remembered reading about Eric Newby and Hugh Carless having a similar experience in *A Short Walk in the Hindu Kush*. They had been walking in the valleys of Nuristan, when one day they came across a dead body with its face caved in by a large rock. On asking for Carless's opinion as to what they should do, Newby was given the answer he hoped for. *Keep on walking.*

Before long the taxi arrived on the outskirts of Herat, a low-lying city, much of which, even as the second city of Afghanistan, was still built of baked earth. Amongst the bazaar, the Jam Hotel rose out of a menagerie of stalls selling car tyres and headscarves.

It had been recommended in an ancient guidebook and I was glad that it still existed.

'*Salaam, salaam.*' I was met by an old man who welcomed me with a toothless smile and a limp handshake that lingered for far too long. Speaking in Dari that was muffled by the escaping vowels of his calcium-free gums, he explained that he would show me to my room personally. There was something about his wink that I didn't like.

A dark corridor with dirty marble floors led to a room over-looking the bazaar. The old man followed me and closed the door behind him. He was perhaps seventy, although from what I had seen so far in this country, anyone over fifty usually looked like they had one foot in the grave. I assumed he wanted a tip, so I got out my wallet before remembering that I was virtually penniless. I shrugged and tried to communicate the fact that I had no money. He shook his head with grinning senility and went to hug me. I was beginning to feel uncomfortable, but didn't want to be too rude; for all I knew this may have been the standard Afghan greeting. He held me in a lingering embrace and kissed me on the cheek.

Slowly pushing him away, I thanked him with a smile, but this only seemed to encourage the randy old geriatric. Before I had a chance to intervene, he put his right hand straight on my crotch and the other for my belt buckle. Well, by now I didn't care much for catering to local custom, so I grabbed him by the shoulders and swung him around, giving him a firm shove out of the door with a foot to his backside so there was no more confusion.

That was my introduction to the more unseemly side of Afghan culture. I unpacked my belongings and thought about what I would need for the forthcoming hitch across Afghanistan.

It was clear from the example of the old man that if I continued to look as I did, I would be inviting unwanted attention and perhaps next time my assailant might not be so decrepit. I decided to exchange my tatty trousers and shirt, which had passed very well for Russian and Iranian garb, but would not be appropriate here.

I went back into the bazaar and found a shop selling an array of *salwar kameez*. I chose a nice bland (and cheap) khaki number, which I took great trouble to dirty with a combination of dust and mud, so that it didn't look too new. I thought about Arthur Conolly, who spent his time in Herat dressed as a wandering *hakeem* – a kind of alchemist – whilst secretly noting down everything of importance about this strategically important city.

Reassured, I continued wandering around the bazaar after changing into my disguise and felt relieved that the locals didn't pay me any attention. I furnished myself with a military-style waistcoat that all the men seem to wear as a symbol of their manhood and I donated my fleece jacket to a particularly ragged child.

That afternoon I had a chance to look around the city. I walked around at ease, invisible and free. Children darted about the little alleyways, shoeless but with big smiles. One group of infants pelted stones at a stray dog too old to care or avoid the battering. It just lay there, flinching with each fresh pebble bouncing off its hollow belly. In the bazaars, musky with spices and goat meat as the Ramadan sun set, the air took on a fragrant wildness.

Fairy lights lit up tiny shops selling bicycle tyres and turquoise jewellery. Fake imported watches from China had travelled across the river Oxus to find themselves pinned to wooden boards at exorbitant prices. There were decaying shops selling plastic sandals and shiny new trainers, smuggled from India over the Khyber Pass. In the background were gaudy posters of Mecca, dangling alongside seductive images of Bollywood actresses. The picture of Ismail Khan – Herat's most persistent warlord – lingered in the dark shadows.

Old men with missing legs perched on the pavements, begging harmlessly from passers-by, but even amongst these poor wretches, there was a sense of pride. They did not pity themselves, nor ask for any. They simply looked down their hawk-like noses rattling a tin pot, demanding attention.

I wandered into the side streets. The drains were clogged with excrement and the resultant smell pervaded the air, which, combined with the aroma of diesel fumes, gave a deathly stench. Some chickens had had their feet tied together and flapped about clumsily, waiting for their imminent execution, and a goat, devil-eyed, bleated in distressed anticipation of his own fate. I walked past the clinking of metal as a blacksmith hammered an old car exhaust into some new unfathomable object.

Open doors gave brief glimpses into the private lives of the Heratis. A few women could be seen half-hidden, shrouded in their full-length blue *burqas* at the back of the rooms. Men, some turbaned and others in white or grey skullcaps, tinkered away in the rotten doorways. Back on the main road, a traffic policeman stood waving his hands around like a man possessed, blowing his whistle brutally at the flow of battered Indian taxis. I jogged across the street, narrowly missing a Toyota minibus that was speeding along with no lights on.

To the north of the old town is the imposing ruin of the ancient citadel, which sits atop a mound overlooking the bazaar. I could barely make out its dark silhouette in the moonless sky.

It is purported to be the original site of a fort constructed by Alexander the Great, but the present walls date back five hundred years to the Timurid era.

By the time of Alexander's conquest in 330 BC, Herat was already the capital of the important Aria district and was described by Herodotus as 'the bread basket of Asia'. The region grew as an important intersection on the Silk Road, and lay – as it still does today – as the western gateway to Afghanistan.

In the Middle Ages, Herat was captured by the Mongols and destroyed by Ghengis Khan in 1221, who killed all but forty of the inhabitants. One hundred and sixty years later, Timur came and ransacked what was left. Fortunately his son, Shah Rukh, was more interested in building than pillage and the city once again became a centre of wealth and commerce and blossomed from the wealth of the Silk Road.

Astonishingly, in the twelfth century Herat had more inhabitants than Paris or Rome and, perhaps because of its prosperity, the city changed hands several times over the next five hundred years. The Timurids gave way to the Uzbeks, and then there were the Persian Safavids and the Mughals. In 1710, the city fell to the Ghilzai Afghans, but was soon overrun by the Durranis who held it for over a hundred years, despite attempts by the Persians to reclaim it.

The British were instrumental in helping the Durranis to repel the Persians, who expected the fall of Herat to herald an imminent Russian invasion – British India's worst fear. Fortunately for the British, and the Afghans, the Russian invasion never came – at least not until much later, in 1979, when the city was used as a base for Soviet 'advisors'. In fact, Herat played an important role in the Soviet occupation, when, after the Afghan army mutinied against the occupying Russians, the communist Afghan Air Force and the Red Army itself bombed the city, killing some twenty-four thousand civilians. Herat was then recaptured by the Soviet airborne forces.

The former army commander and warlord Ismail Khan became a leading mujahideen figure, and when the Soviets finally withdrew in 1989, he regained power and became the city governor. Six years later, he was forced to flee when the Taliban took control of the city, but returned in 2001 after the coalition invasion following the September 11th attacks in New York and Washington D.C.

A few weeks before I arrived, there had been clashes in the city between government troops from the new Afghan army and Ismail Khan's personal militia, the result of which was the death of Khan's son. The Afghan president, Hamid Karzai, was pressurised into sacking Khan as governor – a bold move since Khan was a very well-respected figure, but as a strange concilia-tory gesture, he was appointed Minister of Energy in the cabi-net. I learned quickly that Afghan politics was as confusing as its history.

I seemed to be getting used to Ramadan now and I stuffed myself with rice and lamb stew at sunset from a stall in the bazaar, and got an early night in preparation to move on in the morning. I woke up later than planned, though, as I was oblivi-ous to the change in time zones. I asked the hotel manager, who had only one eye, to take me to where I could find some trans-port to the East.

On leaving the hotel, the randy old man from the previous night was still smarting from rejection, but nevertheless came to offer me a final handshake and a dirty wink. The manager led me through the bustle of the bazaar to a small caravanserai that served as the transport hub to the East. The dusty courtyard would have been more suited to its original purpose of housing camels than the cluster of battered Toyota minivans and Land Cruisers that now clogged the square.

In Afghanistan, there is only one paved road. Highway 1 runs in a vast circle around the four main cities. It was built by the Russians in the mid-seventies, but in essence followed the same trail that had been in use for millennia. Here the traveller has always been forced to choose which of three routes to take to the East. To the north lies the long road through the mountains, by way of Mazar-I-Sharif and the banks of the Oxus. This was where the Silk Road departed for China, and was the route chosen by Marco Polo. I was warned that for now it was totally off-limits due to tribal fighting north of Kabul.

To the south are endless deserts and the lawless city of Kandahar, named like so many others, after the conquering *Iskander* – the Asian name for Alexander. This was flat and convenient for the long camel trains returning from India laden with spices. Back in the winter of 1830, it was the route that Arthur Conolly chose to take on his odyssey to India.

The southern road was not without its own dangers, then as now. Conolly talks of the violence of the people of the south and the dreadful state of the road. Nowadays it's the Taliban heartland and still completely lawless – few things have altered. In 2004, the international coalition hadn't even begun to patrol the vast wilderness and it would not be until two years later that NATO forces felt bold enough to attempt to pacify the notorious Helmand badlands.

The shortest, yet by far the most difficult road, lies directly to the east, following the course of the Hari Rud through the Central Hindu Kush to Kabul.

Conolly wrote of the notorious central route:

Those who have seen such places will not suppose this road to be an easy one ... One old Moolah, who had just come from Caubul this way, when applied to for information regarding the road could scarcely do anything but groan at the very recollection of the journey ... It appears that the inhabitants of this mountainous tract are as fanatical as they are wild.

It appeared I had little choice. Ignoring Conolly's advice through necessity, I chose this way and it would be the last time our paths would converge. Conolly spent a further few weeks on the road before finally entering British India via the Bolan Pass on 14 January 1831. I hoped that my journey would prove as successful.

At the caravanserai, I was given the choice of attempting the road in a shiny white Toyota Land Cruiser, the best of the best as far as off-roaders are concerned (donated, it seemed from the presence of a charity sticker, by a Japanese aid agency), which cost seven hundred Afghan afghanis (every bit of my remaining twenty-five dollars). The alternative was a rather feeble minibus with no front bumper and a smashed headlight at half the price. I had no choice but to take the cheapest option. I reckoned I'd need a bit to get me through to Kabul and into Pakistan.

'We only go to Chaghcharān,' said the driver. 'If you want to get to Kabul, you will have to hitch from there.'

I passed my rucksack up to a skinny boy whose job it was to tie down all the baggage and got into the van. Despite only having eight seats, we somehow managed to absorb eleven passengers, as well as all their luggage. They were all male; there were a couple of young teenagers and the rest men in their late twenties and thirties. They wore an assortment of baggy kameez and brown robes. All of them donned khaki waistcoats and one had a knitted fleece. Only one of the men wore a turban, the rest covered their heads with plain white skullcaps.

I didn't like the look of the driver at all, who appeared thuggish and had cruel eyes. Nevertheless, he offered me the front passenger seat, which I naively took as a compliment. I soon realised it couldn't have been further from the truth – as we drove through the withered poppy fields and across the dusty plains, I realised I had by far the least legroom and had the gear stick squarely up my backside.

The central route has never been popular with travellers, and Herat has always been a kind of junction in the road. The centre didn't have much to offer. The mountains were high and its people were feared and barbarous. Some of the passes are fourteen thousand feet high and the ancient travellers worried that their camels would perish on the way. In the winter, temperatures plummeted and the route was often impassable due to the snow. As a result, the centre of Afghanistan remained largely unknown.

Few foreigners had ever followed the course of the Hari Rud (Rud being the Dari word for river) from Herat to the east. Almost constant civil war and foreign invasion have combined with geographical inaccessibility to make it an unattractive choice. The most famous account of the journey made in recent times was by Rory Stewart eighteen months before I arrived.

Stewart was the first foreigner to walk the entire distance between the two ancient capitals of Herat and Kabul, perhaps since the Middle Ages. Even the locals never made the journey, because of their inherent distrust of their neighbours. He travelled on foot, accompanied in part by suspicious security guards

from the newly formed Afghan secret service, as well as a toothless mastiff that he acquired from a village *en route*.

On his travels, Stewart found himself at the mercy of the
locals; some of whom were Taliban sympathisers, others being
supporters of al-Qaeda. But the majority were simple farmers,
abiding by the Muslim code of hospitality, who treated the
eccentric pedestrian with a combination of awe and wary generosity. I was fortunate enough not to be walking, at least for now.

We set off eastwards, following the winding course of the
narrow river. At first the landscape was flat and unrelenting
desert, the same as it had been since leaving the Khorasan plains
of Iran. The tarmac road diminished as soon as Herat was out of
sight and the track grew increasingly poor, at times unrecognis-
able from the wilderness around us.

A hot haze obscured the distant horizon, but the mountains
to the north rose beyond the sand dunes to an impregnable
magnitude. There was barely any vegetation and only the hardiest of shrubs poked through. The earth was a fine dust, rather
than sand or rock, that engulfed the vehicle whenever we accel-
erated, and because some of the windows were jammed open,
we were soon all covered in a thick layer of grime. The Afghans
muttered incoherently to themselves as we bounced around
inside the sweltering vehicle and I saw in the mirror that they
were staring at me. The hotel manager had told the driver back
at the caravanserai that I was a *farengi* and the passengers were
curious.

'Where are you from?' asked the swarthy driver. His face was
marked by a huge purple birthmark that covered his right cheek
and forehead.

Remembering Conolly and the other Great Game explorers
travelling incognito, I replied, 'Inglistan.'

'Ingees, Ingees,' I heard repeatedly from behind.

'Is that far?'

'Very.'

'Further than Hindustan?'

'Yes, it is beyond Persia and the land of Iskander.'

Ahead, walking parallel to the left-hand side of the track, a lonely tribesman was leading three camels. They munched nonchalantly at invisible grass as the dust flew into their weary eyes. As the morning matured, we gained height. The mud villages became less frequent and the road worsened. At best, it would be four feet wide with deep ruts, and at its worst it was nothing more than a winding footpath around the huge boulders that lay strewn at the bottom of the cliffs – deadly reminders of the threat of landslides. Sometimes the trail ran perilously close to a vast ravine. The drops were terrifyingly sheer and disappeared into the barren, quarry-like nothingness below. There were no fences or barriers here.

The van somehow carried on, sometimes assuming almost impossible angles, where I was convinced it would have to tip over. The wheels clung on with an air of self-preservation, but soon the mountains closed in around us. We had left the vast plains behind now. The midday sun shone above, illuminating the bronze valleys and causing the hill to radiate a faint glow. As the road grew worse, so did the number of times we had to stop. On two occasions the tyre burst and so the driver replaced it with one of the many spares kept on the roof. Several times there was a disturbing amount of smoke emanating from the engine and we pulled over while he examined the damage. Boulders had to be shifted from the track after they had fallen from the cliffs above. Other times, the wheels became so stuck in the dust that we all had to get out to push.

When we did stop, some of the Afghans immediately lay down at the roadside and fell asleep, using their brown woollen blankets as a pillow. Some of them prayed. Others would squat on their haunches, feet flat on the ground. It struck me as a position virtually impossible for Westerners, except perhaps yoga practitioners, and no matter how much I tried to emulate them I never got the hang of it. The men gazed into the distance, apparently unaware of time or space, offering me only fleeting glances.

The teenagers, on the other hand, stared directly at me. One of the boys was wearing a woollen hat, which had the Nike logo sewn badly across the front. It was a cheap import from China or perhaps a donation from some Western charity. I smiled, but they didn't respond. I wondered what exactly the hotel manager had told them. Eventually, whilst we waited at the foot of a huge mountain for the driver to fix a tyre, one of the men approached me to break the silence.

I had already made a mental note of this individual as soon as I got on the bus. He came across as the most confident of the bunch and had the distinctive aura of a pirate, with a huge black beard and rotten teeth. Around his neck he wore a black scarf that looked a little like the Palestinian *keffiyeh*.

'*Salaam*. I am Daoud,' the pirate announced in guttural Dari. 'Where are you really from?' he asked in a conspiratorial whisper.

'Inglistan,' I repeated.

Daoud raised an eyebrow and shook his head.

'No. We think you are Pashtun. You are a Taliban spy.'

I was shocked. I had been called many things, but never a Taliban spy.

'No. I am a tourist from England.' And to prove it I took out my camera, and let the scruffy rogue look through its viewfinder.

'I came to take pictures of Afghanistan.'

At this there were murmurs all around and Daoud was very much impressed and insisted that I took his photograph. This seemed to satisfy him that I was not a neighbouring insurgent, but as he went over to speak to the driver I overheard him ask who he thought I was.

'Oh, it's just some foreigner who comes to fight with al-Qaeda.'

The people here had barely heard of England. 'Inglistan' rang a vague bell for some of them, especially the older ones, who remembered stories from their grandparents about British rule in the early days (the third Anglo-Afghan war was in 1919 and British troops were stationed on the Khyber Pass until Indian partition in 1947). Unsurprisingly, everyone knew about the USA. Most had heard the name George Bush. To them he was simply a beardless mullah from a distant land. They did not understand why the coalition had bombed Afghanistan or why foreigners from strange countries (Portugal, Denmark, Estonia) were rummaging around their villages. They just accepted the latest violence as part of an endless string of foreign intervention.

Everybody, of course, knew of the Taliban, and despite being a predominantly Tajik area, the Taliban had ruled here as severely as in the rest of the country and had left a deep impact. The peasantry lived in fear of the radical mob, but also accepted their presence as a necessary evil. The Taliban brought some semblance of order from the regional and tribal infighting. Al-Qaeda, on the other hand, to the average Afghan, was seen as another belligerent foreign influence – albeit a Muslim one.

When the driver fixed the tyre, we continued the journey for another thirty kilometres or so before breaking down again and going through the whole rigmarole once more. At sundown, we pulled over and the Afghans quickly prayed before producing from their bundles of cloth some delicious flat bread and black *chai*, which they shared with me generously. We drove a little further to find a village. It was pitch black and there was no moon yet; the driver must have been exhausted.

At a place called Chest-i-Sharif, at the outer limit of Herat province near the boundary with Ghor, we knocked on several doors but were turned away. Perhaps other vans had got there first or maybe the villagers didn't like the look of us.

We drove on, up and up through the shale and lime hills, following a narrow and winding path that led over a high mountain pass. In the cold night air and clear sky, it felt as if we had reached the roof of the world. The horizon ceased to be obscured by mountains and stars filled the panorama and reached down to ground level. I didn't know how high we were, but the temperature had plummeted to below freezing. Puddles were covered in ice and a thin layer of sparkling frost clung to the grey boulders.

Inevitably we broke down. A clanking noise had continued since the last repair job, but this time it appeared more serious, and the driver gave a look of solemn concern. With the help of Daoud and one of the boys he removed the front wheel, but to no avail. Something had snapped. The rest of the Afghans merely squatted and stared in complete silence. A couple of hours passed whilst the trio fiddled with greasy axle oil and tied bits of rag around the chassis in an effort to keep things in place, and finally the driver managed to get the wheel back on again.

If not for the cold, it would have been pleasant to bed down in this surreal crater on the mountain top. But by now the temperature had dropped so low that a nearby stream had frozen solid. The heater did little more than suck in the dust from the outside, so we all wrapped up in our brown shawls and shivered together, until continuing the descent from the mountain. This was the Shotor Khūn, the 'camel's blood pass', so named because the ancient travellers thought it was so high that their camels would get nose bleeds.

The ancient Greeks called it *Paropamisus*, 'peaks over which the eagles cannot fly', and saw the mountain range as an important frontier; it was the edge of the known world. Until the conquests of Alexander, beyond here was an anonymous and uncharted wilderness. Sometime after midnight we made it over the pass, and at the bottom of the mountain found another village called Shartak, where the driver pleaded with the headman for half an hour to let us stay.

'We have driven all day from Herat. We have been travelling for fifteen hours,' begged Abdul.

'Who are you?' asked the headman.

'Tajiks from Chaghcharān. We are coming from Herat. With us is a foreigner,' interrupted Daoud.

'What kind of foreigner? Is he dangerous?'

'We don't know, he doesn't speak our language. He says he is from Inglistan, but he looks very poor. But we are bound to show him hospitality and so must you.'

The elder glanced sceptically at my dusty rags and brown blanket, but he invited us in anyway. He was a wizened old Aimaq with clear Mongoloid features, a descendant of the Temuri tribe – followers of Timur's Mongols, who had settled in the highlands eight hundred years ago. He agreed to let us sleep on the floor in an upstairs room. He must have been quite wealthy, because two-storey houses were rare outside of the main towns. His house was well built and he led us inside the compound, where the only light was a flickering candle in the downstairs room. Some steps led us to a room built of hardened clay on the roof.

'You can sleep here,' said the elder, before scuttling off to make tea. He was clearly annoyed at having been woken up, but he fulfilled his duty regardless. I was glad to discover an ancient carpet filled the floor space, though I needn't have worried about being cold. The old man lit a fire in the room underneath and by convection our floor soon became pleasantly warm. I waited to see what etiquette was involved in sleeping with ten Afghan men on a rug, but it was immediately apparent that there wasn't much fuss made. You simply wrapped your blanket around you and lay down to sleep wherever there was space. I was so exhausted that I passed out straight away and slept through the breakfast reveille at four a.m.

There are three main tribes in Afghanistan. The Pashtun are the most numerous and are dispersed across the south and east of the country. The Tajiks are the second largest and make up the population of Herat, the western desert regions, and some parts of the central highlands and the Transoxiana. They are of old Persian stock and speak Dari. The rest of the centre of the country is made up of Hazara, flat-faced descendants of the Mongol horsemen. The majority of them are Shia Muslims in a predominantly Sunni country.

Then of course in the north, things get even more complicated. There are the warrior Turkmen, the beardless Uzbek herders and silversmiths, nomadic Kirghiz, Ismaili Wakhis, Nuristani mountainmen, not to mention the diaspora Arabs, Baluch, Qizilbashi, Brahui, and the Jat.

But now we were in the land of the Aimaq, a semi-nomadic, historically loose entity related to both the Tajik and the Hazara. Both groups inhabited the wild central mountains and

because of their ancient enmity with the Pashtuns, were generally against the Taliban and welcomed the recent shifts in
power. It had let people such as our current host prosper, when
perhaps only five years ago he would have been in hiding,
scared of being persecuted by the brutal regime because of his
ethnicity.

I woke up at five-thirty to the sound of munching. One of
the Afghans was finishing off some flat bread. I went outside to
the back of the house to go to the toilet, and walking around the
garden wall, I found the driver squatting on the ground and
wiping his bare arse with a handful of sand. I had been surprised
when I was shown to the fields in Afghanistan and had never
been given a jug of water with which to clean myself. The
Afghan method was now clear and I could see why town dwellers like Daoud so proudly displayed their pink toilet paper from
their breast pockets.

The morning drive carried on in much the same way as the
day before; dusty, hot and suffocating. We entered the valleys of
the Hazara people, traditionally herdsmen and farmers, some of
whom had been allies of the Russian invaders, whilst others
were staunchly opposed to the Taliban, and many were both.
These days they made their money smuggling opium on donkeys
through the mountains. Finally, as the sun was almost directly
overhead, we ascended a ridge and the town of Chaghcharān
came into view in a wide valley with the Hari Rud running
through its centre. By now I was almost faint with thirst and like
my Afghan compatriots, I could not contain my excitement at
the prospect of arriving at this remote town.

14

Bad Habits

Although it was the first sizeable settlement I had seen in two days since leaving Herat, the reality is that Chaghcharān is a small provincial district centre of no more than fifteen thousand inhabitants. It sits high amongst the westernmost foothills of the Hindu Kush at over two thousand metres tall and at this time of year (I reckoned it was about the fifth or sixth of November), it was cold throughout the day – and freezing at night. The people were expecting snow any time soon. Like everywhere else, the town was built mainly from mud, although I noticed a couple of two-tier buildings made from modern breeze blocks and some rudimentary wooden scaffold. On the far side of the Hari Rud, about a mile away, I saw what appeared to be a runway with a small compound attached to it. On a cliff top behind was an ancient fort with thick walls and towers.

My fellow *musaafir* got off the bus and, dragging their bundles from the roof, dispersed into the alleyways of the bazaar. Only Daoud shook my hand.

'*Khuda hafiz,* traveller.'

'Goodbye, pirate. How will I get to Kabul from here?' I asked, a little concerned that I had made no provision for my onward travel.

'Kabul?' he smiled. 'I don't know, I've never been.' He shrugged, and with an aggravated limp, hobbled off down the street.

I stood in the middle of the bazaar, an open piece of stony waste ground filled with empty stalls and a few mud-brick shacks. I resolved to take a look around the town. As I normally did whenever I was lost or didn't have a map, I made my way to the largest building that I could find. It was just off the main street and I was surprised to discover a recent building, only semi-complete and made of breeze blocks, inside a traditional adobe compound. The United Nations logo was painted clumsily across the wall. I was relieved in a way; maybe there would be someone who could speak English who could help. The gate was closed, so I sat down on my bag and waited.

It was warming up a little now and the clouds had disappeared to reveal a perfect azure sky that seemed to increase the starkness of the surrounding brown mountains. In the street, the few merchants that had bothered to set up shop were settling down for an afternoon snooze and I noticed an old man squatting over by the wall with his head resting in his hands. He wore a long, baggy kameez that enveloped him like a Victorian nightdress and on his head was a stained white turban. Some boys ran past, none of them older than six or seven. They too wore long shirts, some grey and others brown, but instead of turbans they sported little white caps with the front cut away in the shape of mughal arches. They seemed bent on mischief and ran up to the old man and kicked sand over his feet to wake him up before scuttling away in a fit of giggles.

The old man gazed at me through one eye and I saw that he had no teeth. He coughed up a mouthful of phlegm and spat it into the dust before dozing off again. I stood up and went back to the iron gates to peer inside. I could see an open courtyard with a few chickens huddling in the shade of a cotton drape, which was pulled taut from the corner of one of the walls. A wooden bed-frame with a wicker trellis was to the right of the gate, next to a corrugated iron shelter that looked like a guard-room. On the bed, another old man was sleeping soundly. An AK-47 machine gun lay in place of a pillow.

I tapped softly on the iron gate, not wanting to shock the guard, but he snored away unconcerned. I banged harder. Suddenly I felt someone touch my shoulder from behind and I spun around quickly to find a young man standing before me.

'*Salaam alaikum.*'

'Hello,' I replied in the traditional greeting.

I asked if there were any Westerners around. '*Faranj, farengi, afranj?*' It was the best I could do, reciting all the words for a European that I could remember.

He frowned and I got the impression that he didn't under-stand. He cocked his head and looked me up and down.

'Where are you from?' he asked in Dari.

'Inglistan,' I replied, not sure whether or not it was wise to admit, and where the political loyalties lay here.

Osman broke into a childlike grin and offered me his hand. 'I speak English very good.' I was dumbfounded.

'I spent last year studying in Kabul,' he explained. 'I am the first man in my family with an education!'

Osman was nineteen or twenty (he wasn't sure which), but had the hairless face of a young boy. He didn't look like the other Afghans I had seen so far and I guessed he must have been an Uzbek or Hazara. His eyes were narrow and squinting, but his cheeks were full and round so that he could have been easily mistaken for a Mongol. He looked sensitive, effeminate and at the same time very cunning.

'You are English then?'

'Yes.'

'English from America?' He raised his eyebrows as if he had discovered a great secret.

'No, English from England.'

'Good, I like Inglistan and the English. Come,' he said confidently, 'we are friends. I will be your guide in my village and tonight you will stay at my house. It is very small and I am very poor, but I hope you will understand.'

I got up and followed him across the dusty street back towards the deserted market place.

Osman, it turned out, was a Tajik. Or at least that is what he claimed. He was probably more likely to have been a Chahar Aimaq, but they all claim to be Tajiks when it suits them. Osman explained that his family lived in a small house a few miles to the south of the town, in the foothills of the mountains. He told me that he had eight brothers, of which he was the youngest, and that his father, along with the eldest brother, was away from town for a while.

'Working?'

'He is in Iran,' he said gravely. By his tone I understood that to mean not to ask any more questions.

'Would you like to see the new governor?' he asked, changing the subject quickly.

I said that I would and we passed through the bazaar to an open field on the southern bank of the river, near to the bridge, where the reason for the market's emptiness suddenly became apparent.

Outside what appeared to be a school house, a huge crowd of several hundred men was gathered (there were no women), squatting and murmuring to themselves. Some Afghans in suits and dark glasses were busy fiddling with some loudspeaker apparatus that was being plugged into a generator. Looking on from

a distance of thirty metres was a section of Afghan soldiers in the
ragged olive-green caps of the Afghan National Army. They had
their rifles slung haphazardly about their shoulders and looked
bored. None of them wore beards and they didn't look like they
were local. A white pickup truck arrived at the scene and I was
surprised to see two American soldiers get out and start talking
to the suit-wearing Afghans. One of them, a round individual
with red cheeks, looked like an officer, and I guessed the stern
lanky one was his bodyguard.

'What's happening?' I asked Osman, as we sat down amongst
the crowd of Afghans.

'We are waiting for the new governor. This is his first speech,
he was only appointed a couple of weeks ago.'

Some children were led out of the school house. They were
wearing smart, clean white shirts and black trousers and the girls
looked pretty and playful in their colourful headscarves. They
were all carrying flowers and began to dance in a circle to enter-
tain the onlookers.

'What happened to the old governor?'

'He went to Herat.'

'A new job?'

'No, he ran away when the fighters came.'

Osman explained how, four months ago in June, a warlord
called Abdul Salaam Khan had attacked Chaghcharān, because
he rejected President Hamid Karzai and the new government's
plan to disarm regional militias. Osman preferred the word
lashkar; a Pashtun term for warriors. The town was subject to a
fierce siege and eighteen people were killed in the battle. The
old governor, appointed by Karzai, had fled to Herat and the
town was at the mercy of the militia for several days. Khan's
gunmen finally moved on from the town when they heard that

an Afghan Army battalion was *en route* from Herat accompanied by a platoon of American soldiers.

But that wasn't the end of the story. Three weeks later, on the fifteenth of July, more violence erupted when some corrupt Afghan soldiers tried to steal money from some of the townspeople, who had been stopped at a roadblock just outside of the bazaar. It resulted in a fight and the soldiers shot dead two local shopkeepers, who also happened to be militiamen. A crowd gathered to protest the killings and demand the bodies of the two dead people. When the soldiers tried to disperse the rabble, things escalated as the mob marched on the airport and stormed the UN building, the one where I had met Osman in the first place. Shooting broke out and the American platoon rescued seventeen people, mostly foreign aid workers, who were subsequently evacuated by helicopter. Since then, few had returned.

Qazi Abdul Qadir Alam finally arrived in another pickup with two armed bodyguards to a general murmur from the onlooking crowd. The new governor was a small fat man with glasses and a grey turban and he began to speak into the microphone. The speakers didn't work at first and then with an ear-piercing screech his low, mumbling voice burst out across the valley. I could hardly make out what he was saying, but there was much *salaaming* and pleasantries, as you would expect. Osman yawned, he said he was bored and wanted to leave.

'I'll meet you back at the bazaar.' I told him I wanted to stay and listen to the speech, but in reality I wanted to introduce myself to the Americans to see if they knew how I could get to Kabul.

I waited until the governor had finished speaking and made my way through the crowd. I rehearsed the line over and over. The last thing I wanted was for the Americans to think that I

On the banks of the Hari Rud, Chaghcharān, Afghanistan.

'Tajik' Afghan merchants,
travelling by minibus from
Chaghcharān to Kabul. Taken
before the crash.

Aftermath of the crash. The
condition of the injured
passengers remains unknown.

Kabul market. There are few women on the streets, and those that are must wear the *burqa*.

The 'Tank Graveyard' of Wazir Akbar Khan district, northern Kabul.

The Khyber Pass, scene of some of the deadliest battles in history.

Gun factory in Darra Adam Khel, North–West Frontier Province of Pakistan.

The author in Taxila, where Alexander established his most remote city in modern-day Pakistan. Note the Greek-style columns.

Kim's Gun, also known as the Zamzama Gun, outside Lahore Museum. Among the earliest curators of the museum was Rudyard Kipling's father John Lockwood Kipling.

Gonga Saeed, the 'best *dhol* player in the world', in Pakistan.

Badshahi Mosque, Lahore, Pakistan. Mughal architecture at its very best.

Sri Harmandir Sahib, colloquially known as the Golden Temple, Amritsar. The spiritual heart of Sikhdom.

Amritsar by night.

Indian taxis. The chaos of 'the world's biggest democracy' was apparent immediately on crossing the border from Pakistan.

The church of St. John in the Wilderness, McLeod Ganj, before its restoration.

The forests above Dharamsala, India.

View from Ilaka, in the Himalayas.

Goa. Modern silks at the start of an ancient road.

The author, aged 22, on the Silk Road.

was an al-Qaeda mercenary, as word had spread recently that several British Muslims had travelled to Afghanistan to join the jihad.

'Hi, how's it going?' I said, in my best Queen's English.

The captain took a step back and looked at me with a suspicious frown. I quickly offered him my hand and told him that I was a journalist gone native.

'Oh, thank God for that.'

The captain seemed intelligent and very interested in and knowledgeable of local affairs. He confirmed Osman's story about the governor and recent events.

'Hey, why don't you come over to the airbase later on?'

I said yes, but that I would first need to placate my Afghan host. I didn't really want to rely on the US military, but at least I had an offer if things went wrong, so satisfied with that I returned to find Osman in the bazaar.

I found him lounging on a pile of cheap rugs surrounded by a group of six men. Only two of them wore a headdress of any kind. This was unusual in a country where everyone wore a turban, a skullcap or a *pakul* – the pancake-shaped *chitrali* hat preferred by the tribes of the north-east and the mujahideen. It could have meant that they weren't particularly religious, or else that they fancied themselves as urban elite.

'My English friend. Welcome back. How did you find the new governor? A horrible man, no? Meet my brothers.'

He introduced me to each of them beginning with the oldest, a handsome light-skinned forty-year-old with a neat beard called Hamed. Then there was Qasim; muscular, with a strong handshake. Aziz was pear-shaped and seemed like a shopkeeper with saggy jowls and a thin moustache. Nadir was in his mid-twenties and looked thin and hungry, he had dull eyes and appeared simple. Rauf was the most friendly and the only other Afghan to speak English. He was around thirty-five and darker than the rest. I guessed that he wasn't actually one of Osman's brothers, but was more likely to be a cousin or more distant relative. He was less Mongoloid in appearance and had a striking black beard, but with it a humble, genuine smile. Along with Nadir, he wore a white, subtly embroidered prayer cap and over his brown knee-length shirt he wore a thick, leather padded jacket that looked like it belonged to a Hell's Angels biker.

'Rauf will show you around the town,' said Osman with a sense of cockiness that I didn't like. 'I have to do some business, but will meet you later.'

It was clear that despite being the youngest of his family, he was a wily individual and eager to prove himself as an adult. Since I didn't have much choice, I agreed.

'You can leave your bag here. They are good people,' said Rauf. Again, it was either that or walk around the town looking extremely suspicious and so I left it with the gang of brothers. Sometimes you have to trust people.

I was fortunate: as it happened Rauf turned out to be trustworthy. He worked as an interpreter for the charity *Médecins du Monde*, or Doctors of the World, and we walked to its 'office' inside a compound on the north banks of the river.

'I have worked here for a year now,' said Rauf in excellent English. 'I speak French, too.'

I asked if the pay was good and whether the aid agencies were effective. I wanted to discover what the people felt about foreign intervention.

'The money is normally good.' He sighed. 'Since the fighting, the aid agencies haven't been going outside and so they don't need me. In fact, the Americans are the only foreigners in Chaghcharān at the moment.'

'What about the Russians? What did they do here?' I was interested to see where the local allegiances and historical ties lay.

'They stayed at the airfield, too, like the Americans. We worked with them. I was too young, but Osman's oldest brothers joined the communist militia and fought against the mujahideen.'

'But I thought your family are Tajik and would have supported the mujahideen?'

'We are Tajik, but it is very complicated. The Russians lived here for many years and forced the people to work for them. Others liked the Russians – they paid well and brought security.'

'What about when the Taliban came?'

'Because we worked with the Russians, the Taliban saw us as traitors, even though the mujahideen were their enemies, too. They came to Chaghcharān and killed many people. There was a lot of fighting, but some people even joined them. Now that the Americans are here we support them, but if the Taliban come back and the Americans leave, we will have to join them as well. It's the only way we can survive.'

We arrived at the compound and entered through a blue iron gate. Sitting on a wooden stool in the shade of the veranda was the biggest man I have ever seen in my life.

'This is Bafool Khan. He is our security guard,' said Rauf.

I shook his immense hand, which was surprisingly gentle. The giant had a peaceful look in his eyes and a good-natured smile emanated through his thick beard. The man must have been seven feet tall and was built like a gorilla.

Bafool held his hand against his barrel-like chest and insisted that I take his seat. Then he changed his mind. No, no, in fact we must leave immediately and visit his house, he wanted to offer me food, remembering his manners. I looked at the behemoth and noticed a calm serenity in his auburn eyes that reflected the flowing creases of his brown blanket.

Food? I thought. *It was the middle of the day and still Ramadan. This wasn't Iran, they actually observed Ramadan here, didn't they?*

We left the compound with Bafool taking the lead, presumably leaving the security of *Médecins du Monde* to its fate for the time being, and walked to a nearby house. Bafool was unmarried and lived alone; he was in his early forties and couldn't speak a word of English. He went off to fetch some flat bread and tinned jam that was the staple diet of most of the Afghans I had met.

Rauf told me that Bafool had joined the Russians in 1985 and fought alongside them on several campaigns. 'He has killed many mujahideen,' said Rauf, clearly in awe of the enigmatic titan. By his weathered face and colossal hands, I didn't doubt it. Bafool indicated that he wasn't in fact a Muslim at all, patting Rauf on the shoulders sympathetically; he was a communist. He produced from a drawer his Soviet belt, with a large star on the buckle, and proudly handed it to me.

Rauf translated.

'I liked the Russians,' Bafool said with a gentleness that seemed to bring a sense of peace to the room. 'I still like them. They did many good things for Afghanistan. They built many bridges, all the roads and plenty of schools and colleges. And also they brought electricity and fresh water and I supported them. I fought for them for many years against the mujahideen. I also fought against the Taliban during the war in the last decade, but my fighting days are over now. I am happy with what the British and the Americans have brought, they have destroyed the Taliban and hopefully now we will have peace. *Insha'Allah.*' God willing.

I noticed at the end, though, that his voice seemed to trail off and lose its earnestness. Perhaps Bafool did support the Americans, but I don't think he really believed there would ever be peace in Afghanistan.

Suddenly there was the roar of a motorbike pulling up outside and a dusty Osman walked in without acknowledging either Rauf or Bafool.

'Come. It is time to visit my house,' he said with an air of authority. I thanked Rauf and the giant for their kindness and reluctantly got on the back of the bike to go and retrieve my rucksack. Fortunately, it was still there and hadn't been interfered with. We left the bike at the shop and set off on foot.

The walk to Osman's house took a little over forty minutes. His family's compound, which was bigger than any of the others in Chaghcharān, lay a few miles out of town, across a gently rising plain to the south. He told me that all of the land between the road and the mountain belonged to his family. So much for being poor.

'Look, the Hindu Kush.' He pointed at the brown foothills that rose like immense warm sand dunes behind the buildings.

Osman seemed to take an abnormal pleasure in decrying his poverty, despite clearly being one of the richest men in the town.

'See how my buildings are crumbling. He pointed to the southern end of the collection of compounds, where some ancient walls lay in ruins. No one had lived there for generations. 'Yes, we are very poor,' he mused, expecting my sympathy and probably some money. The main entrance was on the southern side of the high perimeter wall and as we circumnavigated the property, its magnitude dawned on me. I thought that the cluster of houses was a village unto itself, but the whole settlement was interlinked by a series of narrow alleyways and dug-out trenches that Osman referred to as 'irrigation ditches'.

The walls themselves were almost a metre thick and at each corner of the compound was a distinctly military looking guard tower. The place was a fortress, designed to keep even the most persistent enemies at bay. Inside the courtyard was a large open space, half the size of a football pitch, in the middle of which was a deep well. Washing hung from a line across the yard, and in the corner nearest to the house, a wooden shed had been built with a kind of thatched roof acting as shade for the family's prized possession: parked under the canopy was a brand new red Toyota Land Cruiser. When I asked him where he had bought it, he told me it was 'donated' by the Americans.

I understood that to mean that his family had been paid off for information regarding the whereabouts of local Taliban factions, or else they had siphoned away cash from a development programme. Osman chuckled.

'They are always coming here asking questions.'

'Who?'

'The Americans, of course. We tell them what they want to know, maybe give them the address of our enemies if we feel like it, but really, we don't help them very much. They are so stupid.'

I noticed a huge white satellite dish poking ignobly from the roof of the main house.

'The last time they came we told them to go away.'

'Why?'

'Because one of them was black. We don't like black ones.'

He led me inside to the reception hall, a musty room ten metres wide filled with handwoven carpets and decorative cushions. There were two small windows at knee height that looked back out into the yard and the walls were adorned with shelves containing brass pots and a silver jug. Hamed lay sprawled out on the floor with a cigarette in his mouth. He grunted as we passed by. Across the hall in another, smaller, yet similarly furnished room, was a huge widescreen television. It looked vulgar and contrasted sharply with the mud plaster walls.

'Donated by the Americans?' I asked.

'Of course,' laughed Osman, as he flicked through the multitude of channels. I wanted to watch BBC World News, because I saw the headline that George Bush had just been re-elected, but he said that it was boring and after lingering for a while on a Hindi music channel, he turned it off.

'Let's go and smoke.'

We climbed a staircase that led to an open roof, where we sat looking out north across the plains towards the town. I asked about his family, hoping to find out how they had come across their wealth, but before he answered it suddenly became clear.

As I looked down to the fields, past the ruined walls and beyond the ditches that contained water pipes, I saw four or five farmers, Osman's workers planting seeds in the ploughed fields. It was opium poppy. Osman confirmed my suspicions quite openly.

'My older brother spent two years in an Iranian jail for smuggling.'

'Drugs?'

'What else? Our family has no choice, there is no work here. We grow it and send it to Iran.'

'Haven't the Americans tried to stop you?'

'Not yet, they only arrived a few months ago, after the harvest. Now we are planting for the spring.'

'What then?'

'The chances are that the Americans will be gone by then.'

'And if they are not?'

'We might kill them.'

Osman took out a pack of cigarettes and offered me one. I declined.

'I don't smoke either.' He winked. 'In our culture, you cannot smoke in front of your elders. My father smokes, but he thinks none of his sons do. Even Hamed, who is forty-one, doesn't dare smoke in front of him. I have to hide up here whenever I want to smoke.'

Despite his conceited nature, he was hospitable enough. I decided early on that it wasn't only because of the Afghan code of hospitality (Osman was far too businesslike for that), and concluded that he probably felt having a foreign guest gave him an elevated status amongst his friends. I was treated and fed well. Along with the brothers, we sat cross-legged eating meals of sticky rice and warm flat bread. There was even some chicken and yoghurt, which arrived by way of a wrinkled female hand sliding the tin platter from the dark recesses of the kitchen, screened by a green curtain.

The only other indication of women in the house was the occasional cackle of the mother, who insisted on cooking me a delicious breakfast of scrambled eggs and tea, which I devoured gratefully, knowing that was all I would be getting for the next twelve hours. For all his show of urbanity, Osman was careful to adhere to Ramadan as far as his mother was concerned and there was no food in the house after dawn. Osman joined in the namaz (prayers), too, when his brothers were around and I sat in the corner sketching them as they prayed.

Back in town, I was disheartened to learn that there were no vehicles to Kabul that day. In fact, no one seemed to know when the next car would be leaving for the East. 'Once a week,' said one man. 'Early in the morning,' said another. So I resigned myself to another day in the company of Osman. I didn't have much choice. I asked him to take me to one of the hills that overlooked Chaghcharān from the south-east, where I wrote up my journal and sketched the views.

Osman sat alongside, quite quiet; until out of the blue he asked if I had 'any work for him'.

'What do you mean?'

'Work. I need work.'

'I'm sorry. I am just a traveller passing through. I don't have any work.'

He sat patiently and stared intently into the ground. Then after a few minutes he came out with what I had suspected all along.

'But I am very poor. I need money.'

I have to admit I was a little disappointed. *So much for the hospitality.* I tried to explain that despite how it may appear, I did not have any money myself. In fact, at that stage I had exactly fourteen dollars to my name – and I wasn't the one involved in selling drugs.

I thought that the best way to get off the subject was to be equally direct and to ask him how much he needed and what for. This seemed to work, as he refused to state a figure.

'Maybe you can give me a present?' he changed his tactic.

'You can see what I have, Osman, and it isn't much.' But I decided that even though I didn't like him or what his family was up to, he had put me up for two days and I needed to stay another night, so I offered him my sleeping bag. He seemed mildly placated and walked back down the hill to his motorbike, leaving me alone on the hilltop to watch the shepherds, with a promise that he would return to pick me up later. I was half-tempted to leave there and then and begin walking to Kabul, but thought better of it now that I was without a sleeping bag. As much as I detested being dependent on him, he was my best hope of getting a lift. I didn't even know which of the desert tracks led to Kabul and my Dari was limited to a few words. Instead I sat and observed Afghan rural life from a distance.

On the opposite bank of the Hari Rud, the land rose in a series of mounting hills for miles to the horizon; a tanned, brown autumn landscape dotted with dusty poplars and crumbling adobe walls. A few thin tracks, accessible only to those on foot or the hardiest of motorbikes, wandered like centipedes into the Hindu Kush. Over all of this a clear, vivid blue sky shed a uniform brightness, reducing height and distance, and making it impossible to tell one mountain from another. I sat and sketched until sundown, when at last long shadows brought the scene to life and a deep red sunset retreated into the mountain passes, reminding me suddenly that I was alone in the heart of Afghanistan with no money, and no one within several thousand miles that gave a damn whether I lived or died.

Out there, somewhere beyond the crimson hills, lay an army in waiting. Hundreds, thousands of illiterate tribesmen waiting for the right time to strike and rise up against the latest foreign invader. Out there, somewhere to the east, was Osama bin Laden and his henchmen, plotting their vengeance. I wondered if Arthur Conolly felt as vulnerable and as lonely as I did that day. It was the sort of place where Rudyard Kipling's Victorian hero in his poem 'The Young British Soldier' would die alone on a stony hillock, with the vultures hovering nearby:

When you're wounded and left on Afghanistan's plains,
An' the women come out to cut up what remains,
Jest roll on your rifle an' blow out your brains,
An' go to your Gawd like a soldier.

To my surprise Osman did return and we went back to his house to eat. I presented him with the sketch of the town to show there were no hard feelings and he wasted no time in proudly showing it off to his brothers, who also seemed to like it. Inevitably the requests came and I spent the evening drawing a covert sketch of Osman and his fifteen-year-old 'girlfriend' from a photograph that he had somehow managed to acquire. She was his cousin and lived on the other side of the river, but he saw her twice a week. It was the only image of an Afghan girl I had seen that wasn't wearing an all-encompassing burqa. She wore a loose-fitting violet headscarf and was quite pretty with deep brown eyes and voluptuous lips. I always hated drawing girls since it's a risky business, but when I had finished I thought it was a very good likeness.

Osman snatched the finished work out of my hand and studied it for a moment.

'My nose is too big,' he whined. I told him he needed to be less vain and that he ought to thank God for being blessed with such an appendage.

I woke up at four to eat breakfast and left immediately afterward in order to catch the truck, which Osman assured me departed at six. It was freezing cold and pitch black. Osman didn't even offer to drive me back to town, probably still smarting over the size of his nose, and so I made my way out of the compound and began to walk north across the plain, following the narrow footpath that snaked across the barren poppy fields.

I could barely make out the few flickers of light in the distant town. The early morning night was almost silent, except for the faraway howls of wolves in the surrounding hills; I imagined them stalking me across the plain and felt the involuntary movement of my hands searching desperately for the penknife in my pocket.

The walk took only half an hour, but thoughts of treachery and murder caused me to increase my pace to a jog and get into the safety of the town as soon as possible. The path was stony and I stumbled on the rocks under the weight of my rucksack. Osman's cunning face flitted through my mind. *They are enemies . . . I need money . . . We might kill them.* I turned around to check nobody was following, but I couldn't see beyond the path in the darkness. I cursed Kipling for his poetry and held my tiny penknife in a vice-like grip.

With a sense of relief, I entered the bazaar through a little alleyway that skirted a crumbling compound and found the place that I had been told was where the trucks departed for Kabul. The populace had only just begun to stir and a lone old man, whose face was still cloaked in the darkness of the night, squatted on the floor.

'I want to go to Kabul,' I said, in slow, deliberate Dari.

'*Ne* Kabul.' He shook his head with a malicious grin. '*Panj.*'

Panj is Dari for five. I had missed it again. I sat resolutely until the sun rose to light up the town in which I had now been stranded for three days.

I went down to the river and took a wash in its cold waters. I was beginning to think that I would never make it out of Afghanistan, never mind all the way to India. I remembered as I looked out onto the far bank that there was a contingent of American troops at the runway a mile or so away, and thought that now might be a good time to take up the invitation to visit. I walked back through the bazaar to the bridge at the western end of town and stuck to the path, wary of mines, as I crossed the open desert to the barbed-wire fence that surrounded the airstrip. Past the burned-out hulks of Soviet tanks and armoured cars, charred from past wars, there was an open gate, where a couple of Afghan guards waved me through without even asking for identification.

'Who the hell are you?' yelled a US Army private with a vicious crew cut, as I walked past a concrete building that looked like the centre of operations.

I introduced myself as a freelance journalist, sticking to my story, but cursing the fact that I had neglected to get the name of the captain I had met two days ago.

'I was told there might be a chance of getting some transport to Kabul?'

'Hang on,' he said, before shouting across the square in the direction of a group of soldiers, who had appeared from inside a building.

'Hey, Sir, know anything about a bird to Kabul?'

'Hell, no,' was the reply from a broad-shouldered cowboy with an unbuttoned shirt hanging scruffily over a pair of shorts.

'Who's this *in-dig*?' enquired the tatty officer.

'Some sort of hack,' said the soldier. 'Says he's a Brit.'

The cowboy introduced himself as Colonel Hank Peterson and looked at me suspiciously. He asked for my journalist's iden-tification card, to which I replied I had lost it but showed him my UK driving licence instead.

'Ain't no planes outta here for a fortnight until the next resupply.'

'I don't want a plane, just a truck or something.'

The colonel laughed. 'A truck? We don't drive in these parts! Never heard of mines?'

He spoke at length about the security issues, whilst a labrador puppy snapped at my feet. He explained how the mixed US unit was struggling to keep the Afghan soldiers at bay and that the hardest part of policing the town was keeping up to date with the local politics.

'It's damn dangerous, boy. It's no place for a white face alone,' he sneered. 'The Taliban aren't the problem here. Although even that's a loose term. It's the warlords and the opium growers, they are all fighting against each other. It comes down to greed here, nothing to do with religion or any of that Muslim bullshit. It's all about the money.'

It seemed that the Americans were mentoring the Afghan soldiers – who were Tajiks from the north – in basic military counter-insurgency tactics: patrolling, looking for minefields and bombs, vehicle roadblocks and above all, searching for weapon caches.

'Problem is, whenever we do an arms amnesty and order the tribes to give us their guns they just go and buy some trash from their neighbours in the south, in Helmand or Oruzgan, which they hand over. It's old stuff from Pakistan; AKs that don't work or Lee Enfields that ain't ever worked – at least not for over a hundred years. They keep the good stuff for themselves. So we have to go looking for it.'

'And have you found anything?' I asked.

'A couple of rusty PKMs and old Russian mines, but the rest are still out there, hidden in caves.'

Another soldier arrived and handed the colonel some papers.

'Listen, I've gotta go. I'm afraid you can't stay here. Security. Sorry we can't help. Wait, I don't suppose you want to buy a bike?' He pointed to a decrepit Honda 125cc that was leaning against a wall. 'We commandeered it from a dead terrorist.'

'Two hundred bucks and it's yours. You'd better wrap up warm, though. It's fucking freezing out there.'

Even if I wanted to, I didn't have the money, so I shook my head and left the Americans to their business and walked back over the river in confounded disappointment.

I discovered Rauf walking alone down the street and he greeted me with a big smile.

'I thought you were going to Kabul today?' He seemed genuinely upset when I explained that Osman had got the time wrong.

'You should be careful around him.' Rauf looked to check no one overheard. 'He's a very dangerous boy.'

'I thought he was your brother?'

'He's a cousin through marriage, but he's not a good person. Come, I know a safe place you can stay tonight and we will find out about a car for you.' I trusted Rauf and was relieved that he had found me after I'd been dismissed by the Americans, so I followed him back into the town.

Rauf took me to the only other two-storey building on the main street. It was a restaurant, where I deposited my bag. He asked around and discovered that a group of merchants were travelling by minibus in the morning, they were leaving at five, but I had better be there at four to make sure there was space.

That afternoon we went for a walk on the northern side of the river, in an outlying village where Rauf lived. Among the mud shacks a re-entrant turned into a valley, which wound away into the mountains. At the base of this was a field and a ruined house covered in bullet holes.

'This house belonged to my uncle. He was a communist and when the Taliban came four years ago they killed him and thirty of his family. I myself lost nine close friends. They took them outside,' he pointed to the wall, 'and shot them all with machine guns. Women, children, all of them.'

I didn't know what to say. I was shocked and thought that my sympathy would be woefully inadequate. He must have sensed my reaction and smiled.

'There is a saying in Afghanistan,' he looked me directly in the eye. 'When the tiger kills, the jackal profits.' He continued, 'Unfortunately it is our way of life in Afghanistan. It is our habit.'

'It's a very bad habit,' I replied, somewhat uselessly.

I woke at three to find the van already waiting. A group of men were loitering in the dark; some were eating bread and a few were smoking. I recognised a couple of their faces. Two of the men had been on the minibus from Herat. We greeted each other with a handshake. Two children, boys of eleven or twelve, were put to work strapping the luggage to the roof and I noticed a pair of dogs, one was a large mongrel and the other a golden retriever, tied to a fencepost.

I approached and told the driver that I wished to join them. This time the bus was even more packed full than the last one I had taken from Herat. There were fourteen of us, which meant two to a seat. I got a place right at the back and as I squeezed in next to a hairy Tajik in a vast grey shawl, I watched doubtfully through the window as the dogs were hauled onto the roof and strapped down mercilessly with bungee cord. They didn't so much as whimper.

We set off and the road began comparatively well. The land started off flat and we didn't break down before sunrise. The first time we stopped was for morning prayers and by now we were high in the mountains. When daylight came, I once again found myself the centre of attention as the other passengers saw my face and tried to figure out who and what I was. There was a soldier amongst them called Ahmad, who was very friendly and insisted on offering me food after I explained that I was a foreigner. Ahmad seemed to be a good mechanic and changed the wheel when we broke down for the first time at the foot of a vast ravine. As we were busy changing the wheel, a colourfully painted lorry, laden with goods bound for the capital, passed us and its driver gave a cheerful wave. It was the only other vehicle I had seen on the road and I wondered how something of its size managed to negotiate the treacherous narrow paths.

Setting off again, the minibus climbed higher into the mountains and over a high pass near to Delak. It was hot inside the van and even the Afghans were sweating. Outside, eagles circled high above the valley. Mini whirlwinds sucked dust up from the valley bottom and sand blew in through the radiator. Nobody said anything and we were all hungry. I don't suppose you ever get used to Ramadan. I was glad to be on the road again though and happy to be away from Osman and his wild gang of smugglers. I thought back to Georgia and those American tourists, and the chaps I'd met in Iran. Well, I went looking for wilderness, and I suppose I got it. It doesn't get more remote than this.

The road got narrower as we reached the summit. It reminded me a little of one of those cartoon passes in a *Boy's Own Magazine*, where even a couple of donkeys would struggle to pass by each other. To the left was a jagged brown wall of crumbling rock, poised, it seemed to avalanche at any moment. To the right a five-hundred-metre cliff edge, dropping into oblivion. From the tight confines of the van, you couldn't see the bottom. I thought the best thing to do was try and sleep. It would all be okay. *Insha'Allah*. As we began to descend, I was woken sharply out of my slumber. There was a loud whirring noise. Something wasn't right. Then came cries of hysteria from the driver.

'Get out, get out!'

He began to shout and wave his arms towards us rear passengers. Surely not! This was my worst nightmare. I was in the middle of a row of packed seats and the man next to me started to push me violently. Although he shouted in Dari, it soon became clear from the speed of the van that the brakes had failed and we were about to lose control of the vehicle. The noise got louder as the gears crunched and sparked, but there was no stopping as the relentless momentum gained. The road bent downwards and I caught a glimpse of the path ahead. On the left the overhanging rocks loomed above us – the road narrowed to an almost impossible tightness – and on the right was a sheer drop into the valley of death below. Was this the end?

The van was speeding up at an alarming rate. The road had so many twists and turns, but the driver somehow stayed at the wheel and veered us around several sharp bends – narrowly missing a cliff tumble each time. 'Get out, Get out! *Allahu Akbar!*' He was still shouting and somehow, someone managed to open the side door. Two of the men jumped free of the hurtling van and crumpled into a roll in a ditch, disappearing into a cloud of dust behind us. I shoved one of the children forward and a man unceremoniously threw him out of the door. He rolled and tumbled and became a speck in the rear-view mirror.

We must have been hurtling downhill at sixty miles an hour by now. The man in the front passenger seat, a bearded old shopkeeper, simply froze in panic. I looked around for a means of escape, but there were too many of us. Onwards we ploughed, faster and faster. I tried the handle of the back door, but it was locked. *Shit, shit, shit* was all I could think. The only thing I could see to the rear was dust and the disappearing horizon, where the road had summited the pass.

Looking forward through the terrified bobbing heads of the other passengers, I saw instantly that the road was about to take a sharp left turn, almost at a right angle. There was no way of making that bend at this speed. *This is the end*, I thought. *What a pointless finale to such a wonderful journey.*

It is incredible what few things go through your head when you think you are about to die. There is no drama or glory, no flashbacks. Just a quick prayer and a vain automatic attempt to try to protect your head.

I remember trying get into a brace position – the kind they tell you to do in the safety brief on a plane – although in hindsight, I didn't see what use it would have been as we went airborne off the edge of a cliff. 'Get down!' I shouted in English, 'Get bloody down', more for my own sake than anyone else's.

All of this, of course, from those first shouts to the moment of clarity when I knew I was about to die, occurred in a few seconds, although I remember every slow moment as if it were a lifetime, and even now the thought of hurtling off a cliff to an unmarked grave sends a shiver down my spine.

Fortunately, the end didn't come there. The lorry that had passed us earlier had stopped, right on the curve, blocking the road. I didn't see it until the very last second and realised there would be a collision. I gritted my teeth and waited for the pain.

Our little van crumpled pathetically against the back of the lorry. There was a colossal explosion and then nothing. Utter silence.

I saw nothing but dust as I opened my eyes, wondering if I was still alive. For a few seconds, or maybe even minutes, I lay there, conscious but in shock. I couldn't quite make out where I was. Slowly I pressed my fingers hard against my face, then my legs and then my left arm, which was trapped under the seat in front. As the sensation came back, I squinted to see if there was any blood. My arm was badly bruised and I had a small cut on the top of my head, but apart from that I felt fine. I prodded the unravelled turban that was squashed at an awkward angle next to the window and the head wrapped inside it grunted. I pushed Ahmad towards the back of the van where the window was smashed through and then wriggled free of the wreckage.

The first thing I saw were the boys who had managed to jump free running down the road. Some of the other passengers had got out and were beginning to dust themselves down. Everyone was dazed and I stumbled on a rock, suddenly feeling violently sick. When we gathered our senses, we immediately set about freeing the others. Most of the passengers were unhurt, except the man in the front, who had been thrown through the windscreen and was lying motionless several metres away in a pool of blood, his face shredded by shards of glass. And, of course, there was the driver, who had received the majority of the impact. The front of the van was crushed against the side of the lorry and the steering wheel was jammed solidly into the driver's abdomen, his legs mangled in the twisted metal chassis. The man appeared dead and had a look of distant serenity in his eyes, but when Ahmad began trying to pull him free he began to groan, barely audible at first, but enough to stir everyone into action.

The men pushed the van away from the lorry and gradually plucked away at the obliterated dashboard until the driver's legs were freed. He was eventually pulled clear and placed at the side of the road. While three of the men went to attend to the unconscious passenger, I attempted to release the dogs, which by some miracle had survived the crash, although one was now hanging limply by its collar off the side of the van. I eventually managed to cut it loose using a shard of glass.

I was amazed at the absence of any sense of panic. Everyone got on calmly with helping everyone else. I rummaged through my bags to my 'Boots' first-aid kit, which had followed me unused around the world for five years, and applied a bandage to the driver. I found some antiseptic cream and rubbed it into the cuts that were on the children. Even those without any cuts demanded the cream, but with the exception of the driver and the front passenger, everyone else was more or less fine.

I took a moment to look at the wreckage. It was covered in blood and it looked like the scene of a massacre. We loaded the driver and the seriously injured man onto the lorry, whose driver explained that he had stopped for a piss break – fortunately for us, because if he hadn't, we would have been in several pieces at the bottom of the valley now. The lorry driver took his sad cargo and disappeared off down the road and that was the last I saw of them.

'They'll both be dead by the morning,' said Ahmad. 'The nearest hospital is in Kabul, over two hundred kilometres away, and the road is like this all of the way.'

The rest of us waited at the roadside. Suddenly the soldier began to laugh and everyone followed suit. It must have been the shock wearing off. I looked at my hand as it trembled uncontrollably and I too started to chuckle. I looked at the ragged children. They hadn't complained or so much as shed a tear throughout. For some reason I had been expecting them to pray, to thank Allah for saving them, but they just squatted and looked at the wreckage. To them it was *insha'Allah*, God's will, whether they lived or died, and none of their concern.

Three long hours passed and without any shade, the midday sun baked the blood-soaked earth. A few shepherds walked past and barely acknowledged the scene. Eventually a minivan pulled to a halt and Ahmad convinced the driver to return and pick us up after dropping off its passengers at the next village. It returned in the early evening, a few hours later, and took us to Lal, a small settlement that we reached by nightfall. We ate thankfully that night in a surreal setting. Ahmad recounted with delight our near miss to the inhabitants of the village and we were invited into the local mullah's house for dinner. I still couldn't believe their stoicism. After asking one of the children if he was all right, he shrugged and said to me, quite nonchalantly, 'This is Afghanistan.'

After dinner, the mullah ordered his servant to bring in a small television set, which was wheeled in on a wooden coffee trolley and attached to an old VHS player. A long cable was thrown out of the window and a generator fired into life. The mullah grinned and inserted a tape into the machine and we all waited expectantly.

The film was *Rambo III*, where the muscle-bound hero fights alongside the mujahideen against the Russians. The Afghans cheered as Rambo rode on horseback firing an explosive arrow at a Soviet helicopter.

Ahmad nudged me with a huge smile, baring his bright white teeth, and pointed at the screen.

'This is Afghanistan,' he repeated, as the helicopter burst into flames.

15

Crossing the Khyber

Waking at four, we managed to get a van to take us the remaining distance to Kabul. Two others attached themselves to the group, including another soldier who was convinced that I was a member of al-Qaeda, but didn't seem to mind too much either way. Just to ensure that we got over our little trauma with speed, the new driver carried on twice as fast, skidding all over the place, much to the group's displeasure, until Ahmad punched him in the back of the head.

I tried to doze off, but as we gained more height throughout the morning, the scenery became awe-inspiring and I couldn't help staring at the surrounding majesty. Snow-capped peaks of the Hindu Kush rose out of the brown hills like jagged white teeth. We stopped a few times for the Afghans to bundle out and pray, which allowed me some time to enjoy the sublime passes. I thought back to Conolly, who had passed over the mountains a hundred and sixty-four years ago, and wondered for a moment how many near-death scrapes he must have experienced. As the day wore on, we passed over more mountains and it was dark before the lights of Kabul came into view. The houses grew in number until we reached the almost metropolitan-like outskirts of the city. Concrete almost outnumbered mud here and I looked in disbelief at the high-rise, Soviet-era flats and apartment blocks. It was another world.

I said goodbye to the chirpy merchants and their children, with whom I had nearly spent my final hours. They were just happy to be in the capital, where they could enjoy the wonders of the twenty-first century for a short while. For me, I was looking forward to having a shower and some decent food. I headed straight to Chicken Street, the infamous old hippy market in the heart of the city, and nearby I found the Mustafa Hotel, a relic of the old days, bustling with wealthy Afghans, foreign journalists and a few shady mercenaries.

'It's a hundred dollars per night,' said Javid, the hotel receptionist. I walked away gloomily.

'Wait!' He stopped me. 'We don't get tourists here anymore, I'm sorry, but I know somewhere cheaper, if you like?'

Javid gave me directions to the Park Hotel, a ten-minute walk through the grim, dark streets. It was eleven dollars, and all the money I had left, but I was finally in civilisation and hoped there would be some way of getting some cash. I got wearily out of my rags and gave them to two mischievous looking boys, who said they would wash them. The shower didn't work and the room looked like a prison cell, but it was my first bed in a week and I slept like a baby.

Kabul is an odd place. At almost two thousand metres it is a high city, and was the only place of any real development in the whole country. The Kabul river runs through its heart, winding its way between the town's high-rise tower blocks, low mud shacks, Chinese-style villas and bustling bazaar. Above it all is the ancient Bala Hissar fortress and a ring of mountain peaks. The next morning the two boys returned with my clothes immaculately clean and pressed, so I set about exploring the city in the general direction of the Mustafa Hotel to look for Javid. Wandering about the ancient alleys, I mingled with the throng of people from across the country. Shadowy figures flitted among the piles of rubbish and NATO soldiers patrolled cautiously along the avenues, while women in blue burqas waddled quickly between the doorways and shops.

Historically, Kabul dates back almost four thousand years, when it was the main centre of both Zoroastrianism and later Buddhism. The Persians settled in the region around 400 BC, before Alexander arrived during his conquests some seventy years later. The Greco-Bactrians and Indo-Greeks ruled the city for two hundred years until the Kushan empire wrested it from them, taking charge until the third century AD. Then followed the Sassanids, the Kidarites, the Hephthalites, and the Turkic Shahi. In 674, Islamic invaders from the west arrived in Afghanistan, but met fierce resistance from the Hindu-Shahi occupants. The kingdom of Kabul was not fully converted to Islam for another two hundred years.

When it finally succumbed, Kabul was successively ruled by various Islamic, Mongol and Persian empires until it became the capital of Afghanistan in 1776. The city was therefore used to foreign invaders and the presence of NATO troops in the city was merely the latest in a very long line.

I found Javid watering the plants that decorated the restaurant terrace. He was in a cheery mood.

'*Salaam*, Inglees,' he waved.

Javid was in his mid-twenties and clean-shaven. He had greasy, slicked-back hair and looked like an Italian gangster made more authentic by his choice of clothes – tight black jeans and a leather jacket, with fake designer sunglasses protruding out of the breast pocket.

'Have some breakfast with me,' he said.

'I'd love to, but I ran out of money,' I replied.

'Don't worry about money, my friend, this is Afghanistan, we are hospitable people. You may eat and drink what you like for free.'

Normally I'd have been suspicious of such hospitality, but Javid was genuine and insisted I sat down. I couldn't believe my luck as I tucked in to a delicious portion of spaghetti bolognaise and a cold glass of beer, and I listened intently as Javid told me about his life.

'I came to Kabul in 2001, as soon as the Taliban fell. I was so excited about the prospect of study and work that I left my family and all my friends in my village and came to the city. It was my first time here and I had never seen such buildings and so many people. I got a job here at the Mustafa, because I learnt English quickly. In the end, I didn't need to study, because I learnt the language through watching TV and reading books. I was so happy to find work. You know, that's all we really want here in Afghanistan – work. Just like everyone else, we only fight so much because there isn't any work. If everyone had jobs and a little bit of money, the fighting would stop. As long as nobody interferes.'

He certainly had a point and I was slowly realising that the only way for Afghanistan to progress was through economic development and financial security. 'But the problem is that Afghans are a proud people and always have been,' Javid continued. 'When foreigners come with their guns and kill Afghans, we forget about the money and want to take revenge.'

Javid offered to guide me around the bazaar. The streets had come to life in the day time and I could hardly believe it belonged to the same country as the barren interior. People occupied every inch of the city. Buying, selling, bargaining and fighting for space.

Javid asked around to see where I could change a traveller's cheque, but people only shrugged. We tried the embassy cantonment in Wazir Akhbar Khan, but the sole ATM in the country was out of order.

'Don't worry,' said Javid, pressing a hundred afghanis into my hand. 'Take this.'

It was embarrassing to be borrowing money, but I resolved to break my golden rule of travelling and ask for a Western Union money transfer from home, in order to pay the kindly hotelier back. I made the rather humiliating call to my parents and a few hours later I was one hundred and fifty pounds richer. I told myself I wouldn't spend a penny more than that until I reached India.

It was a weight off my mind to finally have some cash. I worked out that I'd got this far on a little under four hundred and fifty pounds – that's only around six hundred dollars – which isn't bad for seven weeks and five thousand miles. So I probably shouldn't have decided to celebrate by going straight to the Chicken Street market. There I browsed through its jumble of souvenir and antique shops, where Kabuli shopkeepers, a mixture of Baluchi carpet sellers, Pashtun dagger smiths, Tajik jewellers and Nuristani hat makers were offering all kinds of special tourist discounts. But, of course, there were no tourists; there hadn't been any in twenty-five years. There was, however, a steady trickle of journalists wanting an Afghan rug for their flat in Greenwich or Brooklyn.

One morning I saw a whole platoon of Norwegian soldiers jump off the back of a troop carrier and surround Mr Rafiq (& Son) Lapiz Lazuli shop. I waited excitedly for the imminent raid, only to be a little disappointed to realise that an officer was simply using them as his personal protection while he surveyed the antique rifle collection.

Habibullah Seyyed Umar the shopkeeper was sixty-three, but he looked older. His grey beard was flecked with henna and it glinted in the streak of sunlight that streamed into the dark trinket shop. He looked sad as he sat on his prayer mat and fiddled with his prayer beads.

'I remember the *farangs*,' he said thoughtfully. 'Chicken Street was full of Westerners. English, Australian, French. We would all smoke hashish together and I would listen to their music. Do you know of the Beatles?'

'I've heard of them ...'

'But now of course it's all different. The workers buy things, and we charge them more, but it isn't the same. It's no fun now, they just come in, pay the money and leave. They all think they will be killed in the street.'

'But isn't it dangerous? I heard two Italians were murdered in the park last week.'

'They were journalists or security guards or something. They went out looking for the Taliban. Real travellers – *musaafir* – have nothing to fear.'

I humoured Habibullah by bargaining hard over the price of five pakuls as gifts for my friends. I noticed how he cheered up immeasurably at the prospect of a good haggle and I was satisfied with the price – less than a dollar each.

'Prime quality, made in Pakistan,' said the Pashtun proudly. I was a little disappointed. I wanted a souvenir from Afghanistan. I let him convince me to buy a small rug for fifty dollars. That was almost a third of my cash gone immediately, but I figured that I probably wouldn't be back in Afghanistan anytime soon, and anyway, I'd lasted this long with no money.

'An ancient carpet, maybe two hundred years old!'

And for my father, a Lee Enfield bayonet inscribed with

the crown of George V, dating back to the 1919 Third Afghan war.

'Take it home, where it belongs,' said Habibullah, with the graceful pitch of a wise hermit.

For two days I explored the bazaar on the south bank of the Kabul river, full of piles of steaming rubbish and grazing sheep. The sights and smells were overwhelming, the crush suffocating. I walked along the Jad-e-Maiwand high street to see the famous ruined buildings, devastated in the 1990s when the Taliban besieged the city.

I watched as small children played amongst the dusty ruins; the bullet-ridden carcasses of former homes were a vivid reminder of the recent battles and civil war. But in spite of the presence of the international coalition – British, Norwegian, American and Danish troops at every corner – the city seemed peaceful. As dusk approached, the Afghans scuttled around with more urgency, eager to get home to break the fast with their families. Those that didn't, held impromptu picnics on the pavement and handed bread and apples to complete strangers. The generosity was remarkable. That weekend, I discovered, was the end of Ramadan and the holy feast of *Eid al-Fitr*.

I was reading the morning newspaper at the Mustafa Hotel and I noticed that it happened to be the eleventh of November. I thought that since it was Armistice Day, it would be appropriate to visit the British war cemetery to pay my respects. Javid had never heard of it, but I had read about it somewhere and determined to find it before eleven o'clock. I wandered north through the run-down suburbs, where the lanes became steep and windy, and I began to climb a hill where half-built concrete mansions sat empty amongst the piles of rusting Soviet tanks that had been left to rot, half-buried in rubble. I found the cemetery conveniently located next to the Afghan city graveyard, which spread arbitrarily over the hill to my right. A local mechanic took me to the entrance of the walled compound.

A small plaque was attached to the wall that said that it was the 'Kabul European cemetery of the Sherpur cantonment'.

The small enclosure was filled with skeletal trees, which had flung a covering of brown and orange leaves over the white headstones, but the gravel paths were swept and neat. Sitting on a discarded office chair in the corner was an old man dozing peacefully in the shade of a mulberry tree. He was Mr Rahimullah, who had been the cemetery's keeper and gardener for over thirty years. The old man told me that he came here originally to graze his sheep, but for the past couple of years he had been paid a small wage by the British Embassy to keep the graveyard tidy and, I suspect, his sheep out.

The cemetery was created in the late 1870s during the second Anglo-Afghan war to inter some of the casualties of that campaign, and Rahimullah showed me the weathered graves of a number of British soldiers, including that of Major John Cook VC, of the Bengal Staff Corps, who was killed leading a bayonet charge when the British forces in Kabul were surrounded by an army of ten thousand Afghans. He had earned his Victoria Cross only a year earlier for charging out of a trench under heavy fire 'with such impetuosity that the enemy broke and fled'. His story was hardly unique in this sort of place.

As well as the military ones, the other gravestones were Kabul's European residents up to the 1970s. They told of missionaries, explorers, philanthropists, journalists and even some children –

a reminder of the expatriate families who once used to fill entire districts in the city.

Sir Aurel Stein, the British archaeologist, was buried here in 1943, after moving to Afghanistan to study the campaigns of Alexander the Great. There was an American engineer, who was sent to work on the Helmand irrigation project in the 1950s, a British family killed in a car crash and a woman who was murdered. Other graves mark happier lives. One gravestone dated 1972 proclaimed 'Billy Batman loves Joan' – a reminder of Afghanistan's historic place on the hippy trail; a time when it was more famous for its marijuana than mujahideen.

Large black slate plaques with the regimental badges of the Royal Anglians and the Rifle Volunteers were the most recent memorials to those fallen while in service of the International Security Assistance Force. A wreath of poppies was mounted on either side of the northern wall, which contained the British headstones.

With a glint in his eye, Rahimullah said that once, shortly before the coalition invasion, he was visited by Mullah Omar, the Taliban's supreme leader. The belligerent mullah asked him why he tended the graves of *infidels* – to which the old man replied that, at his age, even a blind man would have more chance of finding a better job – forgetting for a moment that Omar himself had only one eye.

In the evening, I returned to the Mustafa as usual to say good-bye to Javid. He seemed sad that I was leaving.

'Please visit my family,' he implored.

But I felt that I needed to keep on moving; the greenery of India, the draw of lapping shores and swaying palms in Goa was too strong. I gave him twenty dollars as a tip for his help, which he tried to refuse, but I would not take no for an answer. In return, he insisted on giving me a free omelette, which I gladly accepted. As I sat pondering the future of the city, there was suddenly a loud, protracted explosion, followed by a deep grumble that shook the whole building, almost causing my plate to fall off the table. Outside, people were shouting and a woman screamed. I ducked automatically, assuming it must have been a car bomb or a rocket attack.

'What the hell was that?' I asked Javid, who didn't look in the least bit alarmed.

Javid laughed. 'That,' he said, 'was an earthquake. We get them all the time.'

I woke at four thirty in the morning and walked through the blackness to find the eastern bus station. Packs of dogs flitted between the shadows and the dim outlines of groups of Afghans could be seen huddled round the glowing embers of fires in old oil drums. They were as cold and hard as the night sky. Brown stony faces with long, drawn features looked out from unforgiving black beards. They lifted up their knees to their chins and wrapped their heavy woollen shawls across like bats in a cave, their heads covered with beige pakuls or dark turbans, only the black eyes peering out into the cold. As I walked past, they sneered through their thick moustaches, narrow eyes levelled straight, in contempt as much as in curiosity.

I found a cluster of taxis and buses amongst the shacks and a van heading for Jalalabad, the gateway to the Khyber Pass. Sitting on the back seat was Hamid Noori, an aspiring writer who was an Afghan refugee living in Peshawar. He had been in Kabul looking for work with the coalition, but had finally given up and was going back to Pakistan to his family.

The route set off past the military cantonments west of the city, past the United Nations Headquarters and the military airport. For a while the road was made of tarmac and we seemed to float along in peaceful contrast to the vicious jolting I had been subject to in the mountains. The only disruptions to the ride were the occasional old tank tracks, stripped from the Soviet machines and now serving as speed bumps to deter any would-be car bombers. Both sides of the road were littered with charred debris and ruined vehicles. We passed several checkpoints on the way out of the city, but before long we had entered the Mahipar Mountains and we were back in the wilderness again.

It became apparent that the road was snaking downhill after crossing the Puli Charki pass. The view was spectacular as the road wound through the defiles and canyons. Immense crags flanked the Kabul Gorge where the road clung precariously to the cliffside. A narrow stream trickled menacingly at its bottom. I imagined the peaks and boulders as they must have looked to the retreating British army in 1842, as wily Pathan snipers fired down on the heads of the wretched, doomed soldiers withdrawing through the narrow canyons to Jalalabad. Hamid, who had studied history at school, started to tell me the story. I smiled, relaxing, because I already knew it off by heart, but it felt right to hear it again from an Afghan.

'Here is where they died,' he said, shaking his head earnestly. 'It was a very cold winter that year and our Afghan warlords said we would let you British leave, but of course they lied. They couldn't resist wanting to kill the *farengi* soldiers as they ran away.

'You know there were four thousand Britishers and Indians, and something like ten or eleven thousand civilians. You had your women and servants with you, and that was your mistake.

You should have fled and left them. You didn't stand a chance in these passes, look.'

He pointed out of the windows of the van at the rocky precipices, perfect to conceal thousands of the Pashtun warriors. 'There was nowhere for the English to hide, and they hadn't eaten in days. Even your soldiers couldn't feel their fingers in the cold and the guns froze.' Hamid shook his head again. 'Your men gave away their blankets to the women, but they all died anyway, so what was the point?'

Somewhere among the valleys to south lay Gandamak. The final stand of the British army, which took place on the morning of 13 January 1842. It was one of the most tragic episodes in British imperial history. Twenty officers and forty-five British soldiers, mostly of the 44th Regiment of Foot, were all that remained of the column and they found themselves surrounded on a small hillock. The Afghans attempted to persuade the soldiers that they intended them no harm and to convince the British to surrender. 'Not bloody likely!' was the bellowed answer of one British sergeant.

Hamid shook his head once more. 'The British were very brave. But also a little foolish.'

All except a handful were shot or cut down. It is thought that only two British officers and a few Indian sepoys survived the massacre of over sixteen thousand men and women. One lucky chap, Captain Thomas Souter, survived only because he wrapped the regimental colours around himself to save them and as a result was taken prisoner. The Afghans didn't kill him – not because he had done the honourable thing, but mistakenly they thought he must be a rich and high-ranking military official with his expensive adornment, and they reckoned they would get a good ransom. The other was surgeon Dr William Brydon, who made it as far as the British garrison at Jalalabad, after riding his exhausted horse to the limit for days.

Hamid finished the story, 'and when Brydon was asked where the rest of the army was, he replied, "I am the army".'

On the far side of the pass we descended through the village of Surobi, a small collection of high-walled compounds surrounded by fields, which in the spring would be blooming with pink opium poppy. The road followed a dry river bed down a valley, marking the start of a fertile plain that harboured some greenery, rare in this brown country. It was kept watered by the presence of a nearby lake that was dammed during the more prosperous 1950s. We entered another narrow gorge that was filled with stout mulberry trees and here we were pulled over at a checkpoint, where our driver was questioned by a heavily bearded tribesman wielding an AK-47.

The man was not in uniform and was evidently a Pashtun. I quietly asked Hamid who these armed men were. He explained that the area west of Jalalabad was controlled by the militant Hezb-e-Islami group, which was founded by the pragmatic warlord Gulbuddin Hekmatyar – a former mujahideen commander, and one-time prime minister.

'He is an independent ruler,' said Hamid in a whisper. 'He is more interested in protecting his poppy crop than supporting the Taliban, but everyone suspects that he has links with al-Qaeda. He spent many years in Iran and Pakistan and has helped a lot of foreigners – jihadists – come to Afghanistan.'

The driver, cautious not to invite trouble, handed over a wad of afghanis and we were waved through the makeshift chicane out of the far side of the orchard. As we passed by a group of tribesmen, Hamid nudged me, 'Keep low and do not make eye contact with the militia.' I heeded his advice and pulled my brown woollen blanket tightly around my face until we were well clear of the valley and back onto the safety of the main trail.

Soon the mountains subsided and we emerged onto a flat plain. It was green – the first proper cultivation I had seen since the Caucasus. Corn and poppy fields now grew in abundance. Even palm trees sprung out from beside the road and there was an almost subtropical air as we approached the town of Jalalabad. Water buffalo and Brahman cows from the Punjab graced the scene. The buildings were better made, and more modern materials such as steel girders and breeze blocks complemented the traditional earthen walls.

We passed through the lush fields around the city and stopped for a while near the confluence of the Kabul and Kunar rivers. Hamid and a few of the others got out to wash their hands and feet in the frothy waters, before settling into the routine of *namaz*. Whilst the Afghans prayed, I took the opportunity to walk over a bridge, which displayed a small plaque proclaiming that it had been built using funds from the European Union in 2002.

Near to the sign, a small boy leant barefoot against the wall wearing just a filthy salwar with no trousers or shoes. I smiled at him and gave him a pen that I had in the pocket of my waistcoat. He took it cautiously, looking around to check that no one had witnessed the transaction, before hiding it in his sleeve and running away gleefully in the hope that he would not have to share his prize. I looked at the old men who were squatting on their haunches on the far side of the bridge, deep in conversation. They all wore full black beards and were physically quite different from my acquaintances on the bus. We were in the crescent moon of the Pashtun heartlands now, trundling towards Jalalabad.

The Pashtuns, or Pathans as they are known in Urdu, are the tribal group that dominates Eastern and Southern Afghanistan as well as the border regions of Pakistan. These infamous mountain warriors still control the vast, lawless highlands that form the border. Because of the nature of the terrain, with its vast tracts of mountains and deep ravines, it has always been ungovernable by the official governments of either countries. There can be no fences or walls here and that has meant that the hill-dwelling tribal clans have generally been left to their own devices. They speak Pashto and practise *Pashtunwali* – an ancient code of conduct that predates Islam. Many actually believe themselves to be a Semitic race, descendants of Abraham and one of the lost tribes of Israel.

The Pashtuns have long dominated the political scene in Afghanistan and for over three hundred years have held a monopoly of power within the government and society in general. The Pashtun tribes formed the core of the anti-Soviet mujahideen, and now of the Taliban. They were famed during the days of the Great Game for their ferocity in battle and savagery against opponents, as well as their wiliness and pragmatic approach to loyalty. In his famous novel *Kim*, Kipling's character – the paternal Mahbub Ali – warns his boy protégé to 'trust a Brahmin before a snake, and a snake before a harlot, and a harlot before a Pathan.'

After he had finished praying, Hamid gave me a whistle and waved for me to get back to the bus. The driver was eager to make the border for lunchtime and hopefully beat the queues. Soon enough we began another climb and the brown foothills became bigger as we left behind the emerald fields of the Jalalabad vale, heralding the start of the celebrated Khyber Pass. Presently we reached the small administrative outpost at

Torkham. It was a motley collection of mud buildings with one or two concrete shacks. On the wall opposite the customs house was a huge mural depicting pictures of the different kinds of landmines to expect in Afghanistan. Next to it, in bold hand-written letters, was the single word 'Welcome'. I pondered whether or not it was the most suitable greeting to visitors.

In the bustle of the crowds inside the sweltering room, I fought for my place in the queue to the desk. After much push-ing and shoving, I obtained an exit stamp in my passport and crossed into Pakistan by way of a rickety iron gate, which had the green and white flag of Pakistan painted clumsily on a rusty sheet of metal attached to it. On the other side, a soldier looked at my passport and welcomed me in perfect English.

'I trust you are well, sir? You will be requiring an escort, if you don't mind.' An ancient Afridi tribesman with no teeth and a huge beard snapped to attention.

'Private Gulham at your service.'

Hamid said that we had no choice but to accept the escort and so the three of us piled into a taxi.

I felt a shiver of excitement as we sped off, away from the crowds of refugees up into the shale hills of the infamous Khyber Pass – the main corridor connecting Afghanistan and the Indian subcontinent; it has hosted invading armies and trade caravans alike. Alexander trod the path almost two and a half thousand years ago; Kipling called it 'a sword cut through the mountains' because of its bloody history, and it was a famous soldiers' saying that 'every stone has been soaked in blood'.

In reality, it is not one but a series of winding passes served by a narrow road that stretches almost fifty miles through the Safēd Kōh mountains of the Hindi Kush and its summit is just over three miles inside Pakistani territory at the hill fort of Landi

Kotal. The Afridi and Shinwari tribes that inhabit the pass have been its traditional guardians throughout the centuries. They used to levy tolls on travellers and this was their main source of income until very recently. The British wisely employed them during the incursions into Afghanistan by creating a regiment called the Khyber Rifles.

There were several villages lining the route and it was more populated than I had expected. A few cows filed along the sloping terraces and sparse greenery sprouted from the rocks. The road was well maintained and surfaced all the way.

Every so often, Private Gulham would point out a fort – a reminder of those blood-soaked stones. Bleak, mud-walled castles, at least one of which, Kafir Kot – the Fort of the Infidels – dates back to the time of Alexander. There can be few places in the world that have seen such a succession of armies pass through them. From Alexander's warriors to the British brigades whose regimental badges were now carved into the cliffside, this was one of the most historical thoroughfares anywhere in the world. I told the driver to stop at the hill fort of the Khyber Rifles, now a unit incorporated into the Pakistani Army. I wanted to see the headquarters of these celebrated warriors.

The Khyber Rifles were raised as a militia in the 1880s to serve as part of the British Indian army. The unit's main duties were to guard the pass against the Afghan army and any roaming bandits. Soon after it was raised, the regiment was drafted to fight in the mountainous border lands, where the tribesmen were often put in the difficult position of having to fight their own clansmen, making it hard for them to remain loyal. After a number of desertions, the regiment was disbanded, but it wasn't long before there was a renewed need for a permanent presence on the Khyber. More recently, the regiment had been busy helping to track down Taliban fugitives and al-Qaeda militants – most notably the infamous Osama bin Laden.

'Where do you think he is?' I asked Hamid.

'Bin Laden?'

'Yes.'

'He's either dead already – killed by a bomb in the caves of Tora Bora, or hiding out in one of these tribal villages,' said the young man.

Nobody thought for a moment that he was living a life of luxury just outside Islamabad, the capital of Pakistan. I told the taxi driver to pull into the driveway of the barracks.

'We can't go any closer,' said Hamid, worried about driving towards the army base. The Afridi guard was fast asleep on the back seat, resting his head on his rifle.

'Alright, wait here,' I said, and walked up to the main gate. A moustachioed corporal was on duty and I asked if I could come in to view the famous guest book signed by Rudyard Kipling. The corporal looked at my ragged *salwar kameez* doubtfully.

'I think that perhaps you should come back when you are more formally attired,' he said, before saluting and marching off.

It was late afternoon by the time we descended into the Vale of Peshawar and the city rose from the plain like a dark shadow. At its outskirts, we came across a police checkpoint, where Private Gulham got out and started talking to the policeman.

'He says that will be five hundred rupees.'

'What for?'

'Baksheesh, sir. For services provided. Pay him now.'

I fumbled a few haggard notes from my pocket that I had exchanged at Torkham and handed them over. There's a special sleight of hand that's peculiar to policemen around the world: the conjuring trick that palms and conceals banknotes with a skill that experienced swindlers envy. The wiry copper gathered the money with a two-handed handshake, smeared a palm across his chest as if feeling for his heart and then scratched his nose with a practised innocence. The cash had vanished and he pointed towards the city.

After Afghanistan, the city of Peshawar looked strangely modern. The streets were relatively clean, and they were filled with gaudily coloured metal gates and concrete palaces. I gawped in shock through the window at the apparent wealth of the place. Hamid sighed.

'Drugs.'

'Sorry?' I said.

'The money. It's all from the opium trade. That policeman that we passed, he is a big drugs man, he allows it to come into the city. All that heroin on your streets, millions of dollars, all goes through that little checkpoint we just passed. It gets processed here in Peshawar, then loaded onto trucks to Karachi and it's shipped to the West.'

It was time to leave and let Hamid get home to see his family. As I spilled out from the taxi, Hamid shook my hand and bowed formally. He gave me a business card and told me that if I ever had a job for him, he would be most grateful.

'I must go and celebrate *Eid* now, sir. Goodbye'.

I found myself walking along smooth footways, choking on the fumes of passing cars. Clean-shaven young men pedalled rickshaws and many went about bareheaded. I went past glass-fronted shops with neon signs selling watches and mobile phones. The houses were made of concrete and breeze blocks and the buildings had whole upper storeys in varying stages of completion. Streets had names and the trees were tame. There were women. Yes, they were swathed in burqas, but they were there – visible, for all to see, standing outside shops and walking in the streets, leaving their dark eyes scandalously bare. It seemed all too surreal and exciting.

I found a small hotel – recommended as the only place to stay in Peshawar – rather uninspiringly called the Tourist Inn. It was, however, pleasant to enjoy a warm shower and even indulge in a spot of shopping in a rudimentary supermarket that sold bread and sweets. I spent the evening relaxing in the grounds of the hotel and chatting to the owner, a round Pashtun called Bahadar Khan.

There were a few other travellers, including a serious American, an irritating French woman and some Germans, and I could tell from their staring that they were a little dubious about my costume, but I was so relieved to have made it through Afghanistan that I didn't care.

'Do you want to come to Darra?' asked Hans, a curious-looking German, over breakfast.

'I don't know, what is it?' I said.

'Darra, the weapon market – Bahadar says he will take us. I have asked the others, but they are too scared.'

I looked at the emaciated thirty-year-old, who was wearing baggy green fisherman trousers from India and a white collarless shirt. I guessed that he was an aid worker or perhaps a journalist.

'All right. Let's go.'

Darra Adam Khel is a little village twenty-five miles south of Peshawar, off the main road, inside the tribal areas. The entire village is reliant on the fabrication and sale of arms and munitions. It took an hour or so by car along dusty roads that wound through the brown hills, which was made surreal as Bahadar serenaded us with Hindi pop karaoke.

Although technically inside Pakistan, it is beyond the remit of the law and therefore anything can be purchased there without a permit. It started off as a centre of arms production in the late nineteenth century, when the British decided to turn a blind eye to the trade (and in any case thought it better that the tribes make their own inferior weapons rather than steal British ones).

Nowadays weapons are handmade using traditional gunsmith techniques passed down from father to son. The street looked like it was lifted straight from a scene on a Wild West set, except instead of gun-toting cowboys, there was the fleeting presence of salwar kameez-clad tribesmen wearing military waistcoats and black turbans. There were no women here. The clinking of hammer and nail was continuous, broken only by a burst of automatic gunfire from the back of a building. I walked into one of the shops – a small closet-sized room – where a middle-aged man sat cross-legged and barefoot, hunched over a drill press. In his hand were the makings of a gun barrel, which he peered down intently, inspecting for abrasions. He barely noticed our arrival.

There were rows and rows of all sorts of firearms, from the ubiquitous Russian-designed AK-47 and all its variants, to double-barrelled shotguns and rudimentary pistols.

'See what you think of this,' said Bahadar with a grin.

I picked up a small tube that looked a bit like a fountain pen. Yes, that was a gun, too. 'Very popular with the Japanese,' said Bahadar. He went on to boast how these craftsmen could repro-duce any weapon they could get their hands on in less than a week.

'How much do they cost?' I asked innocently.

'This one is forty dollars US,' said Khan, handing me a 'Chinese'-style AK with a folding stock. I grasped the weapon and pulled back the cocking handle to look inside the chamber. It was unloaded, so I felt confident enough to release the working parts forward and pull the trigger. It gave a satisfying click. I looked at the stock – the gunsmith had carefully replicated everything in minute detail, including the serial number of the original.

'They take great pride in their work,' said Bahadar.

I was about to place the rifle back on the rack in favour of inspecting a modified walking stick (that was also a gun), when he asked if I wanted to fire it. I had fired weapons on the ranges before when I was in the Territorial Army, so I didn't suffer from the childish excitement that the German did, but I agreed anyway out of curiosity.

Khan helped himself to a handful of 7.62 rounds from a brass pot next to the gunsmith and loaded two magazines with around ten rounds each. He handed them to Hans and motioned for us to follow him outside. We loaded the rifles around the back of the shed and cocked them.

'Just fire them into the hill over there. But don't kill any chickens or you will have to pay.' I fired off the ten rounds in three bursts of automatic. The German was more carefree and let loose the whole clip in one long noisy rattle.

'They can make over five hundred guns a day,' said Khan, 'if business is good.'

'Five hundred a day? Who on earth buys them all?'

'Oh, sir,' exclaimed Khan, 'there are many customers. Everyone is wanting many guns. All the tribesmen need one, maybe two. If he is a rich man, perhaps he needs rocket launcher or maybe anti-aircraft gun.'

'What for?' I asked, astonished.

'Killing, sir. What else? The tribes they like very much to kill each other.'

'And the Taliban?' asked Hans. 'Do they buy them?'

'Of course, anyone may be a customer. Guns are no problem, they are everywhere. It is the ammunition that is difficult to find. You can't just make ammunition in the same way that you can make the guns.'

I asked him where it came from then, if it was not made here. At this Khan looked away.

As we spoke, the wail of the muezzin pierced the air from a loudspeaker attached to a tall pole in the street outside.

'You are asking too many questions, Englishman sir. Come, it is time to go,' he said solemnly, but with a glint in his eye.

Officially, travel to Darra by foreigners is forbidden; in fact, it is forbidden to leave the main road anywhere between Peshawar and Landi Kotal or Kohat, because where the tarmac ends, so does Pakistani law. Beyond this, in the tribal lands, the gun is the law and it's not a place where outsiders are supposed to interfere.

Back in the city, it was the end of Ramazan (pronounced with a 'z' instead of a 'd' here) and the festival of *Eid* was upon us. The city was as silent as Christmas morning in the Cotswolds, yet the sun blazed down on the empty streets, giving it a surreal atmosphere. Hundreds of buzzards glided through the air in search of something with which to celebrate the festival.

The bazaar in Peshawar has long been a great meeting place of the tribes. It is here that the region's produce is brought to be sold, here that lapis lazuli, opium and counterfeit Chinese goods smuggled over the Afghan border pass into Pakistan, here that news and gossip is passed on and exchanged. Today, though, it was deserted, impossible even to find a *chingchi* (a Pakistani motorised auto-rickshaw). I was a little disappointed to have reached my first city on the subcontinent on the only day of the year it was closed and went in search of solace by visiting the great Bala Hissar fort.

I circumnavigated its vast moat through the empty streets to its arched entrance, but that was shut, too. 'No visitors are allowed,' said the sign in English and Urdu. These days the fort was the headquarters of the Frontier Corps and out of bounds.

Peshawar, which means the city of men, had the feel of a frontier town unlike any I'd visited before, and I sensed that in spite of the silence, it was constantly on edge. Revenge killings, tribal infractions and suicide bombings were frequent occurrences and in 2004 alone some four hundred people were murdered in the city. Much like the Wild West, this no-man's-land was indeed a man's city, where only the hardiest survive. It wasn't a place to hang around.

That said, many don't have the option to leave. It has become the home of a hundred thousand displaced Afghans, most of them Pashtun. As a result, during the 1980s the city served as a base for the mujahideen and more recently a place of refuge for the Taliban. William Dalrymple said of the place during his visit:

> *Violence is to the North-West Frontier what religion is to the Vatican. It is a* raison d'être, *a way of life, an obsession, a philosophy. Bandoliers hang over the people's shoulders, grenades are tucked into their pockets. Status symbols here are not Mercedes or Savile Row suits; in Peshawar you know you've arrived when you can drive to work in a captured Russian T-72 tank.*

But by now I'd had my fill of guns and bandits. India seemed to me a stone's throw away and I was glad to be leaving the barren rocks of Central Asia behind. I had finally reached the start of the 'Grand Trunk Road', that fabled highway that spans the

Indian subcontinent like a throbbing artery through the plains, and I was keen to get on it.

At Peshawar bus station, the official looked me up and down. I had asked for a ticket to Rawalpindi.

'Excuse me, sir, but you don't look like a gentleman from England,' said the young man, wobbling his head frantically. 'I must ask the permission from my supervisor before I allow you to buy a ticket.'

The supervisor, a corpulent man in his fifties, with a tremendous moustache dyed bright red, ordered me into his office and told me to sit down.

'Passport,' he growled with a peevish air.

'Where did you get this?' He suddenly took on a calmer appearance.

'I told you, I'm British. I am travelling overland to India. What, exactly, is the problem now?' I said.

The man blushed and in an embarrassed tone, replied, 'Forgive me, sir, my employee didn't believe that you were English, he mistook you for an Afghan refugee.'

It was high time I bought some new clothes.

16

Land of the Five Rivers

Look! Brahmins and chumars, bankers and tinkers, barbers and bunnias, pilgrims – and potters – all the world going and coming. It is to me as a river from which I am withdrawn like a log after a flood. And truly the Grand Trunk Road is a wonderful spectacle. It runs straight, bearing without crowding India's traffic for fifteen hundred miles – such a river of life as nowhere else exists in the world.

Rudyard Kipling, *Kim*

Brightly painted lorries, or 'jingly trucks' as soldiers call them, are Pakistan's modern-day equivalent to the camel caravan, trundling along the trunk road belching a thick black smoke from their exhausts. They were similar to the ones I had seen in Afghanistan, but there were more of them here and they were even more colourful. Reds, golds and crystalline mirrors depicted idyllic scenes of alpine cottages and mountain streams next to Chinese pagodas and Mughal palaces. Their roof racks, shining like jewelled tiaras, were often curved upwards like a saddle or the seat of a maharajah's elephant, and on the front a pair of painted omniscient eyes would survey the road ahead.

Sometimes, whenever the bus slowed down to pass through villages, or overtake one of these slow-moving monsters, bare-footed children and moustachioed men in mustard-coloured robes bearing baskets of coconuts, bags of fruit juice or nuts, would clamber on the side of the vehicle and thrust their wares through the open windows. The landscape was green now, as the road followed the downward flow of the Kabul river where it converged with the Indus at Khairabad and Attock. From now on I would be crossing the plains of the Punjab – the land of the five rivers – which extends at its western extremity from the southward flowing Indus, cutting perpendicular the watersheds of its tributaries, the Jhelum, the Chenab, the Ravi, the Beas and the Sutlej, where Alexander finally decided to turn around after his conquest of Asia. It might have been the end of his journey, but for me it felt like the final stretch before reaching my goal.

Great fields extended in all directions, as the hills gave way to gently undulating pastureland and fierce agriculture. It was hot as the tropical sun beat down, turning the bus into a dawdling mobile oven.

What made the bus journey more exhausting was the Pakistani passengers' almost perfect command of English and their natural curiosity. I should have been glad of the familiar language and the friendly interest, but the questions were relentless. 'What is your nationality, sir?' 'Are you a Muslim, sir?' 'Will you get me a visa for your country, sir?' When we slowed down to avoid hitting a three-legged goat, one young man with noticeably piercing blue eyes shouted from outside the window, 'Hey you, sir, where are you from?'

'London!' I shouted back, not wanting to complicate things.

'Not Crewe?' he replied, disappointed. I shook my head, slightly baffled, and we moved on.

I was relieved when the bus arrived in Taxila. I was going to have to change here to get to Rawalpindi, so thought I might as well have a look around.

For the first time, I was free to walk across the town at my own pace and take in the sights and smells of a Muslim country outside of the shackling constraints of Ramadan. At a roadside stall, for the only time in a month, I ate, unmolested and unafraid, in the bright light of day. It was wonderful and I felt free. Hot *chapattis*, fried beans and *dhal* were served to me on a small silver plate, which I devoured in no time at all, getting my fingers wet and sticky. I ordered a crispy lamb *samosa* and another *chapatti*, both delicious and a world away from the monotonous flat bread and sickly jam that I was used to.

The ruins of Taxila were heaving with local tourists; another new and strange sight. Large mobs of wealthy Pakistani families on a day trip from the suburbs of 'Pindi shuffled around the *stupas*, Buddhist mound-like monuments. They were wielding cheap video cameras brought down the Karakorum from China on the back of a jingly truck and were now recording scenes of domestic revelry, as smart boys stood side by side with their sisters in bright saris next to crumbling temples. There were a few foreigners, too. I heard the slow dialogue of a pair of men from Birmingham and looked up to find another family, indistinguishable from the locals I had just seen; a testament to the two countries' intertwined multiculturalism.

In fact, multiculturalism has long been a facet of Taxila. I took a rickshaw to the main excavations of Jaulian and Sirkap, where Mohammad, a bearded grave digger-turned-tour guide from a nearby village, told me the story of the ancient city.

'There are actually three ruined cities in Taxila,' said my guide. 'Hathial is maybe three thousand years old. It dates back to the Gandharan period, an ancient bronze age dynasty. We have found many pieces of pottery.' He pointed at a grassy hillock surrounded by what seemed to be dry-stone walls.

'Over here, we have Sirkap. This was the second city and was built by the Greco–Bactrians two thousand years ago. Amazing, isn't it?'

'Alexander's army?' I asked.

'Yes, to begin with, but their descendants stayed behind and many families didn't want go back to Greece at all. Look around, why would they?'

It was, I had to admit, an enchanting spot. It was late afternoon and pillars of dung-smoke rose from the villages that dotted the open plain. At the foot of a hill, below the olive groves, gristly black water buffaloes sat with their legs folded up beneath them chewing at the long grass. Above, there were parakeets among the branches and, as you walked between the ancient slabs, flights of grasshoppers exploded from beneath your feet. I looked out over the undeniably Asian landscape, astounded by what I was seeing.

'They founded a kingdom that intermarried with the locals and became Buddhists.' Mohammad pointed to the stone carvings at the temple, a grey granite *stupa* that had been scrubbed clean and preserved since its declaration as a UNESCO world heritage site. I looked at the statues – many of whom were missing heads, hacked off by unscrupulous tomb raiders – and expected to find the ever-enticing image of the Buddha in one of his many representations. But I was in for a shock. I did find Buddha, but instead of the bald, jolly oriental that one comes to expect after several forays into Thailand and Nepal, another figure looked back. It wore the carefully chiselled stone toga of a classical Greek and the bearded, proud facial features of a European.

At the Jaulian temple (named after the Roman governor Julian, who converted to Buddhism), ornate Ionic columns rose from the Punjabi plain. They were exact replicas of a style that would not be out of place in the Forum or the Parthenon: the ruins had porticoed and pedimented fronts. Classical halls, fonts, burial mounds – all were built in a style immediately recognisable as Classical Greek; yet these were Buddhist monuments, twenty miles from the Pakistani capital, and they dated from the early centuries of the Christian era, long after the demise of Classical civilisation in Europe.

The origins of these extraordinary pieces of rock date back to the autumn of 327 BC, when Alexander the Great swept into the Punjab at the head of his victorious Macedonian army. Intending to conquer even the most distant provinces of the ancient Persian empire, Alexander had crossed the Hindu Kush; and there, high on the Afghan plateau, he had first heard stories of the legendary riches of the Indian subcontinent – of its gold, said to be mined by enormous ants and watched over by griffins; of its men, who lived for two hundred years, and women who made love in public; of the Sciapods, a people who liked to recline in the shade cast by their one enormous foot; of the perfumes and silks, which the Afghans told the Greeks grew on the trees, and even in the cabbage patches of India; of the unicorns and the pygmies, of the elephants and falcons, and of the precious jewels that lay scattered on the ground like dust.

It was the end of the hot season, the beginning of the monsoon, and Alexander had arrived at the edge of the known world. Now he made up his mind to conquer the unknown world beyond. He defeated the Hindu Rajahs of Swat on the banks of the river Jhelum, and prepared to cross the last rivers of the Punjab and conquer the Indian plains. But on the swollen banks of the Beas River, Alexander was brought to a halt. His homesick soldiers refused to go on; the torrential monsoon rain had destroyed their spirits where everything else – countless battles, heat, starvation and disease – had failed. Alexander was forced to turn back, leaving a series of Greek garrisons behind to guard his conquests. On the return journey Alexander died, or was poisoned, in Babylon; his empire fractured into pieces.

In the anarchy that followed, the Greek garrisons of India and Afghanistan were cut off from their homeland. They had no choice but to stay on in Asia, intermingling with the local peoples, and joining Indian learning with Greek philosophy and classical ideas. Over the following thousand years, further cross-fertilisation occurred, as Central Asian influences were brought in by the conquering Kushans, an astounding civilisation that grew up in the fastness of the Chinese Karakorums and built the third and last of Taxila's cities, calling it Sirsukh.

These Scynthian-Greek-Chinese were Buddhist in religion, though they worshipped an extensive myriad of Zoroastrian, Greek, Roman, Hindu and Buddhist deities – Gandhara's principal icon being a meditating skinny Buddha draped in a Greek toga.

Although Alexander only stayed in Taxila for a matter of weeks, his visit changed the course of the region's history. The king of Taxila did not attempt to fight the Macedonian, instead offering him hospitality and food. It was to be a wise decision that resulted in millennia of stability and the creation of a unique culture in this far-flung mountain kingdom.

Visiting the museum at the entrance to the archaeological site, I wandered through the rooms looking at the Gandharan sculptures, some of which dated from nearly a thousand years after Alexander's death. The museum looked in a state of faded decay. Nothing was lit. Broken clay bowls, stone tools and rusted iron arrowheads filled dusty cabinets in the south wing. A plaster model of the site sat glumly in a glass box, with pieces of rough-cut moss taking the place of trees and hedgerows. Fragments from ancient dynasties were scattered in its gloom.

I searched the bearded Buddhas' faces for some undisclosed secret that the people outside had withheld. The Buddha, that defining symbol of Eastern-oriental philosophy, had undergone a process of Hellenisation: his grace and sensuality was thoroughly Indian, yet staring back at me from stolen plinths, the statues were all defined by occidental ideas of proportion and realism. They were wearing togas, the height of European fashion, and their faces were angular, bearded and severe; empires apart from the Buddhism of the east, and even further from the crafty modern-day Pakistanis that were outside trying to sell me fake coins, bronze statuettes and bits of pottery.

At least, I hoped the coins outside were fake. In one dim corner of the museum there was a collection of gold and silver coins that documented thousands of years of history. What was remarkable wasn't solely that the coins were all modelled on Greek originals. It was the names of the rulers: Menander of Kabul, Diomedes of the Punjab, and Pantaleon, King of the Himalayas. The coins showed the strange fusion of worlds that these kings inhabited. They brought East and West together at a time when the British were still running through prehistoric swamps dressed in bear skins. The coins of Heliochles of Balkh represented perfectly the crossbreed society: on one side they showed a Mediterranean profile, with a big nose and imperial arrogance, yet on the reverse the old king chose as his symbol the very Asian contours of a hump-backed Brahman bull.

'Sir, sir. There is one more thing you should see.' Outside, Mohammad led me past the tall hedgerows that flanked the museum to the car park, where a group of long-bearded locals were gathered.

Mohammad, my faithful guide, archaeologist and defender of the relics of Taxila, produced from the under-seat compartment of his friend's motorbike a parcel, carefully wrapped in a white cotton scarf.

'What is it?' I asked.

Mohammad unwrapped the cloth and handed me a beautifully chiselled head of a bodhisattva.

'Original Gandharan art, sir. Two thousand years old. It is yours for twenty dollars.'

'You're a criminal.' I shoved the priceless work back into his hand, told him that he wouldn't be getting his tip and stormed off to the train station in disgust.

I had hoped my outburst would have the effect of teaching these philistines a lesson, but as I walked away I heard the men giggling like school boys.

'Somebody else will buy it by the end of the day,' Mohammad shouted in my wake.

I arrived in Rawalpindi angry and determined to make a dash directly for Lahore. It is amazing how one bad experience lasting less than a minute can affect your plans so drastically. I had contemplated visiting the Karakorum, of seeing the famed natural splendour of Gilgit and Hunza in Kashmir, but because of a moment's disgust, I found myself speeding instead towards the Indian border in a conceited rage.

In the meantime, I made the error of ordering more *samosas* from an anonymous hand that had found a way to penetrate the open window of a moving train. I was hungry and ate them without a second thought, but literally within the space of five minutes I felt my stomach twist. Soon enough my belly was writhing in torment and the short stopover in Rawalpindi was only a taste of the squirming agony yet to come, as I clambered on board the Islamabad express bound for Lahore.

Anyone who has been ill on the subcontinent, and by that I mean the vast majority of travellers there, will know that trains are not a wonderful place to suffer from energetic innards. Granted they have toilets (or perhaps a hole in the floor), which may or may not be accessible, but there is no way to get off. At least on a bus you can lobby the driver with green-faced pleas or threats of a sullied disruption, but unless your train happens to be making a scheduled halt, or you risk undertaking an illicit exit, your fate is sealed.

I recalled being ill in the Sinai desert the year before and spending almost three days lying prone in bouts of alternating sweats and shivers in a miserable shack at forty-five degrees centigrade, followed by a six-hour bus journey to the nearest civilisation. Since then I have contracted dengue fever in Mexico, been treated for bilharzia in Malawi, subjected to a rabies injection in my face (after being bitten by a monkey) in Thailand, and been taken into hospital with suspected malaria from Tanzania; but I still remember that night on the train in Pakistan as being one of the worst in my life.

Beside me was a twitching mullah, whose beige robes were now stained and dirty after many days travelling from his village in Kashmir. He spluttered and spat black mucus onto the floor of the carriage by my feet and muttered to himself, all the while stroking his long, grey beard that was burnt at its extremities. He seemed miserable and complained about having to visit the city.

'... full of devils and djinns.'

His mood reflected mine and I tried to let myself be anaesthetised by his mumblings, but it didn't work. The foul smell of stale urine and dried sweat emanated from my neighbour. I felt awful and the jolting of the train only made things worse. There were no curtains on the windows, and outside, Pakistan was juddering by at an alarming rate.

It was four in the morning when I arrived at Lahore station and I was in no mood for banter with the rickshaw cyclists. My stomach cramps were now so desperate that I was forced to shit myself at the side of the road – much to the amusement of the pedal wallah. I only remember fleeting visions as we weaved through the smoggy night air to the Regal Chowk district in the heart of the city: a barking dog, a fingerless leper holding out a wretched stump, a dozing security guard, and piles of raw sewage in the road.

To make matters worse, the hostel was closed. A sign outside declared that it would be open at eight o'clock.

'Come, I will take you to my brother's hotel. A wonderful place. Many ladies, much boom boom. They will make you feel better, sir.'

'No, thank you.' I hauled my rucksack into the street, but didn't have the energy to lift it. The wallah shrugged his shoulders and chuckled to himself and drove off into the dim half-light of the bazaar. I banged on the gates in vain and thought back to the countless times it had happened before; how in Esfahan I had slept at a crowded bus stop to the bewilderment of onlooking commuters, and how in Estonia, Jon and I spent an uncomfortable night at the base of those castle walls after being chased out of a drug den.

I looked around. There were no people here, only scrawny cats and a few solitary mongrels patrolling the alleys in search of rats, of which I counted three, burrowing into the piles of rubbish that littered the road. The pavement was sticky with the remnants of the previous night's *Eid* festivities. Chicken's blood congealed with the remains of a goat's carcass and a pile of silver bunting had been trampled into the reeking gutter. The smell made me vomit into a pot hole. I wanted nothing more than to escape, and for the first time in four months of travelling, I would have given anything to teleport myself back to a nice cup of tea and a fireside armchair in England. Instead, I found myself lying down on the pavement, where I passed out into a feverish state of unconsciousness.

'Hey, mister. Wake up!'

I felt a gentle prod on my arm and sat up with a start. It was already light and the noise of a city in the morning filtered through the air. I looked up to see a young bearded traveller in a red T-shirt and jeans. He was grinning.

'Do you speak English?' I said, squinting in a semi–delirious state.

'Sure mister, why not? You look like you need a room.' Gregor helped me up the narrow stairway of the Regale Internet Inn, past a disorientated Japanese tourist.

'Malik's not here at the moment, but there's a spare mattress on the floor in our room, you can sleep there.'

I must have passed out as soon as I lay down, because the next thing I remember was waking up and looking out of the window to find that the sun had already set. I had been asleep for almost twelve hours straight. Down below, the bazaar was in full swing and where there had been rats and cadavers in the morning, there were bustling stalls selling vegetables and spices to a throng of Pakistanis. There was no one else in the dark room, but outside on the terrace was a steady stream of Japanese chatter. I looked at the bed next to my mattress and saw that Gregor, and whoever he was travelling with, had left. I hadn't even had a chance to thank him for picking me out of the street.

At first, I took an instant dislike to Malik — he looked like a gaunt vampire, with a sly look and pencil-thin moustache. His floppy hair was greying, and leathery skin was pulled tight across an enormous nose.

'Have some magic tea,' he said, handing me a glass of dark green *chai*. Flaky bits of mint floated around rapidly from where the proprietor had been stirring his potent mixture. 'You will feel much better.'

Malik took a long drag on his cigarette and asked if I was English.

I told him I was.

'I thought so,' he said wistfully at my reply. 'I have met *some* nice ones in my time.' *Here we go,* I thought.

But Malik was only trying to bait me; he didn't hold us in that much disregard, although I suspected that underneath his veneer of banter there was probably an element of animosity.

'I am forty-seven years old, I have been running this hostel for ten years. I have seen a great deal of change in this country – we are still trying to fix what mess you English caused over two hundred years.'

I rose to it.

'What mess? You wanted your independence. You wanted partition.'

He smiled, knowing that he'd got a victim. 'I'm not talking about partition, young man. I'm talking about these tribes – the Pathans. They have always been the problem. It was you who created the tribal areas and you who encouraged their savage lawlessness. The English wanted the frontier to be wild, so that the Russians wouldn't try and come into Afghanistan.'

He looked at me down his nose, his forehead seemed to slope away into oblivion.

'And see what has happened. The tribes are rising again. The Taliban, Osama Bin Laden, all of them are the result of your British recklessness. Mark my words, Pakistan will feel the effects of this new war. As we speak, the Taliban – as you know them – are gathering in the countryside and the cities, waiting and watching. They will recruit from the schools and the *madrassahs* until they have an army of jihadists and then . . .'

He broke off as a youngster entered the terrace and brought more tea. Malik smiled.

'But don't mind me. I'm just an old journalist who can't give up his bad habits.'

He took another sip from the delicate glass thimble before asking me how I had enjoyed India.

'I don't know, I haven't got there yet,' I replied, knowing full well what his next question would be.

'Well, anyway, where have you come from?'

I told him that I was travelling overland and that I had come from Afghanistan.

'*Allahu Akbar.* On my father's grave, I salute you. What were you doing amongst those beasts? No, no, you must be tired of answering those questions. No wonder you are ill. I shall let you off our debates this evening, Englishman.'

He sighed and then continued, 'I'm afraid that you will be disturbed tonight. We have a group of musicians playing in half an hour.'

'That's fine, I'm actually feeling much better,' I said, honestly.

'I told you. It's the magic tea.' He smiled.

Lahore is Pakistan's second city and has been known to travellers for thousands of years. It reached its true zenith when the Mughals gave the city its finest architecture, the impressive fort and the Badshahi Mosque. When Mughal power waned in the eighteenth century, Lahore succumbed to several invasions – firstly by the Afghans, and then by the Sikh ruler Ranjit Singh, who went on to establish the city as his capital. It wasn't long before they were defeated by the British and incorporated into the army of the British East India Company. By the early twentieth century, Lahore was a feature of the emerging Indian independence movement – it was here that the All India Muslim League demanded the creation of two nations, an Islamic Pakistan and a Hindu India. It seemed always destined to be on the fault lines of this turbulent road.

I was determined to see something of Lahore, as I felt that I had missed out on much of Pakistan. This would be my final city of the Islamic world – and the only one I would see in a state of normality outside of Ramazan.

I skirted the vegetable bazaar, dodging the dung fires and relentless traffic; cycle rickshaws, horse-drawn tongas, Suzukis and towering painted trucks. The drivers were bent on killing each other and drove on whichever side of the road they pleased, rickshaws weaving in and out causing a constant menace to pedestrians. It was as if every driver was a novice, acting like a seventeen-year-old who had just passed his test and was determined to show off. I thought how if they drove like this in England, they would end up on the sharp end of First World road rage. But there was no violence here, everyone simply accepted, even embraced the chaos.

Along Lahore's most famous road, The Mall, chicken tikka cooked over fire pits, with whole birds skewered on an iron cage above a clay pot, the coals burning bright red and black. Nearby little plates of rice with black bean curry steamed, and the spices filled the nostrils. I turned down Cinema Road in search of a way out of the madness, but there seemed no escape. Hotels looked abandoned, shops half empty; enormous billboards were painted with Bollywood movie stars, heroes and villains stared down at the madding crowds. Only when I gave up the quest to escape did I stumble amongst the side streets of the bazaar and discovered a quiet little courtyard, where old men reclined on bed frames strung with rope, sipping *chai* with their friends.

An optician's shop displayed a banner offering 'novelty spectacles'. Painted wooden signs hung above the curb; drawings of maligned teeth displayed above a row of small dentistry shops. Their tools in the window sent a shiver down my spine. This was the Southern Silk Road – or the modern equivalent: moustachioed shopkeepers shouted their wares, from leather belts imported down the Karakorum to glass bangles recycled from the rubbish tips of Delhi, and saris made from the finest threads all the way from Beijing.

In the new town, modern mixed with ancient and amongst the donkey carts and rickshaws were suit-wearing businessmen carrying briefcases and talking into mobile phones, whilst queuing to get a burger from the newly built McDonalds.

'Hallo, all right my friend?' I heard a voice say.

I turned around to see a light-skinned young Pakistani.

'Would you like to come to see some dancing?' he said.

Youish was a nineteen-year-old Kalasha tribesman, who worked in the hostel as a general handyman. I'd noticed him when I was chatting to Malik and it turned out he was supposed to be out buying some supplies for the kitchen, but was bored and wanted some entertainment.

'Yes, why not,' I said. Youish led me back through the bazaar and then beyond, following little lanes through the suburbs, where after half an hour we found a courtyard that surrounded an ancient shrine.

Some of the other travellers from the hostel were already there, waiting outside on some waste ground: Fran, a Swiss lady travelling alone; Mark, an Australian overlander; Sato, a bewildered Japanese; Jan, a frantic Belgium cyclist; and Leander, the most laid-back German I had ever met. They were chatting between themselves quietly as crowds of Pakistanis ushered in from the lanes and converged in the open courtyard.

Every Thursday something strange happens in Lahore. Just as in Europe a Friday night is devoted to hedonistic revelry and the start of the weekend, a similar phenomenon occurs on a Thursday night for one particular mystical group of Muslims.

Pakistani Sufis from all walks of life gather from across the city to the shrine of Baba Shah Jamal in the Ichhra district of Lahore. As the sun set behind a skyline of minarets, domes and unfinished red-brick shanty dwellings, Malik appeared out of nowhere.

'Youish,' he frowned. 'You are meant to be shopping.'

'Please, sir, let me come,' he begged the master.

Malik shrugged.

'OK, let us show our guests what "Sufi night" is all about. It is like nothing you have ever seen,' professed the bony hotelier. 'You might feel a bit nervous at first, but don't worry, you won't come to any harm.' He patted Fran on the shoulder.

Crowds of people lined the dark alleys that led from the car park, selling drinks and snacks to the local men pouring in and out of the shrine. Contingents of rickshaws, horse-drawn carriages, motorbikes and donkeys arrived by the dozen. Men greeted each other with long handshakes and warm embraces.

Apart from Fran, there wasn't a woman to be seen. I soon realised that this was no show put on for the tourists.

Youish hurried us along up a flight of stairs to the upper outdoor courtyard, where the display was to begin. Below us was the graveyard itself, where the shrine and tombs were laid out among the gardens. We were pushed right to the front of the crowds that sat and squatted on the floor.

The scene was set with incense burning around two graves. Decorations, red, green and silver bunting and flags hung from every nook, and trellises were linked with dangling ribbons and aromatic candles. There were people everywhere, every inch of space was filled; there were literally hundreds of men and a few children, who were hanging like monkeys from the gnarled branches of a tree that seemed to sprout from the middle of the quadrangle, its branches winding around the inside of the walls like a twisted serpent.

Just as I thought it was impossible to cram anyone else onto the floor, another immense crowd poured out of the stairwell, pushing their way through the multitude, and somehow managing to squeeze themselves into a tiny hole in the swarm. The place reminded me of a rock concert – hundreds of scruffy, long-haired locals shaking their heads to the rhythm of a singer who had just appeared, and then I realised why everyone was so passive.

'Is that what I think it is?' I took a sniff and looked at Youish.

He just smiled. A haze of marijuana hung thick in the air. Almost everyone was smoking it. A man next to me appeared to be the chief pyrotechnic in his group and took wild delight in suddenly igniting five joints in one go. Flames soared upward as the dry leaves caught fire and then the man took an enormous drag and a pentagon of red embers danced in front of me as he handed them out, before blowing a column of thick blue smoke upwards.

The singers became apparent now and I looked at the small arena to find two heavily bearded men singing a *Qawwali* song of devotion. Their eyes were closed and they seemed to be in a trance. I looked around and saw that so were most of the audience, many of whom had begun to chant to themselves and shake their heads from side to side in wild abandon.

As they sang, vendors made the perilous journey back and forth through the crowd selling juice or snacks. They seemed to float above the crowds. Suddenly the singer began to scream an unintelligible mantra that lasted for a solid minute, which only seemed to encourage the mélange of violent head-shaking and mumbled chanting.

But the crowd was getting impatient, they were waiting expectantly for the main event. And as they sensed it was time for a change, two men appeared from the dark recesses of the shrine and began to beat their drums to the rhythm of the singers. It was artfully choreographed, because I barely noticed the changeover, and the singers faded away like a skilfully mixed radio track. The beat of the drum grew harder and faster now and I took a moment to look at the artists.

Both men were traditionally dressed as they stood stone still on the rug, the only movement was the rapid flicking of their wrists, pounding curved wooden sticks against the stretched hide. The man on the left was a skinny boy of twenty called Mithu, said Youish. He wore a plain salwar kameez, but his drum was ornate and colourful, painted with flowers and red lanyards. To his right was a more alluring figure, a dark-skinned muscular giant with long, tightly curled, fierce black hair.

'That,' Youish shouted in my ear, 'is the famous Gonga Saeed. They are brothers.'

'They don't look anything alike,' I replied.

'Well, the Sufis often have many wives,' Youish grinned with a devilish wink. 'Gonga Saeed is the best *dhol* (barrel drum) player in the world.'

Now, I hadn't seen that many *dhol* players in my time, but I could hardly disagree. The man was incredible; he kept the time perfectly, watching his younger brother intently, and would sometimes break into flourishes of breakneck speed and delicacy.

'He is also deaf,' said Youish, following the rhythm by tapping his knees with his thumb.

'What? You are telling me that the greatest *dhol* player in the world is deaf?'

'Yes, sir. He was born deaf, but as a child his father – also a great *dhol* player – taught him to play by beating him across the head with his rhythm stick.'

'Across the head . . .'

My only knowledge of Sufism was of the whirling Dervishes of Istanbul. Malik explained to us above the din that Sufism was not a distinct sect of Islam, rather an inner meaning; a mystical dimension within the human understanding of God.

Gonga continued with a faint thumping of his barrel drum, softly at first, but the rhythm soon got faster and harder and more complex. Before long, hundreds of heads were shaking and screams of pleasure came furiously from the crowd. The chanting would resume amidst the banging and go on for several minutes. The deaf drummer kept the tempo with perfect precision and led his followers into submission.

'The practitioners are seekers looking for a deeper immersion than the normal, traditional methods of submission to Allah,' Malik bellowed.

'Unbelievers think that it is just crazy spinning around,' said

Malik, 'but really it is their way of expressing their love and devotion to God.'

The crowd went wild and I suddenly remembered my dream on that cold December night back in Nottingham and smiled to myself in a state of perfect satisfaction. More joints were passed around and then the beat grew faster and faster. Four or five of the crowd sprung to their feet like exploding grasshoppers and began to spin around. They whirled and whirled; one jumped up like a rocket, his long hair flailing uncontrollably, throwing great beads of sweat in every direction. Others shook their whole bodies as if overtaken with dementia.

Across the floor I saw an incredibly fat man sitting cross-legged with a ridiculous grin across his face and his eyes rolled back in total rapture. He flicked his hands as though he were conducting an orchestra. An hour and another passed and it was well past midnight before I knew it. Several men began to dance; there was no coordination, purely free-spirited abandon. Some were stomping their feet, others leaping around the floor and others spinning around like madmen.

Gonga took centre stage and – without missing a beat – began to spin. He spun around and around, but didn't move an inch from his axis; his long black hair became horizontal and his drumming got faster and faster. He kept it up for thirty minutes – I found it unbelievable that he was still conscious. Perhaps he wasn't. I saw the other travellers; Sato stared in silence, Leander smoked and beamed, Fran smiled nervously, Jan was shaking his head as good as any of the locals, Mark looked on in awe.

'This is freaking awesome.'

We were hot, we were sweaty and squashed, everyone was exhausted, but we were mesmerised.

'It is time to go now,' said Youish reluctantly. 'Things get very messy later on.' It was one in the morning, and the crowd was reaching new levels of spiritual intoxication. I hadn't touched any of the marijuana, save that which was floating already through the air, but that night, I slept better than I had done in weeks.

The twin wonders of Lahore rise out of the city like magnificent jewels. The Badshahi Mosque and Lahore Fort face each other across the peaceful greenery of the Hazuri Bagh gardens and I was torn between which to visit first. I stood admiring the monuments amongst families of Pakistani picnickers and throngs of pilgrims come to see the tomb of Allama Muhammad Iqbal, their national poet.

The wail of the muezzin sounded from the loudspeakers. Friday prayers had begun, and so in deference and curiosity I made my way into the vast mosque built by the Mughals. It is incredible to imagine that what was the largest mosque in the world until 1986 was completed in only two years. It can accommodate over one hundred thousand worshippers, including over five thousand in the main prayer hall alone. To appreciate its size, you need to imagine that the whole of the Taj Mahal could fit easily into the courtyard of the Badshahi. Standing at the entrance gate, I looked across the seemingly endless marble floor to the other side, where vast pink arches rose like flames and I could barely make out the streams of ant-like devotees.

Lahore Fort, which was built a hundred years before the mosque by Akhbar the Great, is equally impressive. It was established by the Mughal emperor on the site of a mud castle that had stood for centuries to protect the city against Afghan invaders. Since then, the fortress has often served – alongside Delhi – as the capital of successive empires that spanned the subcontinent. Each consecutive ruler added to the grandiose design by adding a palace or a new gate. (At present, there are thirteen.) As a result of the multiple extensions, Lahore Fort is considered the world's best-kept example of the whole span of Mughal architecture throughout the ages.

No visit to Lahore, of course, would be complete until you have seen the Zamzama Gun, more famously known as Kim's Gun, after Kipling's child hero. As I stood next to the immense weapon, I felt as though I had already seen it a thousand times and imagined myself as the boy spy sitting under its eminent shade, watching the daily peculiarities of the Raj. The fourteen-foot-long cannon that points down The Mall was cast in 1757 by Shah Nazir during the reign of the Afghan conqueror Ahmad Shah Durrani, to assist in his battles against the Indian Marathi Empire. It was the biggest gun ever made in Asia and was funded by the people of Lahore, who were asked to donate their metallic kitchenware, which could be smelted down into brass and copper to cast the massive weapon.

Zamzama was subsequently used for almost sixty years in successive campaigns and changed hands between the Durranis, Sikhs and Pashtuns several times. But despite its illustrious background, it was Rudyard Kipling who immortalised the gun for posterity by using it as the introductory backdrop for *Kim*, his most emotive work. It wasn't surprising, really, considering that his own father was the first curator of the museum and that the young Rudyard used to play nearby the cannon in his own childhood.

I had been in Lahore for almost a week, and although I was

enjoying the company of fellow travellers and the bewildering allure of the crescented domes, I still felt an air of repression and limitation of spirit. With the exception of what I had witnessed at the Shrine of Baba Shah Jamal, Pakistan was still very much an Islamic state, where religious mores permeated every aspect of society. Poverty was rife and corruption endemic. The people, for the most part friendly and benign, still suppressed a lingering jealousy of Western freedom and wealth, which seemed to clash in an odd way with the natural pride in the Pakistani spirit, producing a bitter taste. Moreover, India – my ultimate goal – was only fifteen miles distant, and when the place you long for more than any other is so close, it gets hard to become attached to anywhere else. It was time to move on, but before leaving, Mark insisted there was one last place that we had to visit.

'But sir, you simply cannot go to Heera Mandi,' said Youish, as he brought some *chai* from the kitchen. 'It is very dangerous.'

'Come on, Youish, you must have been before?' pleaded Mark.

'Oh yes, I have, sir, but I don't like to take good people, you will get the wrong impression of us.'

'That's settled then. We're going.'

Youish looked embarrassed, but reluctantly agreed to take us window-shopping around Heera Mandi, Lahore's infamous red-light district.

Sato, Leander and Jan squeezed into the back seat of a cycle rickshaw.

'He'll never be able to carry our weight,' said the Belgian, speaking of the poor pedal wallah, who could barely push down on his overburdened stirrups.

'Oh no, sir, he can take six men if he wants to, it is his job!' I looked at the red-faced cyclist doubtfully and clambered into a different one. With a mere three grown men in the back of each 'carriage', Messrs Mohammed and Mohammed raced each other through the heaving streets of the bazaar, dodging cars, donkeys, herds of sheep and throngs of Pakistanis with every manner of burden on their heads – from televisions and wardrobes to the decapitated heads of buffaloes, recently slaughtered. A real concern, more perhaps than the prospect of a messy collision with beefy livestock, was the all-pervading threat from low-hanging live wiring. It was everywhere – dangling like vicious snakes from every lamppost and windowsill, ready to electrocute unwary passengers like ourselves at every turn.

Fortunately, we made it through the old city to the notorious district where, in a bid to avert Mark's fascination with the more seedy aspects of the Pakistani underbelly, Youish proudly showed us an outdoor soup kitchen, where bearded philanthropists dished out food to the city's beggars. Nearby were the 'ten rupee stalls', which were exactly that: market stalls where all manner of useless knick-knacks were flogged for the price of a plate of rice. Youish gave us all some betel nut, a mild stimulant that almost every male in Pakistan chewed relentlessly, leaving a trail of foul red spittle across the pavements.

'Very good, no? Makes you a very strong man and good husband!' Youish winked conspiratorially. It simply gave me a headache.

But Mark insisted that we see some women. He assured us that it was for mere academic research purposes, but given the fact that apart from Fran, none of us had seen a girl in weeks, we couldn't resist the sense of curiosity and taboo of at least wandering down the dark back alleys of the district to see what on earth went on behind the veneer of an Islamic republic. Either way, Heera Mandi was a disappointment. It was hardly Amsterdam, at any rate. There were a few downcast prostitutes that lingered in the doorways of a medieval-style side street, with wooden doors and carved window frames, but they were all so heavily made up that they looked like ugly drag queens. Maybe they were; I wasn't waiting to find out.

'Let's get out of here,' I suggested to Youish. 'None of us really want to be here anyway.'

It was all pretty disgusting and even Mark was in agreement. Once we'd seen the melancholy of the poor girls, it was hard to view it as a spectacle. It was all a bit sad. As we left the street to get back onto the main bazaar street, a police pickup truck screeched around the corner and seven or eight officers jumped off the back and ran in our direction.

'Oh shit,' whispered Mark. The realisation set in immediately that we could be in serious trouble. All of us had heard the stories of police brutality, life sentences and even torture in Pakistani jails.

Youish froze and indicated for us to do the same. Luckily the police ran straight past us and barged into one or two of the brothels. I saw one Pakistani man get dragged out into the street in a state of severe undress and then bundled onto the vehicle. The police chief, who had remained standing next to the truck, gave us a friendly *salaam* as we walked past sheepishly.

'What are you looking for?' he asked, with the assumed nonchalance of a practised rogue.

'We got lost looking for the mosque,' said Sato, the diminutive Japanese. They were the only words I ever heard him say.

17

The Golden Temple

I hitched a lift in a minibus heading to my last border crossing, hardly believing that I was almost in India. It felt surreal and magical, after all this time and somewhere in the region of nine thousand miles overland, that I was actually here. Birds chattered in the trees and goats waddled along the roadside and in the distance was the small village of Wagah, my final frontier.

Wagah, which lies halfway between Lahore and Amritsar, straddles the dividing line between the two new nations; it is the only official border between India and Pakistan and it remains a remarkable frontier. By the time I had hitched out of Lahore to the border, it was late afternoon and the smell of dung smoke lay thick in the air. The moon had risen above the Punjabi plain and sat facing the heavy globe of the late Indian sun. The Pakistani authorities thanked me for my visit and wished me a safe passage through India. Outside the immigration office, a few entrepreneurial money changers offered to sell me Indian rupees 'for a very small commission, sir'. With a stamp in my passport and a singing heart, I crossed the threshold underneath a sign that welcomed me to the world's largest democracy.

'Do you have any contraband?' asked a particularly hairy Indian customs officer, with a broad grin.

'Like what?' I asked, suddenly remembering that I'd stuffed the antique Lee Enfield bayonet down the back of my bag, which was intended as a present for my father.

He flashed his teeth. 'Whisky?' he breathed closely, looking around as he whispered in my ear. I shook my head and explained that the Russians took it all, which only gained me a quizzical frown.

'Never mind. You can buy whisky here,' continued the man in the huge blue turban. 'I just wanted to see if you had any for me, that's all. I suppose you haven't had any good whisky in a while coming from Pakistan. You must be very fed up of the Pakis, eh?'

I just smiled, and put his racism down to neighbourly rivalry. He shoved my backpack towards me and nodded that I could go.

'Welcome to India, the biggest democracy in the world.' He repeated the slogan automatically, as though it were a line rehearsed for foreign tour groups. But as I looked around, I realised that I was the only foreigner crossing; in fact, I was the only person crossing. Apart from a few porters carrying goods to and from their counterparts on either side of no-man's-land, the crowds of people weren't here to cross the border – merely to see it. Outside I took a moment to savour the atmosphere as I stepped onto Indian soil. I turned around to see the huge green gates painted with the white crescent of Pakistan and took a final parting glimpse of the realm of Islam that I had traversed.

'Sir, please do follow me, you are late for the show.'

'The show?'

'Oh yes, sir, the lowering of the flags, it is about to begin.'

Ranjit took me by the arm and rushed me through the throng of daily visitors to an enormous grandstand on the southern side of the grand trunk road, beyond the Indian customs building.

The small Punjabi Sikh wore round glasses and a cream-coloured shirt that reached his knees. He led me to a reserved seat behind the 'VIP' area about halfway up the stand, from where I could look across the road and back into Pakistan, where a similar stadium had been erected.

'My father studied at Lahore University,' said Ranjit. 'He used to talk so fondly of the place, but of course, after 'forty-seven he never went back.'

He looked across the border with a sense of wishful longing and I noticed a melancholic look in his eyes.

'Do you come here often?' I asked the rather pointless question, more to avoid the awkward silence than any other reason.

'Oh yes, sir. I live in a village to the north of Amritsar, but sometimes I come here to look at my father's country. He has told me about Lahore so many times, I feel like I know the place already, but it is very sad – I will never be able to see it with my own eyes. What I would give to see the Anarkali bazaar – tell me – is it wonderful?'

I told him it was a bit rough round the edges, but was interesting to visit.

Only a tall metal fence separated eight thousand Indian spectators from about half as many Pakistanis, who had begun to wave immense green flags and shout friendly abuse across the Radcliffe divide. At least it wasn't bullets. In fact, there was something of a carnival repartee about the place, and as I sat down, most of the seats were already taken by rowdy Indian families returning the insults with even fiercer banter. A loudspeaker was blaring droning religious chants, much to the delight of the Pakistanis, who contributed their chorus of *Allahu Akbar* at every opportunity.

As if to extinguish the Muslims' religious zeal, the Indians started up their own music – ear-bursting Hindi pop songs, which after weeks spent in the subdued Islamic world sounded outrageously wicked and secular to me. The Pakistanis began to shout in a heroic chorus from their paddock; the Indians replied, singing with growing abandon. They were jumping and dancing and beat the Pakistanis hands down for sheer weight of volume.

Suddenly there was a piercing scream and everyone was hushing each other to silence. An Indian sergeant major marched out into the middle of the road, right in front of where I was sitting, and faced the crowds. It was his voice that had caused the high-pitched screech, but now he began to bark incoherent orders that had the Pakistanis in hysterics. The sergeant major took no notice; he was the main attraction at this show and had the look of supreme arrogance on his face. He completed a ridiculous about-turn, spinning like a penny on the spot to face his platoon.

All the Indian soldiers of the Border Security Force were dressed outrageously in khaki dress uniforms adorned with red and gold neckerchiefs, sashes and medals, and bright white puttees. On their heads, they wore black hats with enormous fan-like crests sprouting from them to create the impression of a mating cockerel. The sergeant major – to complete the caricature – sported the most magnificent moustache I have ever seen; a twelve-inch twisting *Rajasthani* that threatened to conceal the greater part of his face.

His orders resounded round the stadiums, in spite of the Pakistani crowd's best efforts to shout above him. On the far side of the gate, the Pakistan Rangers were dressed in a similar fashion, although their uniform and crest was all black, except a red sash. A pair of soldiers from each side started to goose step towards the gate, slamming their steel-tipped drill boots into the concrete to create a resounding clatter. All of them were immense individuals, probably nearing seven feet tall with cockerel fans taken into account.

The Pakistanis both swung their arms with such a ridiculous swagger that the crowds broke into roars of adoration and waves of cheering rose from the masses. The Indians fought back with a swift about-turn and flick of their wrists, and what could only be described as a wiggle of their backsides. More shouts from the sergeant major and the Indians were dancing again. Another pair of soldiers took centre stage and continued the oddly bellicose performance, finishing face to face with their international counterparts.

It seemed that in this spectacle of frontier diplomacy, the victory was in the detail – who could slam their feet the hardest, raise their legs the highest or shout their commands the loudest, but in one part of the ceremony it seemed that cooperation was key. A soldier from each army took their position at the foot of their flagpoles and unwound the cord before lowering their respective country's colours. This was done with remarkable precision, so that they were lowered at exactly the same time, neither wishing to create an international incident over such a trifle.

As the flags reached the bottom, they were snatched out of their neighbour's reach with a peevish rapidity, before the highest-ranking soldiers conceded the briefest of salutes and a momentary handshake to conclude proceedings. With their backs turned to each other, the double gates were slammed shut with a vicious clang and the soldiers marched off with their heads held high. Their job was done until the whole spectacle repeated itself the next evening, as it has every night without fail since 1959.

It took some time to make my way through the crowd, since many of them wanted to get to the gates and take a photograph through the iron bars of the country next door – a place that almost none had ever been allowed to visit. The Pakistanis tried to do the same, but the border guards were stricter there and ushered the audience away from their neighbour's advances. I wondered at how it must feel for either side to look through the painted railings at their foes and see, if only very briefly, another human being, not so different from themselves.

It was almost dark and the happy mob, satisfied with their victory, dispersed back to their cars and minibuses. For many it would be a trip of a lifetime, as close to Pakistan as they would ever get. Ranjit offered to give me a lift into Amritsar.

'I thought you lived in the countryside.'

'Oh, but I do, sir,' he said with a fantastic head wobble. 'But how can I let you come to India from Pakistan and not make you feel welcome? It would be a terrible crime to my country, sir.'

We trundled slowly through the evening half-light in Ranjit's yellow and black Ambassador, India's iconic car, with the dying redness of the sun giving a surreal glow to the green lushness of the surrounding countryside. I had truly reached the plains of India, which seemed to me like a heavenly apparition after the cold wintry gloom of Russia and the Caucasus, and the lonely, barren deserts and mountains of Iran and Afghanistan.

Here, leathery buffalo and the distinctive hump-backed Brahman cows grazed lazily in the fields, whilst dark-skinned women dressed wonderfully in colourful saris finished off their day's labour. Palm trees and gnarled Indian oaks sprouted from the roadside, where painted Hindu shrines offered prayers to a thousand gods. One-legged beggars and smart Sikhs with tremendous beards sat at the roadside watching, as cars swerved to avoid roaming holy cows, donkeys and the occasional monkey preening itself on a branch before bed.

Ranjit left me at the side of the road outside of the bazaar. I asked him which way it was to the Golden Temple, to which he replied, in a way that I found flattering and bewildering in equal measures, 'In India, sir, you may never be lost. Follow first your nose, and if that doesn't work, then follow your heart. Whatever you do, never follow your head – it will only get confused.'

I wandered through the dark but bustling streets and at first found it hard to ignore the constant pleas of the beggars and rickshaw wallahs, but I was content to walk for a while. I wasn't disappointed. It was filthy and overcrowded in a way that made Pakistani cities look sterile, but what it lacked in hygiene, it made up in sheer abundance of character.

I wanted to find one of India's most iconic and holy places – the spiritual heart of Sikhdom. in 1805, after the Sikh ruler Ranjit Singh had consolidated his kingdom in the Punjab, he declared himself a Maharaja and decided to take on Amritsar. It was an act of pride. Singh saw Amritsar, with the local Hindu chiefs who owned the famous Zamzama gun, as the last uncon-quered bastion in his new Sikh Empire. It took him a further fifteen years to fully gain domination, but by the early 1820s, he had conquered the city and built massive walls and a moat around it. Amritsar became his second capital, after Lahore, and he provided ample funding for the construction of the city's many palaces and domes, the most famous of which was the gold-plated Sri Harmandir Sahib that became known forever after as the Golden Temple.

Ranjit was right, the temple wasn't difficult to find; every-body seemed drawn to it like a magnet. Rising from the madness of the night bazaar, I saw the bright white, domed clock tower of Ghanta Ghar Deori looming above the perimeter wall that marked the entranceway to the famous shrine.

The whole place was lit up with glowing bulbs and fairy lights and in-between the arches and porticoes, small orange flags fluttered to give the sense of having arrived in the midst of a festival.

'Can I come in?' I asked a colossal Sikh guard, who was draped in a long orange robe and wore a deep blue turban on his head. In his belt was a traditional curved dagger and in his hand was a long wooden spear, tipped with ten inches of steel.

'Of course you can come in,' said the guard, almost offended that I had needed to ask, raising his hand in salute. I left my shoes in a huge box on the steps and found myself in the massive enclosure that surrounds the holy lake. I was met by Mohander, a slender youngster of seventeen, who was in charge of looking after foreign visitors.

'Anyone can come in here,' the boy explained. 'Foreigners are very welcome.'

'Even non-Sikhs?' I asked.

'Why, of course. Ours is a very open religion, you can stay if you like?'

I wasn't expecting to be offered a bed, but it seemed that Sikh hospitality was a rival to the Afghan's code of generosity. Mohander led me past the enticing view of the holy shrine, through a gate into a large open courtyard. It had the appearance of a kind of caravanserai, similar in many ways to a Turkish *han*; the precursors to the Silk Road hotels. This one had three storeys of arched porticoes flanking three sides of the courtyard, in the middle of which was a round public ablution block, where women in brightly coloured saris flocked to drink from the complimentary water, like flamingos in a Serengeti watering hole.

Inside each of the whitewashed arches was a wooden door that led into the bedrooms. These had mainly been reserved for

'rich Sikhs', said Mohander, although they didn't seem particularly luxurious from the quick glimpse I was allowed. The more
economical pilgrims, it appeared, were simply bedding down
wherever they could find a space on the floor of the yard, and I
picked my way through the multitude of sleeping devotees,
trying to keep up with my guide. Being a tourist, I was led to a
special dormitory reserved for foreigners, which contained three
beds, all of which were empty. The room was spartan but clean
enough, although the paint was peeling and the bedside table
looked like it harboured more than one fearsome cockroach.

'You are our only *Gora Inglandi* today, *sahib,*' said Mohander,
using the traditional Indian expression for a white-skinned
Englishman. 'Normally we have many. Did you know the
Golden Temple attracts more visitors than the Taj Mahal?'

'All the more room for me, I suppose.'

'It is the Sikh custom to allow pilgrims to sleep as our guests
inside the *gurdwara* (temple), but only for three nights. You are
free to walk amongst the beautiful grounds and enjoy our food,
our only rules are that you may not drink alcohol, eat meat or
smoke inside the temple. Meals are served at every hour, just
join the queue, but be prepared to sit on the floor, we do not
make exceptions.'

'Of course,' I said.

I dropped my bag on the squeaky mattress; there was no lock
on the door, but Mohander assured me that no one would dare
to steal in such a holy place – especially not from a foreigner. I
was about to submerge myself into the heaving tide of humanity
that was in various states of consciousness and undress outside of
the dormitory door, when Mohander came running to me from
his 'office' – an old wooden desk, the kind found in Victorian
schools, complete with inkwell and hinged opening.

'*Sahib*, please don't forget your headwear.' He thrust a bright orange bandanna into my hand, before bowing gracefully and darting off back to his administrative chores.

Looking like a doubtful pirate, I went to explore the Golden Temple.

There are entrances on all four sides of the temple, quite unlike the bottleneck security gates of Mashhad, or even the tiny entrance doors to any Christian church. Immediately the place feels welcoming to people of all faiths. The internal walls are filled with hundreds of shrines to past gurus, saints and martyrs. But there was one similarity to a Christian church and that was the hundreds of memorial plaques lining the walls, dedicated to great patrons, significant donors, as well as the thousands of Sikh soldiers who died fighting for the British Empire in the two world wars.

There are even trees inside the ground – each one dedicated to saints or holy events. On the opposite side to the main entrance is a museum dedicated to the Sikh faith. In the middle of the quadrant is the holy pool itself which is over 150 metres wide, and in the centre, rising like a glimmering jewel, is the gold-plated pavilion, the holiest of the holies for Sikhs around the world – an architectural masterpiece completed in 1604. Now I realised why the place was so busy – it was the anniversary of its completion and a grand celebration was underway, in conjunction with the several other Sikh holy days that happened to coincide at the end of November.

The temple was originally built in 1574 on an island in a small lake in the middle of a forest. When the Mughal emperor Akbar the Great visited the village to meet the Sikh Guru Amar Das, he was so impressed by the shrine that he granted it as a marriage gift to the Guru's daughter Bhani, on her marriage to Bhai Jetha, who later became the fourth Sikh Guru Ram Das. He, in turn, enlarged the lake and built a town around it. A few years later, in the last decades of the sixteenth century, a fully fledged temple was constructed on the site.

In December 1588, the great Muslim Sufi Saint of Lahore, Hazrat Mian Mir, was asked to lay the corner stone. Legend has it that a pedantic mason then straightened the stone because it was uneven, and received the personal admonishment of the fifth Guru Arjan, who stated that the man had undone the work of a holy man and who knows what disaster would befall the temple in the future. Future generations reason that the shrine's tendency to be attacked may be attributed to the unfortunate mason, and indeed the Harmandir Sahib has witnessed several bloody assaults by Mughals, Afghans and even the Indians themselves in the infamous 1984 battle.

Thousands of Sikhs, male and female, packed the walkways. Some were performing their ablutions, the ritualistic as well as practical washing of the feet before they entered the shrine. Others prayed, and some swam in the waters of the pool. Old men wearing only their turban and a loincloth dipped themselves into the limpid waters as tranquil hymns rolled across the waves.

I joined the throng of pilgrims crossing the two-hundred-yard causeway that leads across the water to the shrine. The glimmering masterpiece appeared to float on the waves as it grew nearer. The queue to get inside the Harmandir Sahib was long, but it kept moving as the faithful pilgrims touched the shrine with humble veneration, before dutifully moving on past the scripture readers.

The stream of believers and the singing of hymns by the holy men ensured a mood of serenity inside. But the canopy suspended over the holy book was coloured a garish pink and fringed like a bedcover, giving the impression that Sikh aesthetics are not what they once were.

I looked up to see that some restoration work was going on. Nishkam Singh, one of the temple's custodians, told me that the whole complex was being renovated.

'For almost ten years, people have been working on the temple, but it is taking a long time.'

'Why? Surely you must get a lot of money.' I imagined that an architectural masterpiece such as this would receive a great deal of government grants and international support.

Nishkam just laughed. 'All the work is done by volunteers, even this,' he pointed to the copper plates that held the temple together. 'All of the gold leaf encrusting is done by untrained and unpaid amateurs. Many of them are foreigners and have no understanding of our heritage. Every year it looks worse and worse. So vulgar.'

'Foreigners?'

'Yes, expatriate Sikhs, in fact many are from England – your city of Birmingham.' Nishkam looked melancholic. 'But they don't know any traditional skills and are destroying the temple from the inside. Nobody has any control over them.'

'What about the temple authorities?'

'They don't do anything to stop them. Just last year, do you know what they did to the Gurdwara Baba Atal?'

He pointed across the lake to a two-hundred-year-old, nine-storey octagonal tower that rose up from beyond the southern corner of the complex.

'They scraped off the beautiful frescoes and covered it in plaster and green bathroom tiles. It's a bloody disgrace.' The Akal Takht is the other holy spot in the complex, the building to which the holy book, the Granth Sahib, is ritually carried every day. The original structure, a delicate white-brick pavilion, was blown apart by Indian army artillery in 1984, during Operation Blue Star, when Indira Gandhi demanded that the Sikh separatists who had seized it should be killed. The resultant damage was irreversible and the pavilion pulled down and rebuilt – but the replacement is a bulky whitewashed concrete building, with none of the sublime grace of the original.

'The problem is the way the gurdwara is run. The committee is disorganised, and there is much infighting between different groups, and they refuse to employ conservation experts.'

I left Nishkam to his sadness and I felt a sense of shame, too, at the way vulgar modernism and haste had paved the way for the destruction of such beautiful monuments. And this was one of the most famous and beautiful in the world. What chance did the smaller places like Taxila have?

After a peaceful two-day rest in the surroundings of the temple, dipping my feet into its healing waters, I said goodbye to the impotent guardians of this incredible wonder and walked out into the Indian countryside. Despite the renowned crowd-edness and bustle and aversion to personal space that is associated with India, I had never felt more at peace in my life. The concept of the three-day hospitality rule struck a chord with me, and I have adopted it ever since, never abusing someone's kindness for longer, even if they insisted.

I had reached a juncture in my journey. From Amritsar, I could go anywhere. My Silk Road had almost come to an end. Here the path diverged into a thousand smaller ones. In the olden days merchants, camel trains and wandering horse traders would meet here before setting off to the west, and so I was faced with a choice. South, to the deserts of Rajasthan, following the coastal route to Mumbai and beyond which, Goa? Or north, towards the thrones of the Himalayas. Or straight to Delhi? I remembered my dream. First, the mountains.

Like Kim, or a rather sunburned Don Quixote, I wandered north-east on the Pathankot road, sometimes hitching, sometimes walking, until I reached the border of Kashmir. From there I went uphill into the foothills of the greater Himalaya, past Nurpur and Shahpur, until a narrow winding lane that followed the upper reaches of the Kangra valley, flanked by alpine rhododendron and coniferous pine, led me to Dharamsala, 'the pilgrims' sanctuary'.

Another few hours' walk beyond that, at the foot of the White Mountain and in a state of blissful contentment, I reached the tiny mountain village of McLeod Ganj, home of the Dalai Lama.

18

Himalaya

McLeod Ganj is about as close as one can get to Tibet without donning crampons, and sits at a cool altitude of over two thousand metres; the Dhauladhar range of the western Himalayas form a stark natural barrier only a few miles to the north. It used to be a British hill station and I could see why it became a popular playground for the ruling classes during the days of the Raj.

Nowadays McLeod Ganj was filled with another type of expatriate. Everywhere I turned were backpackers and tourists; long-haired hippies in tie-dyed fisherman's pants and dreadlocks. They sat around and drank and smoked and played cards on the terraces of dingy little cafés. Some had come to catch a glimpse of the Dalai Lama, others purely to soak up the culture from the exiled Tibetan population.

I arrived in the village in early afternoon, just in time to see the sun set over the forests. Gaudy neon signs lit up the marketplace that sold miniature Buddhas (beardless here), wooden masks, and an array of religious jewellery made from yak bone and semi-precious gems hewn from the mountainsides. Kiosks offered bus tickets to Delhi, train rides to Shimla and guided treks around the foothills. Restaurants advertised not only Tibetan *momos*, a type of dumpling, but also falafel, pizza and steak, presumably for the benefit of the intrepid Israeli, American and British voyagers, who had come all this way in search of a cuisine to match their own.

I was no longer on the overland trail; in fact, I was no longer in India, it seemed. Many of the locals were wearing fake designer fleeces and technical down jackets hauled over the mountains from China and sold for five per cent of their market price. Was this the Shangri-La I had been searching for?

Seeking solace in the shelves of a small travel bookshop in the 'shopping mall' – a tunnel of dilapidated shops, where a round-faced Tibetan greeted me with a friendly *tashi delek*, hello – I discovered that the bookcases were packed with dubious titles about growing olives in Tuscany and cycling around Brittany with a copy of the Kama Sutra. Is this what travel had become? A middle-aged hobby and an excuse for a circus stunt? What had happened to Newby and Lewis, Dalrymple and Byron? Or the English amateur, who finds himself accidentally exiled to some distant and savage land? Or even Arthur Conolly? I suddenly felt a longing to be away from the bustle of the resort, back in the hills of Afghanistan or the plains of Persia.

My immediate reaction was to escape, like I had done so many times before, but where to? I had reached my destination; where was there left to go? So instead I stayed, I let myself fall into the languid zen-like rhythm of ghetto life. One by one, I shed my snobberies and prejudices and ideals and embraced the inexorable trappings of commercial tourism. I feasted on a fat roast chicken and drank my first beer since an overpriced Heineken in Kabul. I splurged on a five-dollar room (en suite with a balcony). I wrote postcards, used the internet and backed up my photographs. I even washed my socks. The days passed by, slowly at first, but before I knew what had happened almost a week had vanished.

Andy, a balding middle-aged Englishman, approached me in the PeaceTime restaurant. He was a paunchy, sedentary fellow, who saw travel as a lamentably arduous means of moving between hammocks. He sat down with a strained *humph*.

'Been here long?' he mused, picking up the cocktail menu.

'Not really,' I answered. I didn't know whether five days was long or not, I had lost all sense of perspective as my energy levels relentlessly declined. The pines rustled in the breeze and the sun turned a fabulous orange.

'I was going trekking, but I've done my knee in, so I think I'll just wait here while the wife goes,' said Andy with a snort.

I sipped my *lassi* yoghurt drink and looked down into the misty valley, where coloured prayer flags fluttered from the trees. I didn't blame him.

The days were hot, but the evenings cool and clouds would gather, foreboding a storm. Despite my growing indolence, I was determined to walk in the mountains sooner or later and regretted for a moment having given away my sleeping bag to the irascible Osman in the hills of Afghanistan. One afternoon, after getting my sandals repaired, I ambled down the hill to the temple of his holiness the Dalai Lama, who had lived here in exile since 1959.

It was a modest bungalow, not at all what you would expect of a national leader. It was devoid of any beauty, save a simple grace and serenity that belied the awesome natural surroundings. Monks clad in maroon robes wandered about, smiling ceaselessly. They looked incongruent, though, as they got in and out of sparkling Toyota Land Cruisers and carried briefcases and designer sports bags to and from the complex.

'Where are they going?' I asked a trinket seller I recognised from the bazaar.

'They are going to meetings,' replied the man, who explained that these priests were the jet setters of the religious world, on a par with the cardinals of the Vatican, who regularly journeyed around the world lobbying for support for the government in exile.

In 1959, after a failed uprising against the Chinese occupation, the Tibetan government led by the Dalai Lama arrived in Dharamsala. They soon established a thriving community of over a hundred thousand men, women and children. There were schools, hospitals and all sorts of economic development projects, as well as the many Tibetan handicraft centres dotted around the Kangra valley. The Indian government allowed the Tibetans to exercise their own democratic rule and the government in exile has its parliament and prime minister, with the Dalai Lama remaining solely a figurehead for the organisation. Despite his exhausting schedule of global advocacy, he describes himself as 'semi-retired'.

It was pleasant to sit on the leafy terrace watching the Indian tourists and the busy little monks. An opportunistic Dutch film crew arrived on the scene and I looked on with the trinket seller grinning as they were told that His Holiness was not at home. The producer looked distraught.

'But we organised this weeks ago,' he bellowed. 'We need to do an interview.'

A graceful monk smiled, 'Well, I am afraid that you will have to wait. He isn't here.'

'Where is he?'

'That,' he said, still smiling, 'is none of my business.'

It seems that although the Dalai Lama is semi-retired, he still found the energy to disappear off and meet his people every now and again.

Later I went to my usual restaurant, overlooking the centre of the village, and sat alone. A group of travellers came in, and I noticed a couple of English girls who were carrying a crate of beer and some local whisky. With them were some French hippies, one of whom was dressed in a Buddhist toga and then, behind them, three familiar faces.

'Lev?' cried Gregor across the room. It was the Slovenian who had carried me up the stairs of the Regale Inn in Lahore, after I'd passed out in the gutter. He was with his friend Luka and Leander, coincidentally the German with whom I had explored the bazaars of Lahore.

I should have been surprised, I suppose, but experience had taught me that the world – especially the traveller's world – is a very small place. I kept bumping into people all along the overland trail, whether by design or just good fortune.

'You're alive!' He patted me on the shoulder. 'Sorry we had to leave you in Lahore, but you were fast asleep and we had a bus to catch into the mountains. We figured you were in good hands with Malik.'

'Yeah, he looked after me,' I said.

'Did he give you any of his magic tea by any chance?'

I chuckled.

'He certainly did.'

We embraced each other like old friends and sat down to drink. It wasn't long before everyone was recounting their tales of serendipity and chance encounters on the road. Gregor and Luka asked me if I had perchance met two stoned French men in Iran.

'David and Pierre?'

'Yes, those were their names. Real weirdos.'

The two new French hippies, No-No and Bagpuss as they called themselves, burst out laughing.

'Shit man, we bumped into them in Istanbul!' said the 'professional spiritualists'.

'You *have* been all about the place, haven't you, you've *done* the whole world?' said Toni, the young English girl with bright red hair. I cringed.

Soon enough we were all quite drunk on cheap whisky and Godfather beer. The girls and the French longhairs disappeared off to smoke *charas*, while Leander ordered a round of *lassi* and the Slovenians tried to convince me to leave with them to Delhi in the morning. They were leaving at six.

'Not a chance,' I said. 'I need a lie in. No doubt I'll see you there, though.'

I staggered back to my hotel, only to find it locked shut. Ten minutes of solid banging failed to wake up the sleeping night watchman and in my inebriated state, I decided it would be a good idea to climb up the drainpipe onto the third floor of the adjacent building, jump across the two-metre gap onto the roof of my guesthouse, and shimmy back down two balconies to get to my room. I remembered the time that I'd had to escape in the same way from Gocha's house in Georgia. It was a good idea in theory, but where my persistent banging had failed, the noise of my legs clattering against windowpanes on my descent succeeded in waking up the angry manager, who seemed to take exception to the possibility of a tourist corpse on his property.

'Please get down, sir, you will surely die,' he begged with a hint of rage.

'I'm fine,' I said confidently, as I swung on one hand over a ten-metre precipice. Eventually my acrobatics were victorious and I navigated my way to bed with only a few minor bruises. In the morning, though, the manager proved to be unimpressed and asked me kindly never to return.

With a rude hangover and sheepish embarrassment, I decided it was finally time to head for the hills. It seemed like the only thing to do. I'd spent a week staring at the mountains, which were only a stone's throw away, but not managed to get beyond the edge of the village. It was time. Armed with only a cotton shoulder bag and my Afghan shawl, I set off out of the village and into the forest. I had been malingering for far too long and I wouldn't forgive myself if I didn't at least reach the snowline of the Himalayas.

Depositing my main rucksack in the custody of the two English girls Toni and Toyah, who were content to while away another week smoking hash, I strolled a couple of kilometres northwards along the pine-lined road past the church of St John in the Wilderness, a glorious mock-Saxon, Victorian folly with stained glass windows, looking like it had been transplanted by the British straight from a parish in the home counties.

I wandered inside the dusky chapel, and suddenly felt nostalgic for home; I had never been to anywhere that quite encapsulated the idea of a small corner of England in a faraway land. I stood trying to make out the lonely inscriptions on the plaques that lined the wall; colonels, rectors, diplomats and spies that lived and died in this remote mountain wilderness. One told the story of Thomas William Knowles who 'met with his death by an attack from a bear' in the forests above. Suddenly an old man in his late seventies coughed deliberately; I had thought I was alone.

'Please welcome, sir. You are most welcome,' he said politely.

'Sorry, I didn't know anyone was here, I thought it was abandoned.'

'Abandoned? No sir, I am the rector for St John.'

'But why is it in such bad shape?'

The old rector looked as sad as the guardians of the Golden Temple in Amritsar.

'We don't have any money, sir. All the old people who used to come here are dead now. In the old days, many Britishers used to support the church, but now there are no Christians left, and the tourists don't come here – they prefer to see the Buddhists down the valley.' He sighed, and I couldn't tell if it was because he was sad with the decay of his building, or at the lack of Christian spirit in his parish. I gave a small donation, which seemed to cheer him up, but it wouldn't make any difference to the crumbling relic.

I took the middle path directly north and followed the course of an idyllic valley, passing wooden villages that contained beautiful flowers and gushing streams. Everywhere I went, children ran out to wave at the stranger before them. Toothless grandmothers sat and stared through wizened eyes, with a permanent smile etched on their ancient cheeks. One shack was perched precariously on the edge of a cliff, overlooking the forests below that seemed to vanish into the shrouding mist. A lonely teenager offered me Coca Cola and bags of crisps to take with me on my journey.

'Just some *chai*, please.'

'You want to buy a toothbrush?'

'No thanks, I have one, just *chai*.'

'How about a prayer wheel?'

'Just *chai*.'

'I have *charas*, the best in India.'

'No.'

'Sir, I am very poor, you can buy me if you want.'

He gave me a lewd wink and made a coarse gesture, at which I got up and carried on, despondent and thirsty.

Travel has its ups and downs, I thought to myself. I'd realised that on a journey like this you see the very worst of people at times, and yet I knew deep down that sooner or later I'd see the very best too. That was how it worked.

I gained height quickly as the trail rose, winding its way through the alpine forests. Habitation became less and less frequent and the only evidence of life was the distant columns of smoke that rose from the villages far below. The trees grew small, until only the hardiest of shrubs and the occasional bare skeleton of a dead cedar marked the limit of vegetation.

An eagle soared high above the scree slope and disappeared beyond a ridge. A waterfall crashed nearby, cutting a gorge into the open slope, and the trail narrowed to a breaking-up footpath that flitted in between boulders. After several false peaks, I caught sight of a lone hut sitting oddly at the top of a plateau. I hadn't seen another soul in hours, but there were figures, Indians sitting around a fire looking back across the valley.

'*Chai*, sir?' said a boy.

Luckily this one was actually selling tea and nothing more, and I gladly accepted the sweet milky brew. He was the owner of a mischievous puppy, which took great delight in chasing after crows and annoying a lone cow that I found hard to believe had made it this far up the slope.

'Where are you going?' he asked.

'Up the mountain,' I replied.

'You had better wait a while, it is going to be very wet.'

I looked up and saw that although the sky was darkening, it didn't look like it was going to rain any time soon, but before I had time to disagree, I heard an ominous clunk on the tin roof, and then another. He grinned with a look of wise sanctimony as massive hailstones started to pummel the mountainside. I grabbed my bag and ducked inside the shelter and looked on as the poor cow got thoroughly battered. *Always listen to the locals.*

I remembered back to the summer, when I had ignored local advice whilst hitching and ended up lost in the fields of Europe, and chuckled to myself. I thought of running through the rain in Volgograd, wishing for sunshine with Winfield. I wondered what he was doing now. I thought how I would have given anything for rain in Iran and Afghanistan. I suddenly thought back to that rainy weekend on Helvellyn in the Lake District when the idea to travel the Silk Road had come to me in the first place. My mind wandered back even further – to that fateful day when I was sixteen and lost my wallet at Alton Towers, and how Second Lieutenant James Whitehurst R.A. had written me that letter. 'Above all, travel,' he'd told me. *Well, I thought to myself, I've certainly done that.* The hail stones danced around in the mud and formed pools of brilliant white as I smiled to myself and thought about my Silk Road journey. I thought of all the little things, of trying to understand Russian signposts, sleeping rough on roundabouts, drinking vodka on Gocha's farm in Georgia, surviving that car crash in Afghanistan, getting ill in Pakistan, and the splendour of the Golden temple. I thought of the people I had met along the way. Kurt, Christian, Marc, Marta, Lasha, Wim, Gregor, Osman and the rest. It all felt so long ago.

It was almost four in the afternoon by the time the hail abated, so I said goodbye to my young friend to carry on climbing up to the vantage point of Triund, where a glimmer of blue in the sky above illuminated one of the Himalayan peaks that had so far been invisible. Back down the valley, though, the mist had turned black and it was like peering into a thick, dark soup.

After another forty minutes walking, I decided that it was getting late and I had better find somewhere to sleep. I had been expecting more huts and maybe an invite onto a warm floor, but there were none in sight and as the muted sun disappeared behind a hidden peak, I was beginning to get a little worried. I didn't have a sleeping bag and my food consisted of a couple of chapattis and a chocolate bar that had somehow made it all the way from England. It was an army-issue ration, one that under normal circumstances I wouldn't have given to a dog. But here, in the middle of the Himalayas, it was the ultimate luxury.

It was getting dark now and I scrabbled around a hillside covered in boulders, until I came across the opening to a small cave. It was hidden from view from the footpath, but its mouth overlooked the valley, which dropped away sharply to the south. I climbed cautiously onto the ledge and into the narrow opening and was surprised to find that it looked like it had been used before. There was some old straw on the rock floor and a stack of twigs at the back. I used my lighter and some of the straw to make a torch, and there on the walls of the cave I saw some paintings of flowers and Hindu script, flickering with the dancing flames. I had no idea how old they were, or who the cave belonged to. I imagined an angry shepherd or solitary hermit coming out of the darkness at any moment. For a minute or two, I considered moving on. But as I looked back outside, the trees were swaying in the wind and the blackness was closing in all around. *If they were coming, they'd be here by now*, I thought to myself.

I decided to take the risk and sleep there for the night. I gathered some fresh wood outside, not wanting to steal the shepherd's stockpile, and made a fire. I wondered what it must have looked like to the villagers down below in the valley floor. Perhaps somebody looked up at the mountains and saw the distant flickering of my fire and gave it a moment's thought. Maybe they didn't. I wondered how many times Arthur Conolly had slept in a cave. It wasn't long before the night chill set in and as I glanced out into the night sky, I noticed that the clouds had dissipated and a full moon lit up the mountain peaks of Dhauladhar and Dharamkot. In spite of the warmth of the flames and my Afghan shawl, I knew I was in for a cold night.

The shepherd never came, but visions of bears and wolves

filled my dreams, after remembering the fate of Thomas William Knowles laid to rest in the eerie cemetery somewhere hidden in the forest below. The fire had gone out by the early hours and I slept fitfully. When the first light of the sun came to warm the earth, I emerged from the cave, chilled to the bone, but happy. Frost covered the ground and the puddles outside the cave had iced over. Smiling, I removed any trace of my having been there and scattered the ashes off the cliff and set off at a jog towards the plateau of Ilaka, the place where the snow starts.

Sometime later I took a bus to Shimla, where, amid the steep terraces and tall deodar cedars, the town rises out of the forest like an unexpected jewel, with gothic cathedrals and a mock-Tudor post office. From there, I left the mountains and took a steam train down the steep slopes to Kalka. I arrived in Delhi after three or four days by 'general class', ignoring the pleas of my Indian friends, who despaired at the idea of me being packed into the luggage compartment with a thousand others. But I arrived nonetheless. In the backpacker street of Paharganj, I bumped into Gregor, Luka and Leander once again. This time I almost expected it, and for the next three weeks we journeyed together throughout the country. Ajmer, Rajasthan, Mumbai and Goa; fleeting visions of jungles and deserts, and finally the lapping turquoise waves of the Indian Ocean.

With my new companions, travelling in poverty towards the coast, into the past; and deeper in India, into the future. I tallied up my journal and worked out that I had travelled over ten thousand miles overland. I was with friends, the sun glinting into our eyes, everything on earth was green and beautiful, and I thought, *I never want this adventure to end.*

Epilogue

The minibus screeched to a halt, kicking dust against the pavement. 'It's here,' I said out loud, grinning in satisfaction that I had actually remembered the place. I paid the driver a couple of laris for the ride and squeezed past the other passengers to jump out onto the roadside. The door slammed shut and the van sped away, leaving the pair of us alone. I saw that the main road led off into the foothills of the Caucasus, but to the right was the path that I remembered.

'Are you sure?' said my guide.

I looked up at Lasha. He seemed unconvinced.

'I'm sure,' I said. 'It's this way.'

He shrugged and flicked his head down the smaller road. It was paved these days.

How could I forget? I thought to myself.

I looked around. It was almost how I remembered it, the sound of crashing water in the river to my right, and the rolling brown scrub of the hillocks off to the left. Ahead there was a scraggy set of cliffs and as we rounded them I looked up. There it was. Khertvisi castle. The ancient fortress that had seen the armies of Alexander and Genghis Khan pass by.

I patted Lasha on his shoulders.

'Told you.'

It was as mighty as I remembered and virtually unchanged in thirteen years, except there was now a proper road instead of a gravel track, and a small car park at the base of the cliff, where a tourist sign explained a little of the history of the fortress.

'And you slept there?' he asked me, raising an eyebrow. He couldn't believe that I'd actually made it to Tbilisi, let alone all the way along the Silk Road to India.

'No, no, it's a bit further down, on the right if I recall. Although it was dark then.'

I closed my eyes and imagined walking down the same path in 2004. I remember being young and reckless, unafraid of the wolves or bears that inhabit the caves and crags of this wild land. I took a few paces forward and sensed that we were close. I looked over to see a concrete bus shelter at the side of the road by some willow trees.

'There it is.' I nudged him, and ran over to it. I remembered that in my memory it had a tin roof and was held up by wooden poles, but that was a long time ago and it must have been refurbished. Either way it was covered in graffiti and bird crap. I dumped my bag on the floor and stretched out on the wooden bench. Lasha came over and chuckled. 'You look like a homeless!' he roared.

I couldn't quite believe I was back. Thirteen years later, lying on the same bench where I'd once spent the night, or at least some of the night, when I hitchhiked the Silk Road.

I'd always promised myself that I'd return to Georgia since that formative expedition, and now I'd made it.

In the spring of 2017, I set out to cross the Caucasus mountains on a journey from Russia to Iran, following in my own footsteps of a journey that had left a lifelong impression. I'd begun in Sochi a month or so before, on the shores of the Black Sea and travelled East, through the troubled North Caucasian states: Karachay-Cherkessia, Kabardino-Balkaria, North Ossetia, Ingushetia, Chechnya and Dagestan, before traversing Azerbaijan and sweeping back west into Georgia to pick up the trail where I'd left off. Here I was reunited with Lasha, whom I hadn't seen or spoken with in well over a decade.

'I tried to write to you many times,' he said. 'But I lost your address, and no matter how many times I tried to guess, I couldn't remember how to spell your name.'

I laughed. I'd tried to track him down, too. I wanted to write and thank him for his help, and to keep in touch in case I ever returned. But it was to no avail. I just got emails bouncing back at me. This was before the days of video messaging or Facebook, and even when social media became popular, the only Lasha I could find in Poti had a blank profile and only three friends. I sent a message in any case, but there was no reply. I'd almost given up until a couple of weeks before setting off, when, by a stroke of luck, I connected with him on Skype. He couldn't have been more excited to meet up and join me for the Georgian segment of the journey, and I was simply glad to have found him again.

We travelled through Tbilisi, which had transformed itself (with a lot of EU money) from the grimy provincial town of my memory, into a bustling city of culture and excitement. Hipster bars, shisha-coffee combos, and post-modern mirrored museums clashed wonderfully with the original churches, cathedrals and medieval alleys of the old town. Gone were the rusting Ladas at the side of the road missing their wheels, and the tower blocks with no running water or electricity; the charred remains of the state-run hotel had disappeared to make way for a fancy Marriott, which looked out across a bustling city centre.

There were plenty of tourists now to feed a booming industry, and people even did day trips out to the ski resorts of the Caucasus and the cave city of Vardzia. It had changed enormously, and for the better. I was glad that more people were appreciating the legendary Georgian hospitality – not to mention its delicious food, vodka and wine.

Since we'd said goodbye in 2004, Lasha had quit football, become an oil-rig inspector and settled down to get married. He even had a couple of kids that he chatted to endlessly on Skype, telling them all about 'Uncle Left'. He'd also been a soldier, evidenced by a scrawling tattoo on his skinny arm, and fought against the Russians in the 2008 war that saw Putin's tanks roll over the mountains. The new Cold War, it seemed, was being fought out right here, in fits and starts on the fringes of Europe – on the pathways of the old Silk Road.

But for now, it was peaceful. I'd been treated warmly in the least likely places. Even north, in Russia, which I'd remembered as inhospitable and difficult as a backpacker, had been good to me this time round. I'd ridden with Cossacks, partied with Chechens and trekked across Dagestan with shepherds. I'd even been taken in by members of the jihadist families in these notorious badlands. Everywhere, I'd been looked after, and that's why I wanted to return to the Caucasus – and to Georgia in particular. It was every bit as friendly as I recalled, and the wine and vodka, every bit as potent.

This time I was thirteen years older and wiser, and looking back, there's no way I'd want to try and hitchhike all the way to

India again on a budget of £500. But at the time, it was the ultimate in freedom and I relished the challenge.

'Come on then,' said Lasha. 'You've seen your castle and your bench, let's go get some lunch and get to Vardzia. I've never been myself and want to see the caves.'

I got up. 'Wait,' I said. 'There's one more thing I need to do here.'

I closed my eyes again, and tried to remember the night.

I'd been dozing off when three men came over, they were drunk and I was worried they would rob me. One of them spoke to me in German and insisted I follow him home.

I tried to remember how far we'd walked that night to his house. It couldn't have been far, a couple of hundred metres at most.

'Come on,' I motioned to Lasha.

'Where are we going?'

'We're going to find Gocha's house. That bastard holed me up and made me drink homemade vodka for two days solid.'

'Do you think he still lives there?' Lasha asked.

'I have no idea. I had to do a runner and I didn't even get his surname.'

I looked at the row of farms on the left-hand side of the road. They were set back from the path and separated by a series of wire fences and orchards.

The middle one looked vaguely familiar.

'It's here, I think.'

Peering through the gate, I saw the garden and the garage that I'd scuttled over during my bid to escape the epic moonshine binge of yesteryear, and the window that I must have climbed out of in order to avoid getting chomped at by the big grey and white sheepdog with his evil teeth. I

345

wondered if the dog was still around. But no, there was only silence.

'It was a long time ago. He's probably moved away,' said Lasha.

Suddenly a woman appeared from the street behind us. She must have been curious as to why we were staring into her property.

'Can I help you?' she asked. 'This is my house.'

'Sorry,' I said. 'I was just looking for an old friend.' Lasha translated.

'Who?' she said with a kind smile.

'Gocha.'

'Come with me.' She led the way. I couldn't believe it. 'He's my husband.'

We walked across the garden and onto the veranda. There lying fast asleep under the porch was an old sheepdog. Most of his teeth were missing now and he was half the size that I remembered, but it was unmistakably the same beast that scared the living daylights out of me all those years ago.

Up a few steps we found ourselves standing by the front door, which slammed open. There stood a man in a white vest squinting into the afternoon sunlight. He looked at me for a solid few seconds.

'Hello, Gocha. Do you remember me?'

His eyes widened for a moment, before he broke into a wry smile.

'English.' He jabbed me and chuckled before closing the door and disappearing. I looked at Lasha, who just shrugged.

A minute later, Gocha returned with a huge bottle of home-made vodka and three glasses clenched in his enormous hands. He was as big and brutish as I remembered him.

'Welcome back,' he said in broken German. 'You escaped last time. My neighbours saw you running across their roof ...' He chuckled. 'Now, we must drink.' He flashed his teeth and raised the bottle.

Oh no, not again ... I thought to myself.

London, August, 2017

Acknowledgments

This journey took place thirteen years ago, at a time before smart phones, Google Earth and omnipresent Wi-Fi. I was twenty-two years old and it was probably the most carefree time of my life. I didn't really plan very much, or organise logistics too far ahead, so in that respect there isn't an exhaustive list of partners to thank.

That said, there were many people but for whom this trip would have been rendered far less pleasant, were it not for their company, advice, support and sofas.

Firstly, Jon Winfield, who came with me from Nottingham to Vladikavkaz. His company and sense of humour, not to mention insistence on visiting Russia in the first place, made the adventure all the more wonderful.

Thanks also to Christian Abstein, Kurt Seitz, Marta Zawistowska, Marc Engberg, Gregor Bobnar, Luka Mali, Rob Newnham and Lasha Samushia for their kindness and hospitality. There were of course hundreds of others that put me up, fed me and offered me a kindly beer (or vodka) along the way. But also in the weeks, months and years afterwards and when I finally got around to writing it: Dr Ross Balzaretti of the University of Nottingham, for his inspiration and guidance, Will Charlton, Seb Bourn, Toby Truscott, the late Alex Coutselous, Ruthie Markus, Alberto Cáceres, John Copeland and Emma Challinor, who took me in and read the first drafts of an embryonic story; Shwetank Verma, who hosted me in India in 2011; Ceci Alonzo for her support during some of the more frugal times; and my parents, who encouraged me to always travel.

I owe the book to Rupert Lancaster at my publishers, Hodder & Stoughton, and all the team involved, especially Kerry Hood, Cameron Myers and Caitriona Horne. Thanks also to Barry Johnston and Charlotte Tottenham for their help in editing the drafts and Neil Gower for the maps and cover art.

Of course, I could not have done any of this without my wonderful agent Jo Cantello, who yet again has kept me on the straight and narrow.

Finally, my gratitude to the people of the modern Silk Road for their generosity and kindness.

Further Reading

Marco Polo, *The Travels of Marco Polo*, c.1300
Ibn Battutah, *The Travels of Ibn Battutah*, 1829
Arthur Conolly, *Journey to the North of India*, 1834
Rudyard Kipling, *The Man Who Would be King*, 1888
Rudyard Kipling, *Kim*, 1901
Robert Byron, *The Road to Oxiana*, 1937
Fitzroy MacLean, *Eastern Approaches*, 1949
Eric Newby, *A Short Walk in the Hindu Kush*, 1958
Patrick Leigh Fermor, *A Time of Gifts*, 1977
William Dalrymple, *In Xanadu*, 1989
Peter Hopkirk, *The Great Game*, 1990
David Tomory, *A Season in Heaven: True Tales from the Road to Kathmandu*, 1996
Rory Stewart, *The Places In Between*, 2004
Rory MacLean, *Magic Bus: On the Hippie Trail from Istanbul to India*, 2006

Picture Acknowledgements

Index

'Levison Wood has breathed new life into adventure travel'
Michael Palin

LEVISON WOOD

WALKING THE
HIMALAYAS

**WINNER OF THE 2016 EDWARD STANFORD
ADVENTURE TRAVEL BOOK OF THE YEAR AWARD**

Following in in the footsteps of the great explorers, WALKING
THE HIMALAYAS is Levison Wood's enthralling account of
crossing the Himalayas on foot. His journey of discovery along the
path of the ancient trade route of the Silk Road to the forgotten
kingdom of Bhutan led him beyond the safety of the tourist
trail. There lies the real world of the Himalayas, where the ex-
paratrooper encountered natural disasters, extremists, nomadic
goat herders, shamans (and the Dalai Lama) in his 1,700-mile trek
across the roof of the world. WALKING THE HIMALAYAS is a
tale of courage, stamina and the kindness of strangers that will
appeal to the adventurer in us all.

9781473626263 | £9.99 | AVAILABLE NOW

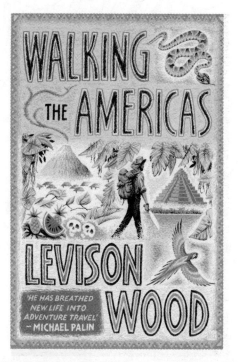

SUNDAY TIMES TOP 10 BESTSELLER

WALKING THE AMERICAS chronicles Levison Wood's 1,800 mile trek along the spine of the Americas, through eight countries, from Mexico to Colombia, experiencing some of the world's most diverse, beautiful and unpredictable places.

His journey took him from violent and dangerous cities to ancient Mayan ruins lying still unexplored in the jungles of Mexico and Guatemala. He encountered members of indigenous tribes, migrants heading towards the US border and proud Nicaraguan revolutionaries on his travels, where at the end of it all, he attempted to cross one of the most impenetrable borders on earth: the Darién Gap route from Panama into South America.

9781473654099 | £9.99 | 18 January 2018

HARDBACK AVAILABLE NOW

An invitation from the publisher

Join us at www.hodder.co.uk, or follow us
on Twitter @hodderbooks to be a part of
our community of people who love the very
best in books and reading.

Whether you want to discover more about a book
or an author, watch trailers and interviews, have the
chance to win early limited editions, or simply browse
our expert readers' selection of the very best books,
we think you'll find what you're looking for.

And if you don't, that's the place to tell us what's missing.

We love what we do, and we'd love you to be a part of it.

www.hodder.co.uk

@hodderbooks

HodderBooks

HodderBooks

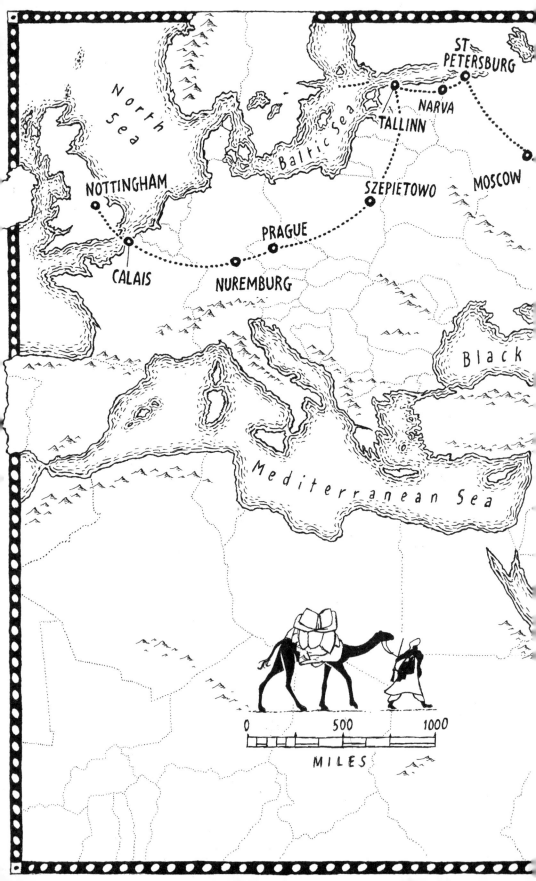